STOLEN IDENTITY

No one has worked harder than Peter Jones to make Christians in our generation alert to the very real and present dangers of ancient Gnosticism. By being aware of the struggle the church has waged throughout her history in defense of the one true Jesus, Christians today can more effectively understand and answer the postmodern confusion about the so-called "historical" Jesus.

JOHN MACARTHUR,
PASTOR OF GRACE COMMUNITY CHURCH, SUN CITY, CA,
AND BIBLE TEACHER OF THE RADIO PROGRAM *GRACE TO YOU*

Dr. Peter Jones stands in the honorable tradition that runs from the great early Christian theologian-apologist Irenaeus of Lyons. Here is a New Testament scholar who understands what lies behind books like *The Da Vinci Code* and who can clearly distinguish fact from fiction, truth from invention. *Stolen Identity* convincingly exposes false claims about early Christianity and clearly explains the significance of the Jesus of the four gospels. It will be a sobering eye-opener for anyone likely to be taken in by sensational page-turners, and, at the same time, an invaluable help to many Christians. We owe Peter Jones a considerable debt for having the courage to speak in a way that is deeply prophetic to the times in which we live.

SINCLAIR FERGUSON
SPEAKER AND PROFESSOR OF SYSTEMATIC THEOLOGY,
WESTMINSTER THEOLOGICAL SEMINARY, DALLAS, TX

Two worldviews, two spiritualities, two views of Jesus, mirror images of one another and yet diametrically opposed to each other. Historic Christianity and Gnosticism—one true and the other a fraud. Peter Jones has laid these out in a way that is clear, concise, and compelling with a conclusion as simple as it is decisive: Choose this day whom you will serve!

DAVID F. WELLS
ᴊGUISHED PROFESSOR OF
SYSTEMATIC THEOLOGY,
ʜEOLOGICAL SEMINARY

The first problem with the approach of Dan Brown (and of others who follow him) is not theology, but history: Dan Brown is an incompetent historian before he is an incompetent theologian. Sadly, in an age when careful probing of historical documents is displaced by love of novelty, Dan Brown is cherished by many not so much as a novelist but as a prophet, someone who leads us to truth. Here Peter Jones provides a helpful remedy. Though he writes in a provocative style, his own doctoral research was in Gnostic literature, and his antidote to the painful nonsense mushrooming around us is to let the ancient texts speak for themselves. This book deserves the widest circulation.

DONALD A. CARSON
NEW TESTAMENT RESEARCH PROFESSOR,
TRINITY EVANGELICAL DIVINITY SCHOOL

As a pastor I am always looking for books that help me to help my congregation understand and address challenges to the faith. Peter Jones has hit the nail on the head by tackling attacks on the identity of Christ. Here is a well-documented, readable resource to add to your library and give to your flock.

ALISTAIR BEGG
PASTOR OF PARKSIDE CHURCH, CLEVELAND, OH,
AND HOST OF THE POPULAR RADIO PROGRAM TRUTH FOR LIFE

PETER JONES

CO-AUTHOR OF CRACKING DA VINCI'S CODE

Stolen Identity

Victor®

The Bible Teacher's Teacher

COOK COMMUNICATIONS MINISTRIES
Colorado Springs, Colorado • Paris, Ontario
KINGSWAY COMMUNICATIONS LTD
Eastbourne, England

Victor® is an imprint of
Cook Communications Ministries, Colorado Springs, CO 80918
Cook Communications, Paris, Ontario
Kingsway Communications, Eastbourne, England

Stolen Identity
© 2006 by Peter Jones

First printing, 2006
Printed in the United States of America

3 4 5 6 7 8 9 10 11 Printing/Year 11 10 09 08 07 06

Cover Design: BMB Design

Library of Congress Cataloging-in-Publication Data

Jones, Peter, 1940-
  Stolen identity : the conspiracy to reinvent Jesus / by Peter Jones.-- 1st ed.
     p. cm.
  Includes bibliographical references.
  ISBN-13: 978-0-7814-4207-7
  ISBN-10: 0-7814-4207-9
  1. Jesus Christ--Person and offices. 2. Bible. N.T. Gospels--Theology. 3. Jesus
Christ--Gnostic interpretations. 4. Nag Hammadi codices. 5. Apologetics. I. Title.
  BT205.J66 2006
  232--dc22

                                                              2005023764

*To the memory of my father-in-law, Edmund P. Clowney
(1917–2005) whose long and faithful ministry as
teacher, scholar, and preacher was dedicated to the
celebration of the centrality of Jesus, the Christ,
in the whole of Scripture and in the whole of life.*

CONTENTS

*A study guide for personal or group study is
available for free download and reproduction online at
www.cookministries.com/stolenidentity.*

PREFACE

The murder scene grabs your attention. In the foreboding semidarkness of the after-hours Louvre museum, the corpse of the curator, Jacques Saunière was discovered, spread-eagled on the floor of his inner office, in the shape of the *Vitruvian Man.* Before expiring, Saunière had deliberately arranged his naked body in the shape of Leonardo da Vinci's famous anatomical study of the human form—the perfect human body, arms, and legs outstretched, touching the edges of a circle. The murder victim left a silent, coded message that would eventually unlock the mystery of the crime. This is how Dan Brown's novel of codes and symbols, *The Da Vinci Code,* gets off to a fast-paced beginning.

The biblical Gospels, too, present a crime scene—at the end. The successful movie, *The Passion of The Christ,* provides an obvious cultural counterpoint to Brown's novel. Mel Gibson's substantially accurate reproduction of gospel accounts of the physical suffering and gruesome death of Jesus of Nazareth leaves little to the imagination. The disfigured corpse of the hero hangs limp, arms outstretched from iron spikes driven through the bones and sinews of his mangled hands and piercing a wooden crossbeam of an ancient scaffold. However, though the perpetrators are readily identifiable, the mystery in this gospel story is no less intriguing.

Will the real Jesus please stand up? Is he the idealized human figure of the *Vitruvian Man,* now in an androgynous form,[1] or the Man of Sorrows, Savior of the World? This question has rarely been asked with such urgency in the history of the West as it is now being asked in our time.

It may be safe to say that more has been said and written about Jesus than about any other religious figure. Many imagine a blond-haired, blue-eyed Jesus with clear skin and impeccable fingernails, amiably mobbed by equally impeccable children. Such images decorate the walls of squeaky-clean suburban churches and jump off the pages of Sunday school manuals written for white, Anglo-Saxon middle-class children. At the other end of the spectrum, another Jesus smiles from the cover of Matthew Fox's book, *The Coming of the Cosmic Christ*,[2] expressing the sexual ambiguities of today's new spirituality. With the baby features of an adolescent boy, this Jesus looks like a "Christian" version of the pagan Greek *kouros*, the feminized pinup homosexual youth found on ancient Greek vases, so attractive to that pedophiliac culture. A comparable version for third millennium Roman Catholics is the all-inclusive "Jesus of the People," on the cover of the *National Catholic Reporter*.[3] The artist, Janet McKenzie, a "devout atheist" with an interest in many faiths, used a black woman as a model, saying, "My goal was to be as inclusive as possible."[4] This inclusiveness is both sexual and spiritual. Jesus is presented against a pale pink background whose details include a yin and yang circle representing perfect balance, and a feather symbolizing American Indian spirituality.

It seems there are as many images of Jesus as there are people who write about him: the Cuban with a rifle over his shoulder, looking suspiciously like a bearded sixties Marxist revolutionary; the successful CEO; the poverty-stricken peasant; the mystical practitioner of the Jewish Kabbalah; or the husky NFL linebacker. Jesus has been described as a guru, sage, cult leader, miracle-working end-time prophet, or as a social critic of the status quo. Jesus, you might say, is the original "man for all seasons."

The present interest in the so-called Holy Grail surely reflects this agelong fascination with Jesus. Will the finding of the cup used at the Last Supper contain the truth of his person, or will some well-kept secret about the love life of Jesus finally prove that Jesus was merely an earthly prophet, not God in the flesh? Endless books and movies in recent times have fanned these speculative flames, but the issues are still unresolved.

In spite of the apparent endless variety of options, the choice for Jesus narrows down to two: *The Da Vinci Code/Vitruvian Man* Jesus, or *The Passion of The Christ* Jesus. Though in no sense exhaustive, these two images are convenient contemporary cultural symbols to evoke two views of Jesus that have persisted down the centuries.

Why do I say that there are only two?

In Brown's novel, Jacques Saunière died, laid out in the form of the *Vitruvian Man*, to preserve a deep religious secret: "ritual sex" for spiritual enlightenment. Just fiction? Not at all. Brown knowingly promotes the spirituality of the *Hieros Gamos*, or sacred marriage, which is central in the ancient Gnostic texts, as we shall see in what follows.[5] The other picture of Jesus, the Jesus of Gibson's *The Passion*, depends on the time-honored witness of historic biblical Christianity. This Jesus died not for ritual sex or secret knowledge, but for the sins of the world. The "ritual-sex" Jesus and the crucified Jesus go back respectively to the ancient Gnostic texts or to the biblical Gospels. In the resolution of the "Jesus controversy," only these two options can make any kind of claim to historical reliability.[6]

We are just discovering the Gnostic texts, so let me provide some background for readers unfamiliar with them. In 1945, while everyone was watching the allied assault on Germany and hoping for a quick end to World War II, an Egyptian peasant quietly made another kind of history. Muhammad Ali dug up the first fragment of "secret scrolls" that came to be published as *The Nag Hammadi Library in English*.[7] When the sand had been brushed away, scholars had fifty-two scrolls written in an ancient dialect called Coptic. The "library in the sand," unearthed near the Egyptian village of Nag Hammadi, were original Gnostic texts, from the second and third centuries (some would claim first century) AD. Their message was perhaps even more earth-shaking than the events of the Second World War.

Thirty-two years after the Armistice we found ourselves in another world conflict—a battle for Jesus. In 1977, when the translation of these Gnostic texts appeared in English, a war over Jesus began in earnest, and the stealth weapon introduced in the form of the Gnostic texts meant that defending biblical faith would never be the same again.

One of the most influential American New Testament schol-ars of the twentieth century, James Robinson, reared in a Bible-believing home, started the hostilities with a number of incendiary claims. As director of the English translation of the Gnostic texts, Robinson wrote the official, scholarly introduction. In it he referred *seven* times to the church fathers as "myopic heresy hunters,"[8] and maintained that, for the first time in mod-ern history, the *real* Jesus could now be known—a composite Jesus made up of elements from the Gnostic and the biblical Gospels.

In this book, I would like to examine the two pictures of Jesus emerging from these two ancient gospel collections. It is high time that fair-minded people look at the evidence and judge for themselves which of these two pictures is the right one. Which Jesus deserves our allegiance? Readers will also have to decide if, following Robinson, they can be merged.

I have tried to write a book that can be used by a variety of people. You should be able to read the text through without using the footnotes, but if you are interested in extra material, resources, or proofs of what I state in the text, keep the footnotes handy.

I have treated these two collections of ancient books as wholes, expressing in each case a common view of the world and spirituality. To be sure, each Gnostic text is slightly different, as various points on a continuum, but the essential worldview of

Gnosticism binds them all together. In the same way, the New Testament Gospels have their own individual perspectives but also collectively witness to the biblical Jesus.

Different kinds of people can read this book for different reasons. Here are a few who may benefit from this work:

COMMITTED GNOSTICS

If you are a Gnostic, you have decided to find security in spiritual *gnosis* [knowledge]. You may have grown up as a Christian, but long ago rejected Christian orthodoxy as "old hat," dismissing the Bible as a mere collection of unrelated human stories. But the Bible has proven resilient over thousands of years, and it has a profound spirituality and deep theological consistency from start to finish that should force you to take it seriously. As a "progressive" spiritual quester, you need to examine the consistency of the biblical account before dismissing its Jesus as a projection of later church dogma.

"OPEN" BELIEVERS

Maybe you were raised in the church, are dissatisfied with what you have been taught, and believe that a composite picture of Jesus, with elements from both the Gnostic and the biblical accounts, will produce for you a viable faith for the modern world of pluralism and inclusiveness. A growing number of mainline Christians are exploring Buddhism, for example, while seeking to remain within the Christian tradition. But there is a downside to this spiritual search. The emerging Jesus becomes merely a reflection of your current spiritual preferences. Before you try to mix and match pieces of each Jesus, you need to observe the two complex pictures, each with its own consistency. This will preserve for you the possibility of meeting the real historical Jesus, be he Gnostic or biblical.

CAREFUL THINKERS

If you've been on a long road, and feel confused, you may

have decided to reject biblical Christianity and the Jesus of the Gospels in favor of agnosticism. This book may help you take one more look before slamming the door shut for good.

HONEST SEEKERS

If you are trying to resolve the dilemma posed by the modern debate, you need to examine the two basic kinds of Jesus on offer before giving up the search or deciding that all solutions are the same. One such seeker sent me the following e-mail:

> I have read many accounts of the Gnostics and so many other religions that I now consider myself not only a Recovering Catholic, but a Recovering Christian as well. What is so odd about Christianity, something that has bothered me for so long, is that how do you truly know you are more right than anyone else? ... For every "fact" in support of Jesus, there is an opposite and equally valid proof against a historical Jesus. Remember, we are all in this together weather [sic] we like it or not.

> J. ____, IOWA CITY, IA.

YOUNG CHRISTIANS

If you are a newly converted Christian believer, you may still feel somewhat confused about who Jesus is. You need to understand the nature of the Jesus to whom you have committed your life, in order to mature in your faith and to resist the allure of "other Jesuses" on offer in our culture. Many new Christians have "met Jesus" through a "born-again" experience, but they have only seen a piece of the picture. They need to understand exactly who this Jesus is. A young bride still has a lot to learn about the character of her husband. "Gospel preaching" can have great emotional power but remain somewhat superficial. A fuller understanding of Jesus brings understanding of the biblical worldview, so essential for witness in today's confusing world.

A further important question to answer is the place of emotional experience in Christian life and worship. Looking at these two views of Jesus will tell much about how to answer that much debated question in our time.

BIBLICALLY COMMITTED CHRISTIANS

If you are a committed Christian, you might wonder why you should read about any other Jesus than the one you know and love. You may be tempted to think that all you need is the Bible, and everything else is superfluous. This is to forget that the Bible is a book of arguments. It is a book that reveals truth in the context of a world pursuing an opposite "truth." Christians need to understand the cultural beliefs in which they live if they are to follow the example of the Bible. To explain why you feel the biblical Gospels present the real Jesus, it is helpful to show why any other Jesus is less than satisfying.[9] Since the discovery of the Nag Hammadi texts, another ancient literary source purports to give us the real Jesus. Christians should be prepared to meet this challenge.

Thousands of books on Jesus offer thousands of interpretations. The advantage of this book is the simplicity of its overview. I propose for your consideration the thesis that only two sources can make some kind of historic claim to authenticity and thus have the right to define the Jesus of history. In this exercise there is one advantage for all—a religious clarity that emerges from an honest look at the two competing views of the greatest religious figure in human history. The choice between them may be easier than you thought.

CHAPTER 1

THE GOD OF JESUS

*There are two generically different views about Jesus, and they are rooted in
two generically different views about God and the world.*
J. GRESHAM MACHEN (1930)[1]

E*cce homo:* "Behold the man." These were Pilate's famous
words, spoken at the trial of Jesus. Pilate's fascination with
this helpless prisoner jumps off the page, and ever since that
time, people have been looking at Jesus with a similar fascination. Western history has often considered him to be the most
significant human being of all time. You can tell Jesus made an
impression on Pilate because, almost in the same breath, Pilate
asked, "What is truth?" *Quid est veritas?* (Now you know five
Latin words—with no extra charge!) Pilate linked Jesus' identity
to the definition of truth. The question, Who is Jesus? still raises
the fundamental question of truth. Whoever defines Jesus
defines ultimate religious truth. But to define Jesus (as the above
quote by Machen so eloquently shows) we must identify the God
Jesus served. If Jesus said, "Whoever has seen me has seen the
Father,"[2] it is also true that the God of Jesus will tell you everything about Jesus—and will provide answers to Pilate's question
of truth. This is a critical time to raise these questions concerning
Jesus and Jesus' God, for in our day there are essentially two
coherent answers—the Gnostic and the biblical.

THE GOD OF THE GNOSTIC JESUS

If you want to know lots about "God," the Gnostic texts have many answers for you. Much of the content of the Gnostic scrolls is dedicated to the nature of the "unknowable" God. Gnostics wanted to know who God is in his ultimate being. Jesus is their favorite, though not their exclusive, revealer of God. The Gnostic texts also define God by clearly identifying the false God.

THE TRUE GOD OF GNOSTICISM

The Gnostics call God "the Father of the Entities," or "the Father of the All." In their texts, Jesus declared that the true believer must believe in the oneness of "the All,"[3] and he said about himself, "It is I who am the All."[4] This statement sounds something like what Jesus said in the gospel of John: "I and the Father are one," but the Gnostic version is much more complicated. Gnosticism affirms that it is easy to know "the Creator of all creatures," but it is impossible to know the true God.[5] The Creator is an impostor. The true God stands behind the false, clothed in mystery. Such is the mystery of God that the Gnostics end up saying only what he is not. "He is neither divinity nor blessedness nor perfection." He is better than that. "He is neither boundless nor is he bounded by another. Rather, he is something better."[6] In order to express the mystery of God, Gnostic speculation about God deliberately chooses nonsense statements like, "He has nonbeing existence," or "He is limitless and powerless and nonexistent."[7]

The God of this Jesus, often revealed in female form as Sophia, makes similarly bewildering statements. God is the "First Father," unengendered. He is either male or female or both. As the Goddess, he/she states, "I am androgynous. [I am both Mother and] Father since [I copulate] with myself."[8] This juxtaposition of contradictory notions also seeks to express the divine mystery. In another text, Sophia says:

> I am the prostitute and the venerable one ... I am
> the wife and the virgin ... the barren one and many

> are her sons ... the bride and the bridegroom ...
> knowledge and ignorance ... war and peace ... com-
> passionate and cruel ... senseless and ... wise ... I
> myself am godless and it is I whose God is mani-
> fold, I am the immutable essence and the one who
> has no immutable essence ... I am without mind
> and I am mindless.[9]

This unknowable God, who is everything and nothing, is the ultimate life source. Everything *emanates* from him.[10] "Emanate" is a crucial verb. "God" does not *create* anything, and there is a reason for it. True existence cannot be *created*; it always *is*. If it is true life, it has always existed. So God shares his life with every-thing. God is only the source from which everything emanates and to which everything returns. Everything, including God, shares the same nature.

The Gnostics use various images to keep God as high above or as far away as possible from what we immediately perceive in the illusion of our "created" reality. He is separated from the cre-ated world by various levels of personal spirit beings and/or worlds, sometimes as many as 365. It can get very complicated and virtually impossible to decipher. The following example indicates the level of speculation to which Gnostic writers were willing to go:

> This is the five-aeon [world] of the Father which is
> the first Man, the image of the invisible Spirit; it is the
> Pronoia which is Barbelo, the thought and the fore-
> knowledge and the indestructibility and the eternal
> life and the truth. This is the androgynous five-aeon,
> which is the ten-aeon, which is the Father.[11]

The Gnostic texts are full of passages like this. This God, wrapped in silence and mystery, denouncing the created struc-tures, is still in every part of the universe.

Such a view of God is called either *pantheism* or *monism*. Pantheism means, "God is in everything" or "everything is

God." According to monism, since everything shares the same divine nature, everything is ultimately "one" (the meaning of *mono*). Together these two terms capture the Gnostic view of God. Some texts make this clear. The female manifestation of the ultimate God states, "I move in every creature … I am the life of … every power … and every soul." In the most well-known of the Gnostic texts, *The Gospel of Thomas*, which is also considered the most "Christian," Jesus makes a clearly pantheistic statement: "It is I who am the All. From me did the All come forth.… Cleave a piece of wood, and I am there. Lift up a stone and I will be there."[12] A modern Gnostic "believer" gives expression to this pantheism:

> This Father, uncreated, does not create … [he] is everywhere.… All living beings are part of the Totality—trees, branches, and fruit—but he is the root that draws up the water of life from the unfathomable depths.[13]

Pantheism is not just an interesting theological option. It is the essence of religious paganism. "Paganism" is not a term of insult. It means the worship of nature, and the forces of nature, as divine. (*Paganus* is a Latin term meaning "of the earth.") If the Gnostic God is everything, then the God of the Gnostic Jesus is the god of paganism, a time-honored form of human spirituality. The church father Hippolytus (AD 170–236) made that connection long ago. He documented that the Gnostics of his day sought "the wisdom of the pagans."[14] He noted that "Christian" Gnostics attended the ceremonies of the Isis-worshipping mystery cults in order to understand "the universal mystery."[15] One of the original, recently found Gnostic texts confirms the testimony of Hippolytus. Sophia declares, "[I] am the one whose image is great in Egypt."[16] Isis, the pagan Egyptian Goddess of Wisdom and Magic is the one "whose likeness is great in Egypt."[17]

Who is Isis? According to her worshippers, she is "the still point of the turning world"[18] who proclaims, "I am Nature, the Universal Mother ... single manifestation of all gods and goddesses am I."[19] An expert in the study of Isis claims that when the Egyptians called her "great in magical power," they believed that she gave them "insight into the mystery of life and death."[20] The "universal Mother" revealing "the mystery of life and death" is almost word for word what Hippolytus says about the Gnostics he knew: They worshipped the Goddess to understand the "universal mystery." The statement of Sophia and the testimony of Hippolytus that Gnosticism was a "Christianized" form of paganism are confirmed by a contemporary pagan priestess of Isis who notes, "Gnosticism serves most admirably as a bridge for paganism to infiltrate Christianity."[21]

In principle, all the Gnostic texts hold to this view of God. One text goes as far as to call God Abraxas.[22] In the subsequent history of Gnosticism, Abraxas, the supreme Gnostic deity, is represented by the image of a man with the head of a cock and with feet made of serpents, holding a shield and whip. Some mythologists also placed Abraxas among the Egyptian gods. The Swiss psychoanalyst Carl Jung, who was fascinated by Gnosticism and practiced occult spirituality,[23] wore a ring bearing the image of Abraxas and described him as:

> Truly the terrible one ... the sun and also the eternally
> gaping abyss of emptiness ... magnificent even as
> the lion at the very moment when he strikes his prey
> down. His beauty is like the beauty of a spring
> morn.... He is the monster of the underworld.... He
> is the bright light of day and the deepest night of
> madness.... He is the mightiest manifest being, and
> in him creation becomes frightened of itself.[24]

This esoteric view of God is only a logical extension of the many texts that identify the voice of the true God with the words spoken by the serpent of Genesis. The "Female Spiritual

Principle," the heavenly Eve, who has the true knowledge of God, enters the snake, called the "Teacher,"[25] and teaches Adam and Eve the true way of salvation. The snake is the true prophet, the revealer of divine truth. He is "the one who is wiser than all of them."[26] It obviously follows that Jesus, the final teacher of Gnostic wisdom, brings the same kind of revelation as that brought by the serpent.

THE FALSE GOD OF GNOSTICISM

Consistently, in all the Gnostic texts, the false God who leads believers astray is the Creator God of the Bible.[27] Because he created the physical world, the God of the Bible is consistently called a fool. He thinks that, as Creator, he is the true and living God, but he is not.[28] He is rather a cosmic fool. Thus he is called Samael, the "blind one." He does not know that Sophia is the "Mother of the Universe."[29] Thus Jesus in *The Gospel of Thomas* reveals the real truth: "My [physical] mother [gave me falsehood], but [My] true [Mother] gave me life."[30] The physical world is illusion, as the Hindus and Buddhists believe. In the Gnostic texts, the God of the Bible is "ignorant, arrogant,[31] conceited, disdainful, stupid, mad,[32] assassin ... a perfect object for Gnostic hatred and contempt."[33] He is a joke, because he makes the statement, "I am the LORD and there is no other,"[34] not knowing that the Father of the All is above him. More than that, he is a demon who creates fellow diabolical beings, one of which is Belias "who is over the abyss of Hades."[35] He even looks like the Devil himself, "a lion-faced serpent with glittering eyes of fire."[36] Finally, Gnosticism affirms that the Old Testament God is the Devil himself. He is the great demon who rules over the lowest part of the underworld.[37]

Yahweh got what any devil deserves—hell. The feminine goddess, Zoe, Sophia's daughter, reprimanded him for his blind arrogance in thinking that he is the one true God. "She breathed upon his face, and her breath became an angel of fire and that very angel shackled [him] and threw him down into Hell, under the abyss."[38]

One would imagine these ancient myths to have passed into the black hole of abandoned primitive lore. But this ancient view of God continues today, with different terminology. A Presbyterian scholar, Lloyd Geering, declares, "The time for glorifying the Almighty God who supposedly rules from on high is now over."[39] A Jewish feminist, Naomi Goldenburg, in 1979 made the bold prophecy, "We women are going to bring an end to God."[40] She describes religious feminism as "engaged in the slow execution of Christ and Yahweh."[41] Episcopal Bishop, John Shelby Spong confesses that "life has taught us that theism is dead."[42] Finally, a Lutheran scholar dismisses the Creator God of the Bible as "insane,"[43] "pathologically violent,"[44] and suffering from "multiple personality disorder,"[45] conditions that resulted from "an archaic first-century understanding of God as a theistic being living in the sky."[46] Until recently, hardly anyone in America questioned the reality of the Bible's view of God. Now, we see a poster in a San Diego gay pride parade aimed at the Christian view of God: "He's your God; they're your rules; you go to Hell."

These modern rejections of the God of the Bible demonstrate the resilience of the old Gnostic views. One has to admire the deep consistency with which these ancient radical thinkers developed their religious understanding of existence, which may partially explain why Gnosticism is still a live option for intelligent people as we begin to structure the religious thinking of the third millennium.

THE GOD OF THE BIBLICAL JESUS

We enter a different world when we open the pages of the biblical Gospels. The birds are singing, happy that the heavenly Father is feeding them. The yellow and purple lilies of the field catch our eye, more resplendent than well-dressed kings. Bread

and wine, children and families, marriage and health are all celebrated. Gone is the polemic against the Creator. Everywhere is
an appreciation for the astonishing beauty of his work. In one
very real sense, to quote an old English hymn, "God's in his
heaven, all's right with the world." I'm not trying to paint a cock-
eyed, optimistic Disney version of yesteryear, with Jesus in the
starring role, birds flying around his head, and laughing children
at his feet. But the biblical Jesus clearly accepts the physical
world as a good place to be, made by God, the good Creator who
causes the blessings of sun and rain to be given to all people,
deserving or not.[47] According to Jesus, the gift of physical life is
itself a wonderful thing, to be enjoyed by everyone. Frankly, for
a man who ended his short life the victim of unspeakable human
cruelty, reduced to fleshy pulp before dying in excruciating pain
on a Roman torture machine, such optimism is breathtaking.
What kind of worldview can explain this enigma?

Jesus' God is the God of Old Testament Judaism. According
to the well-known New Testament scholar, N.T. Wright:

> The Jews believed their god, *YHWH* [Yahweh], was
> the only god, and that all others (including the "one
> god" of Stoics and other pantheists) were idols. …
> Jesus shared the belief that Israel's god was the only
> true god.[48]

According to the biblical Gospels, as a young boy, Jesus
amazed the teachers of Scripture by his knowledge of God's
Word.[49] Arriving at adulthood, Jesus based his life's goal on an
Old Testament text about the God of Scripture. He was called to
"prepare the way of the Lord."[50] At the end of that "way" as he
arrived in Jerusalem, "he came in the name of the Lord."[51] Jesus
revealed the essential principle of his life, based on "the great
and first commandment," namely, "You shall love the Lord your
God with all your heart and with all your soul and with all your
mind."[52]

Who is the God Jesus serves and worships?

The Bible begins, not with an abstract speculation about the unfathomable inner nature of the unknown God or even with the reassuring promise that Jesus is our Savior, but with a programmatic declaration of God as Creator of the universe. The Bible talks about where we come from before it tells us how to be saved from the mess we have produced. In the ancient pagan world, people worshipped nature or the forces of nature as "god." That is why they made idols of natural things. Through Moses came the ringing counteraffirmation, unique in that world: No! "In the beginning, God created the heavens and the earth." The heavens and the earth did not create themselves, or always exist. They are the product of a free and determined act of God. They are in their good and rightful place as mere creatures; only God is divine. The Bible's opening salvo says it all. In a certain sense, after the first verse of the Bible, everything else is commentary.

The God of Jesus is the Creator of heaven and earth. For instance, the biblical Jesus understood historical, human time as beginning with God's act of creation. To situate an event in history, he used the words, "from the beginning of the creation that God created until now."[53] When asked about the goodness of marriage, Jesus immediately deferred to the early chapters of Genesis: "Have you not read," he asked his questioners, "that he who created them from the beginning made them male and female?"[54]

As we have seen, no Gnostic text would honor the God of the biblical Jesus. Interestingly, present-day Hollywood never, with a few exceptions, begins a film with "In the beginning God ..." In *Star Wars*, "the Force" is the Buddhist notion of spiritual energy. In *Pocahontas*, the spirit of nature inhabits all things. In *The Lion King*, God is the impersonal spirit joining everything together—stars, earth, animals living and dead. In *The Matrix*, physical life is an illusion. How different is the God of the Bible!

So different that the prophet Isaiah in the eighth century BC must have had a sneak preview of *The Lion King*, for he says, "He [God] sits above the circle of the earth."[55] To be sure, God is lovingly concerned with his creatures, but in his essence, God is not part of the circle of life. He is transcendent above it as its Creator, as Jesus says, "heaven ... is the throne of God ... earth ... is his footstool."[56]

Such is the God of Jesus. Forty-three times in the gospel of Matthew Jesus referred to God as Father. At one point, Jesus prayed, "I thank you, Father, Lord of heaven and earth."[57] Here, "Father" clearly means "Creator" or generator. But in the mouth of Jesus, the God of the Old Testament had never been made more personal. In the Old Testament, Israel is called God's "firstborn son" when she comes out of Egypt,[58] and once in a while God is called "Father,"[59] but these references are few. Jesus, however, moved our understanding of God to a new level. There is nothing more intimate than the deep relationship revealed in the Gospels between the Father and the Son. Just before his death, Jesus cried out, "Abba, Father [literally, 'Daddy'], all things are possible for you. Remove this cup from me. Yet not what I will, but what you will."[60] Yet in spite of this intimacy, twenty-two of Jesus' references to the Father place that Father as the one "who is in heaven." Why did Jesus emphasize this so much?

He is teaching and respecting the *transcendence* of God, that is, the fact that God is different from the creation he made. God is not to be found within creation as some kind of energy, but is distinct from it as a potter is different from clay. God's transcendence does not make him a deadbeat or absent dad. On the contrary, Jesus asked, "Are not two sparrows sold for a penny? And not one of them will fall to the ground apart from your Father. But even the hairs of your head are all numbered."[61] In this very text, where Jesus taught the close presence of God in his care for his creatures, he also said that anyone who wishes to be associated with him as his disciple must know and acknowledge "my Father who is in heaven."[62]

Jesus' teaching on prayer made the same point, as we shall examine in more depth. He did not encourage people to seek "the god within" in order to "pray like the pagans," but to address the personal Father-Creator who is in heaven.[63] When Peter declared who Jesus is, Jesus made it clear that the truth comes to Peter not by some deep intuition or inner search. "Flesh and blood," said Jesus, "has not revealed this to you, but my Father who is in heaven."[64] In other words, Jesus made the point that this revelation concerning his true nature did not originate from the created order, but from the God who created it.

On earth, the disciples of Jesus did good works to give glory to the Father in heaven.[65] What Jesus demanded of his disciples he practiced himself. "When the crowd ... saw the mute speaking, the crippled healthy, the lame walking, and the blind seeing ... they glorified the God of Israel."[66] Earth or nature is not worshipped as divine, but serves to glorify its Creator. Earth is the God-given place where we are to serve him. The temptation is always present to find in nature all that we need. This, said Jesus, is the great spiritual struggle. "No one can serve two masters, for either he will hate the one and love the other, or he will be devoted to the one and despise the other."[67]

Who are these two masters? Jesus gave the answer: God and earthly things.[68] Thus Jesus answered the Tempter with an unambiguous statement from the Old Testament: "You shall worship the Lord your God and him only shall you serve."[69]

Paul, one of the apostles whom the risen Jesus appointed, speaks of only two ways to be religious. Each involves worshipping and serving. Paul saw the spiritual struggle, and defined it in a manner similar to that used by Jesus. Writing to the first-century church in pagan Rome, Paul described the human condition of rebellion against God the Creator in the following way: "They exchanged the truth of God for the lie, and worshiped and served created things rather than the Creator—who is forever praised. Amen."[70]

Notice a number of similarities:

- Paul's "created things" recalls Jesus' "earthly things"
- Paul's "the Creator who is blessed forever" recalls Jesus' "God"
- Paul's "the truth and the lie" recalls the immediate teaching of Jesus about "light and darkness"[71] and the teaching in the following chapter about "the broad way" and "the narrow way"[72]
- Paul's "they worshipped and served" recalls Jesus' "You shall worship the Lord your God and him only shall you serve"

In other words, both Jesus and Paul associate a certain kind of worship or service with a certain concept of God. In fact, both identify only two. One kind of worship or spirituality is false and leads to destruction. The other is true and leads to life.

Both for the biblical Jesus and for Paul, as for Bob Dylan, "you've got to serve somebody." But how do you choose whom to serve, in a bewildering variety of options? In the early 1990s, my wife and I hosted a lovely woman from Moscow, who spent three weeks with us while doing research in her field of deaf education. The first time she entered a supermarket with us, she stood paralyzed at the sight. "How do you decide what to buy?" she exclaimed. At home, she had two choices: meat was there, or it was not there. Paul and Jesus indicate that the myriad of spiritualities come down to two options: worshipping and serving the Creator of the created order, or the false "god of this world."

Just as Gnosticism in its purest and clearest form describes the Creator God of the Bible as the Devil, and worships the Serpent, so Christianity dismisses the Serpent as the epitome of evil and worships the Creator as blessed forever. As Jesus faces the Tempter, he declared, "Be gone, Satan! For it is written, 'You shall worship the Lord your God and him only shall you serve.'"[73] Jesus came to disarm and bind this false claimant to divinity, and one day will cast the Accuser of the brethren, the Dragon, into the great abyss.[74]

What the Goddess is supposed to do to Yahweh, Christ actually does to Satan. In the end, neither system avoids the ultimate states of heaven (God's domain) and hell (those who oppose him). They simply differ wildly over the identity and nature of the inhabitants. Such antithetical views of God lead us to expect two equally different accounts of the message Jesus brings about God's kingdom.

CHAPTER 2

THE MESSAGE OF JESUS

If those who lead you say to you, "See, the Kingdom is in the sky,"
then the birds of the air will precede you. If they say to you,
"It is in the sea," then the fish will precede you.
THE GOSPEL OF THOMAS 3

And Jesus said to them, "Truly, I say to you, there are some
standing here who will not taste death until they see the
kingdom of God after it has come with power."
MARK 9:1

In our global push for democracy, we hardly remember the word "kingdom." It appears in computer games and mythic movies. Those few kings and queens that still remain as heads of state are mere figureheads, not powerful rulers who dictate the laws of their kingdoms. So, it is hard for us to identify with Jesus' constant kingdom theme in the Gospels. The word "kingdom" appears fifty-four times in the biblical gospel of Matthew alone. The term "kingdom" is used twenty-two times in the Gnostic *Gospel of Thomas,* and relatively often in other Gnostic gospels as well.[1] That both the Gnostic and the biblical traditions emphasize the "kingdom of God" indicates the centrality of this theme in the message of the historical Jesus.

THE MESSAGE OF THE GNOSTIC JESUS

In the Gnostic *Gospel of Thomas* a number of kingdom sayings
have no obvious Gnostic connotations and sound like versions of
those of the biblical Gospels. Readers of the New Testament
would recognize sayings that sound surprisingly "orthodox."
This is why some scholars argue for an early date for *Thomas*. The
kingdom is like "a mustard seed";[2] the kingdom of heaven is
"for the poor";[3] the kingdom is like "a man who has found a
good seed," or "a pearl";[4] it is like "man who found a treasure in
a field and became rich";[5] it is like "leaven concealed" in
dough";[6] it is like "a woman who lost all the meal from her jar
without knowing it";[7] like a man "who has a hundred sheep who
cares for the one more than the ninety-nine";[8] and those who
"enter the kingdom of my Father" are "those who do the will of
my Father [who] are my brothers and my mother."[9]

THE KEY TO THE GNOSTIC KINGDOM

Doubtless, part of the attraction of *Thomas* is the seemingly
"mainline Christian" orientation of much of its material. But, there
is more here than meets the eye. The key to the hidden "interpretation"[10] of these kingdom teachings is found in the sayings that
convey clearly Gnostic truth. No one has yet claimed to break the
code of the entire structure of *Thomas*, but the book consistently
juxtaposes canonical and Gnostic sayings. Biblical sayings are set
in the context of and interpreted by Gnostic teaching.

A superficial rational reading of this gospel will miss the
point entirely. Modern day Gnostic teachers understand this and
meditate on *Thomas* as mystical "holy scripture." James
Robinson, editor of the translation of the Nag Hammadi texts,
exhorts modern Gnostics: "We scholars have completed our
work, it is now time for a Gnostic to write about the Gnostic
scriptures."[11] Today there are many such Gnostic writers.[12]

One is Tau Malachi Eben Ha-Elijah, an "elder" in the Sophian
Tradition of Gnostic Christianity. Malachi has a long experience

in Christian Gnosticism, Rosicrucian philosophy, and the holy Kabbalah, as well as in the Eastern spirituality of Buddhism and Sufism. In his meditations on *Thomas* he explains how to find the interpretation that Jesus promises. One draws not only from the well of the text but also from the well of one's own soul. Initiates in the mystical spirituality of Gnosticism apply their own deepening experience of gnosis to open up the depths of the written text. In *Thomas* Jesus declares, "He who drinks from my mouth will become like me. I will become he, and the things that are hidden will be revealed."[13] To become like Jesus is to draw out the mystical layers hidden in the text and in one's own soul. "Only in this way," says Malachi, "are 'the things that are hidden' revealed."[14] Malachi is proposing that *Thomas* be read as a text for mystical transport.

His treatment of the canonical saying about the kingdom as a mustard seed, found in *Thomas* and mentioned above, seems to point us in the right direction in understanding how the book is to be read and understood. Malachi proposes a "spiritual" reading and hearing of this text. Seeing the kingdom as a mustard seed is to understand it as a sort of atomic spiritual energy, what he calls "the power of Keter."[15] This power or "light force" is both imperceptible yet "everywhere in Creation secretly waiting to be realized and actualized." It is the "smallest thing, which is the most powerful thing."[16] Also, a "shift in consciousness [to an awareness of this reality] is the smallest movement whose effect is incredible."[17] In this way, Malachi successfully interprets all the above-mentioned biblical canonical sayings about the kingdom.

At the beginning of the book, in Saying 3, right after the introduction, Jesus gives teaching on the kingdom. The saying seems to be programmatic for all that follows and employs the procedure mentioned above. Jesus makes a most unusual statement about the kingdom, with *no* parallel in the biblical Gospels. This statement then determines the interpretation of a well-known biblical phrase about the kingdom that follows. To that is then appended another Gnostic comment. Notice how it works:

> If those who lead you say to you, "See, the Kingdom is in the sky," then the birds of the air will precede you. If they say to you, "It is in the sea," then the fish will precede you.

In essence, *Thomas* begins with a polemical argument against the "leaders." Since, as far as we know, the Pharisees did not speak about the "kingdom," *Thomas* is doubtless referring either to biblically oriented teachers or even the gospel writers, Matthew, Mark, Luke, and John themselves. Such "leaders" claim to know about the kingdom but actually teach falsehood. The falsehood they teach is found in their material and earthly view of the kingdom. *Thomas'* Jesus corrects this, asserting that those who seek the kingdom in the sky or in the sea are inferior to the birds and the fish. That is, those whose false perception of the kingdom includes the physical cosmos have become blinded to a deeper, exclusively spiritual sense of the kingdom and are more ignorant than beasts.

THE KINGDOM IS INSIDE OF YOU

Here is the technique. This Gnostic saying now reinterprets the well-known phrase from Luke 17:21, which is then quoted: "Rather, the kingdom is inside you." According to the Jesus of *Thomas*, people who identify the kingdom with the physical, external cosmos fail to see that the kingdom is an internal, spiritual affair by which we come to know ourselves.[18] The Gnostic gospel finishes off the explanation: "And it is outside of you. When you come to know yourselves, then you will become known." This further Gnostic commentary introduces the theme of "knowing yourself" as the key to the mystery[19] of the kingdom, as we shall see below.

Here is the key to the kingdom message of the Jesus of Gnosticism: "The kingdom is within you." That is to say, the kingdom is not an observable but a purely interior and spiritual phenomenon. So Jesus declares later in *Thomas*, "Do not ask when the kingdom comes … it is spread out on the earth and men do not see it."[20] The kingdom does not *come* in the sense of a historical event. It is deliberately esoteric, hidden, purely spiritual, and, by definition, has no outward, visible, or temporal form. It is discovered not by looking around but by "going within."

This may seem a little abstract and unimportant, but the theory has practical implications. I received an astute e-mail around the time I was writing this section that made this very clear. "Dear Dr. Jones," it read, "you make a big distinction between monism and theism, between understanding God as the divine force within the world over against God as the transcendent Creator above it. But it seems to me," continued the note, "that Jesus was a monist because he says quite clearly in Luke 17:21, 'the kingdom is inside of you.'" I will discuss this text in its biblical context later in the chapter. My correspondent, like the Gnostics, took the "kingdom" concept as a symbol of human potential, understood by an elite few. The Gnostic Jesus reveals a "gnosis" and endows believers with personal power that changes them and changes the world. As revealer, he brings to the "ignorant," to "creatures of oblivion" empowering knowledge about the inner kingdom. This explosive kingdom teaching is expressed in a myriad of ways in the Nag Hammadi texts.

GNOSIS AND THE KINGDOM

In *The Secret Book of James*[21] Jesus reveals that the Gnostic believer is "equal" to him,[22] and that having this "gnosis" is the equivalent of "receiving the kingdom."[23] Knowing yourself in this way, as the very equal of Jesus, is to be "filled with the kingdom."[24] It's like being told by the President, "Make yourself at home. You have the run of the White House and can sign documents in my name, because you and I are one and the same. Feel free to use even the War Room!" To know yourself is to discover in yourself "the incomprehensible, inconceivable ... Father, the perfect one."[25] This definition of the kingdom makes it a symbol of pure spirituality and human power. Believers who have "received the kingdom" are those who have received the knowledge of their original higher selves that existed in God before the mistake of the creation of the physical cosmos. The Gnostic Jesus reminds them of their "heavenly origin." Since they possess all the attributes of God, they are from the imperishable light, way beyond the Creator and his angels. Jesus brings to them the knowledge of their "faultlessness," for, like God, they are sinless. Like God, they are "limitless and immeasurable," "indissoluble and eternal," "holy, imperishable spirits."[26] Like the ultimate, unknowable God, whose nature they share, Gnostics understand themselves as "solitary ones,"[27] unencumbered by earthly ties. Being a "solitary one" means finding the ultimate kingdom from which you emanated and to which you will return. The kingdom is made up of those who share the divine nature. One becomes a "passerby" or a "freeman" with no entanglements with the physical world. The kingdom is redefined as the original spiritual unity of all immortal divine beings.

To enter the "kingdom," a Gnostic must deny[28] or renounce the world.[29] This is not the "world, the flesh and the Devil,"[30] — the world of moral evil. This is the world of created reality, of sexual and moral distinctions, of marriage and family, of anything that reminds you of the Creator's "evil" work. To enter the kingdom, you must destroy the works of the "false god," by joining the opposites[31]—an internal affair that you do to yourself. Being like a child (in the genderless sense) entitles you to entrance into the kingdom.[32] Thus, to enter the kingdom, declares the Jesus of the *Gospel of Thomas*, Mary must divest herself of her femaleness and make herself male.[33]

The Gospel of Philip gives the full measure of the knowledge Jesus brings: "You saw the Spirit, you became spirit. You saw the Christ, you became Christ. You saw [the Father, you] shall become Father."[34] The Gnostic Jesus brings secret knowledge that awakens people from the sleep of ignorance and brings them to an awareness of their innate godhood. One is "no longer a Christian: one is a Christ."[35]

THE SERPENT AND THE KINGDOM

As noted above, this Jesus brings the message that was already revealed by the Serpent.[36] The Serpent is not the evil Tempter. He is the Instructor, "more crafty than ... all."[37] Simply put, the message of Christ or the coming of the kingdom is the declaration of the Serpent, who, in as many words, reveals that man is God and God is man. The "kingdom" in the Gnostic gospels is the one promised by the Serpent.

For this Jesus, it is folly to "seek first the kingdom" in the context of the history of the world, or to identify the kingdom as the fulfillment of biblical and human history. Such a false route would only lead to ignorance and destruction. No miracles of healing or miracles over nature herald the kingdom's arrival. The natural world is not worth saving, and the kingdom is a purely spiritual inner reality. Remember: "The kingdom is inside of you."

THE MESSAGE OF THE BIBLICAL JESUS

To many of us history was a boring subject we took in school, but we all have an insatiable appetite for true stories. As I write these lines, President Bill Clinton's *My Life* has just hit the stores. The prepublication orders paid for the immense advance of ten million dollars the ex-president was able to negotiate with Knopf. We all want to know what really happened with the blue dress and the Somalian aspirin factory.

THE KINGDOM IN TIME AND SPACE

This kind of factual history is essential to understanding the biblical Jesus and his message about the kingdom, for two reasons: (1) The biblical Jesus is truly human and participates in time-space events, and (2) the biblical Jesus is the Son of God, the Creator, who creates the biblical view of history! If this is true, then the biblical Gospels are not mystical texts, but are historical accounts of real events, and the kingdom, though spiritual, is also physical and historical.

According to the Bible, God created history, and so it is good and worthy of our attention. According to the Bible, history is not just a series of meaningless events—atoms randomly colliding in space—but divinely appointed occurrences. This is also true of our individual lives. Essentially, the Bible begins with the statement: "In the beginning, God created" history, that is, the history of the cosmos, "heaven and earth." If history in this large sense has a beginning, made by a personal, intentional divine being, then history has meaning and will arrive at a meaningful end. Each event is full of significance in relationship to God's rule over the world. Each individual is significant in his role as a divinely appointed steward, overseeing the good order of things. This was the idyllic arrangement of the original cosmic kingdom, with Adam and Eve as vice-kings, but it did not last.

In the Bible, God remains King,[38] but humans rebelled against his rule, betraying their Creator in the fall. Subsequent history contains both the failure of human kingdoms and divine initiatives to restore a righteous kingdom on the earth. Having lost their place of privilege in God's ordered cosmos, humans must hope in the action of God to restore what has been lost and what they so desire.

THE KINGDOM IS GOD'S

In the Bible, the kingdom is not "within you"—it comes from God, from the outside. Jesus taught his disciples to pray: "*Your* kingdom come ... for *yours* is the kingdom."[39] Thus God, not fallen humanity, established Israel as a "*kingdom* of priests" and said they are his "treasured possession among all peoples, for all the earth is mine."[40] In other words, God, in establishing Israel, showed to a world in rebellion what the true kingdom looks like.

Thus he promised to King David, "I will establish the throne of his (David's line) kingdom forever."[41]

Alas, like Adam, Israel also failed; so God, through the prophets, because of his original promise to David, announced a final kingdom that will not fail. The birth of a child whose name will be "Wonderful Counselor, Mighty God, Everlasting Father, Prince of Peace" will usher in a "kingdom of justice and … righteousness,"[42] a kingdom "that shall never be destroyed … and shall stand forever."[43] Such a perspective takes into account both human sin and God's indomitable intention to save. The kingdom will come.

It is therefore inevitable that in the biblical gospel account, Jesus' ministry will have to do with this history of the kingdom and its fulfillment. Luke records the birth of Jesus as that of the promised child who will sit on David's throne and who establishes this righteous and everlasting kingdom.[44] This emphasis on the *history* of the kingdom is also to be expected. From the start, Jesus called his kingdom message "gospel," which does not mean a gem of spiritual wisdom but a piece of history-making news.

THE INAUGURATION CEREMONY

Jesus' kingdom inauguration ceremony was not public or auspicious. With a five-week-old beard, a filthy body and clothes, matted hair, and a skeleton-thin frame, the Jesus who emerged from the foreboding backcountry after five weeks of spiritual conflict and physical deprivation was not your well-groomed TV newscaster or your classic crown prince, paraded in glory before his adoring people. But Jesus could not *announce* the good news of the kingdom until he had *made* the news, and to make it, he had to get down and dirty, even bloody. At the beginning of his public activity, Jesus could have said any number of things: "Three square meals a day is not all it is cracked up to be," or "the view from the top of the temple is not worth the hike." What he did say was earthshaking, headline news: "With me and what I have just achieved, history has reached its point of culmination; the final reign of God's kingdom is about to begin."[45]

The extent of Jesus' claim here must not be missed. He was claiming that, on the basis of what he had just achieved in the Judean wilderness, the final utopian state of earthly affairs and the culmination of human history had just arrived. As C. S. Lewis said, "Either this man was, and is, the Son of God: or else a madman or something worse. You can shut Him up for a fool, you can spit at Him and kill Him as a demon; or you can fall at His feet and call Him Lord and God. But let us not come with any patronizing nonsense about His being a great human teacher."[46]

Let's back up the gospel tape. The gospel of Mark began the story of Jesus by citing three Old Testament prophecies about preparing for the end of history and about the coming of the Lord. In Mark, John the Baptist helped "prepare the way" both by calling for repentance and by identifying Jesus as the "chosen one." The people also "prepare the way" by coming out into the wilderness, being baptized by John, and repenting of their sins. This represents a break with the past for those repenting, but Jesus is also breaking with the past in a more dramatic way.

He "prepared the way" by doing two things. First, he got baptized by John, as a representative of the people. Second, he prepares the way by defeating the Devil in the wilderness. This "binding of the strong man," as he later called it,[47] cleared the way for his astonishing declaration about the fulfillment of history. In other words, this private battle with the Devil, the only truly successful one in history to that point, allowed him to begin his public activity with his astonishing claim about the arrival of the end-time kingdom of God. Probably, he alone understood the significance of that desert encounter, which allowed him to proclaim and to begin the culminating event of human history.

Essential to that event was his defeat of evil. The message brought by the biblical Jesus is about God and the meaning of history. His amazing good news is that God is in the business of saving history by bringing it to a high and morally satisfying climax. The kingdom is integrally related to the defeat of evil.

LIFE IN THE KINGDOM

Jesus was intent on showing what life in God's righteous kingdom looks like. In the synagogue in Nazareth at the beginning of his public ministry, he read a text everyone knew:

> The Spirit of the Lord is upon me, because he has anointed me to proclaim good news to the poor. He has sent me to proclaim liberty to the captives and recovering of sight to the blind, to set at liberty those who are oppressed, to proclaim the year of the Lord's favor.[48]

What blew everyone away were the words he uttered as he sat down. "Today this Scripture has been fulfilled in your hearing."[49] Everyone knew he meant it. The time of the final kingdom had arrived. This was the reason for Jesus' miracles of healing. He was not performing magic tricks or trying to wow people with his spiritual prowess. He was showing the character of the kingdom of God that had arrived with his coming.

At the beginning, even John the Baptist was stunned by the implications of Jesus' ministry. Not sure he was really understanding, he sent some of his disciples to ask Jesus, "Are you the one who is to come, or shall we look for another?" When they arrived they saw Jesus healing "people of diseases and plagues and evil spirits, and on many who were blind he bestowed sight."[50] Jesus' reply to them picked up the text he cited in the synagogue in Nazareth: "Go and tell John what you have seen and heard: the blind receive their sight, the lame walk, lepers are cleansed, and the deaf hear, the dead are raised up, the poor have good news preached to them."[51]

These miracles show Jesus' interest in the physical well-being of those who come to him. His other miracles also indicate that the arrival of the final kingdom has also material, cosmic implications. He calmed the stormy sea, walked on water, multiplied a lunch of bread and fish to feed thousands, and changed water into wine. Though all these miracles teach deep spiritual truths, they are not just imaginary myths. Those who received the bread and fish were so full that the disciples had to pick up the leftovers.

Of course, there are also social implications. In Jesus' utopian kingdom, he raised the downtrodden, celebrated and blessed children, honored and taught women, fed the hungry, shared a table with sinners and social outcasts, offered mercy to tax collectors, gave hope to the poor, comforted the grieving, sheltered the widows and the orphans, strengthened marriage, ennobled parents, humbled the proud, secured an inheritance for the humble, satisfied the spiritual hunger of those who come to him, and was "no respecter of persons."

The blend of healing and nature miracles with righteous actions, and the defeat of evil and the Devil, stops us from reducing the message and kingdom of Jesus to a mere political, social or ecological program for revolutionary this-worldly change. There is so much more at stake in Jesus' message, as is indicated by the complexity of his kingdom teaching. I ask you humbly to "hang in" as I speak of complexity. It is so important to understand the rich, complex ministry of Jesus. Your understanding of what Jesus did will affect the way you live, even if you are already a Christian believer.

THE TWO SIDES OF JESUS' MESSAGE ABOUT THE KINGDOM

The confusing thing about the kingdom according to the Bible is that Jesus makes seemingly contradictory statements about how and when it will come. I sometimes tease my wife because her very helpful ability to see all sides of a question *can* become a handicap. She says, "On the one hand ... but on the other hand ..." until sometimes she doesn't know what to decide. But my wife can't be completely wrong (and is right most of the time!), since Jesus has an "on the one hand" and "on the other hand" approach to the kingdom.

On the one hand, he says that the righteous rule of God, "the kingdom," *has already arrived.* On the other hand, he clearly affirms that *it is still to come.* He is certainly not dithering, or in two minds, so we need to understand what he means.

With regards to its *present manifestation,* John the Baptist declared that, with Jesus, the kingdom is about to appear.[52] Jesus himself, right at the beginning of his public ministry, stated, as noted above, that his defeat of Satan in the wilderness causes the reign/rule of God to draw near. His works of liberation and healing made the same point.[53]

With regard to the kingdom as a *future event,* Jesus taught his disciples to pray, "your kingdom come," clearly indicating that it is not yet fully and finally here. The kingdom is the future gift for those who, on this earth, are presently persecuted[54]—like Jesus himself, as the persecuted one *par excellence,* who declares at the Last Supper: "I will not drink again of the fruit of the vine until that day when I drink it new in the kingdom of God."[55] The kingdom is clearly a future reality. Jesus thus speaks of the Son of Man who will return in kingly glory to bring in the final kingdom.[56]

Which one is true? Present or future? The Gnostic texts solve the problem by getting rid of the future. Everything spiritual is already here. There is no future for the physical creation. The biblical conundrum has often been resolved by arguing for one or the other—*either* Jesus proclaimed the presence of the kingdom in this spiritual sense, and notions of the future are out-of-date Jewish ideas in the process of being ditched, *or* he announced only the future of the kingdom and the presence of the kingdom was a later addition by the gospel writers who wanted to make the earthly Jesus more impressive.

ALREADY AND NOT YET

The most satisfying answer to a problem is the one that does the most justice to all of the facts. It seems obvious that Jesus, in citing the high hopes of Old Testament prophecy, spoke about the future coming of the kingdom as a great and glorious event. However, the other fact is his undeniable references to the kingdom's present arrival in his own ministry of healing and deliverance. The two aspects can be resolved by understanding that the future, glorious kingdom is mysteriously *present* in the person of Jesus, its King.

Jesus affirms the presence of the kingdom in the text, Luke 17:21, that my e-mail correspondent used as a trump card against the biblical gospel. In the famous phrase, "the kingdom is within you," the preposition "within" is ambiguous in Greek. It can mean either "inside," in the sense of something internal, or "among," like a soldier in his company, or "in the middle" like a lake in the middle of a forest. The specific meaning must be decided by the context.

In Luke 17, Jesus was arguing about the kingdom against his opponents, the Pharisees. They skeptically demanded extravagant signs as proof that Jesus was authentic and that the kingdom had come (v. 20). For demanding such signs, Jesus called these opponents "an evil and adulterous generation."[57] Jesus could not tell this "evil and adulterous generation" (who had already determined in their hearts to kill him)[58] how spiritual they were by possessing the "kingdom within." Far from possessing deep inner spirituality and insight, the Pharisees were demonstrating willful spiritual blindness.

For those with eyes to see, however, Jesus was revealing the mystery of the *presence* of the long-expected kingdom.[59] Though the Jewish leaders failed to see it, the kingdom had come and was present among them, right under their noses, because Jesus, the king, was present among them.

In the light of this context, the phrase should be translated, "the kingdom is in your midst," as Jesus said without ambiguity elsewhere, "But if it is by the Spirit of God that I cast out demons, then the kingdom of God has come upon you."[60] We do not find the kingdom within us. It comes upon us by God's action through Jesus.

"I have come to realize," my e-mail correspondent admitted, having heard my arguments about the passage, "that I prefer being a pagan monist." For him, the Bible was not decisive. Though superficially suggesting a monistic notion of spirituality, this teaching of Jesus actually teaches the very opposite. "Going within" according to the Bible will not bring the kingdom, but rather spiritual blindness, for when we go within, we discover our hearts, which are "desperately wicked."[61] The kingdom is among us only because God has come to seek us out in the person of his Son.

A specific event in the life of Jesus puts it all together. Just after Peter's confession outside a town called Caesarea Philippi, Jesus made a significant declaration about the kingdom: "There are some standing here who will not taste death until they see the kingdom of God after it has come *with power*."[62] Here Jesus unambiguously states that there will be a future, glorious coming of the kingdom, it will be a massive demonstration of power, and some of those listening to him would see it happen. A week later, Jesus took Peter, James, and John to a mountain where he was transformed before their eyes, and his clothes became radiantly, intensely white. At that moment Elijah and Moses appeared and talked with Jesus. The disciples, already terrified, then heard a voice from heaven, like the one at the baptism, which rang out: "This is my beloved Son; listen to him."[63]

THE KINGDOM COMES WITH THE KING

On the mountain, the disciples experienced the glorious presence of the kingdom that broke out in the person of Jesus. They saw him for who he really was, the King of the kingdom that soon will dawn with immense power. They saw both the present kingdom (for they saw who Jesus is) and a glimpse of the kingdom in its future form (Jesus' transfiguration is a hint of his glorified state after his resurrection).

This complex of ideas—the presence and future of the kingdom, its periodic breaking through and its future appearance with power, plus the veiling and the unveiling of the person of Jesus as both simple prophet and all-powerful king—constitute what Jesus calls "the mystery of the kingdom."[64] In other words, the person of Jesus becomes clearer as we understand the nature of his message and mission.

In dealing with the subject of Jesus' kingdom, we see once again that the Gnostic version and the biblical version are in direct opposition. The Gnostic kingdom stands for a mystical state of super-consciousness in which you receive gnosis about the transcendent nature of your being. The biblical kingdom is an event in time, seen in the person of Jesus, which occurs to bring about the redemption of God's good but fallen creation.

If there is mystery surrounding the kingdom, it is because there is mystery in the person of Jesus, the King. Both the Gnostic and biblical Gospels give us important information about Jesus, both with regard to his humanity and to his divinity.

CHAPTER 3

THE HUMANITY OF JESUS

For my mother [gave me falsehood], but [my] true [Mother] gave me life.
THE GOSPEL OF THOMAS 101

We believe ... in one Lord Jesus Christ ...
Who was made man,
and was crucified also for us under Pontius Pilate;
he suffered and was buried.
THE NICENE CREED

I love to meet new people, and ask, "Where are you from?" Their background helps me know something of what has influenced them as I situate them in their context. With a good friend, I recently coauthored a book entitled *Cracking Da Vinci's Code*, which engendered quite a bit of public interest. A reporter for *The Observer* of London called me from England and wanted especially to interview *me* rather than my coauthor, because he had heard I was English. Immediately, we were on the same wavelength. He knew where I was from.

Imagine asking Jesus, "Where are you from?" He might answer with a smile, "Do you want the long or the short answer?" His "short answer," about his birth mother and ethnic background, will depend on which Jesus you are asking—the Gnostic Jesus or the biblical Jesus.

The Gnostic Jesus

Birth

Asking the Gnostic Jesus, "Where are you from?" will eventually receive the "long answer," about his journey through the 360 aeons that separate the human scene from the domain of the Father of the All.[1] Were you to insist, in good reporter fashion, on the details of his ethnic and family background, he will not have much to say. In all the Gnostic texts we have, there is no mention of his birthplace, his family, or his youth. Jesus appeared from nowhere, fully formed, uttering impenetrable mysteries.

The fifty-two Gnostic texts offer a variety of opinions about the birth of Jesus, but they all agree on one thing—Jesus did not have a truly *physical* birth. Jesus in *The Gospel of Thomas* specifically declared that one should prostrate oneself before him because he was *not* born of a woman.[2] Such an unborn, uncreated state is the sign of his true spirituality. In another text Jesus declares that he is eternal, "having no birth."[3]

An early form of Gnosticism was known as Docetism. Docetists believed that Jesus only appeared (the Greek verb, *dokeo* means "to seem") to be human, because the "spirit" has no dealing with evil flesh, made by an evil Creator. For them, Christ was all spirit all the time and could not be a truly physical human being. Some held that Jesus passed through Mary as through a funnel, so that he was not touched and thus affected by her physical humanity.[4] *The Gospel of Thomas* goes even further, expressing repugnance at the idea that Jesus was physically born to human parents. Jesus declares in no uncertain terms, "The one who is acquainted with father and mother will be called the son of a prostitute."[5]

One other saying in *Thomas* relates to Jesus' parents. When asked about his family,[6] the Gnostic Jesus repeated the well-known text from the gospel of Luke: "If anyone comes to me and does not hate his own father and mother and wife and children and brothers and sisters, yes, and even his own life, he cannot be my disciple."[7] But the Gnostic text adds: "For my mother [gave me falsehood], but [my] true [Mother] gave me life."

UNCLEAN FEMININITY

This remark about motherhood is not an insignificant, throwaway line. Motherhood, femininity, and sexual intercourse are major themes in other Gnostic texts, which teach that the "mother" of all the demons is physical matter,[8] and that sexual intercourse, even in marriage, is evil: "Up to today sexual intercourse continued due to the First Archon."[9] The "First Archon," literally, "First Ruler" is the God of the Bible, portrayed by the Gnostics as the evil Creator. Thus physical intercourse produces beasts, so Gnostic believers must "abandon bestiality,"[10] that is, sexual intercourse. The Gnostic Jesus commands, "Annihilate the works which pertain to the woman (that is, childbearing) ... so that they (the works of creation) may cease."[11] Gnostic teaching denigrates the physical body: "The body came from sexual desire, and sexual desire came from ... matter."[12] The language gets very colorful. Femininity is "unclean" and is called nature's "dark vagina."[13] Sexual intercourse is called the "intercourse of Darkness which will be destroyed at the end of time." The Gnostic believer must "flee from the insanity and fetters of femaleness, and embrace instead the salvation of maleness."[14]

BEGONE THE BEGATS

The Gnostic writers systematically despise motherhood as the work of the Devil. To have children and accept the role of motherhood is to fall into the evil Creator's trap. It is little wonder that the Gnostic Jesus tells us nothing about his family and that there are no endless "begats" in the Gnostic gospels to tell us the genealogy of Jesus. Gnostics believe that the alien, unknown God (of whom the Bible is ignorant) suddenly reveals himself through Christ.[15] They also see Jesus as appearing from nowhere, teaching the wisdom of pagan religion like an ancient guru. Jesus appears fully formed, unannounced by the Old Testament prophets, none of whom knew he was coming.[16] Thus the Gnostic Jesus explicitly teaches not to believe what Moses says, for the Old Scriptures are the work of a false God.[17]

In rejecting any physical family ties, the Gnostic Jesus is effectively rejecting any ethnic Jewish roots and, by the same token, any place within the national history of biblical Israel. Again, such a rejection of physical lineage is not an incidental fact of little importance. In some Gnostic texts, the rejection of biblical history reaches the level of outright mockery.

BACKGROUND: JESUS, SON OF SODOM?

The Gnostics mocked the Old Testament God as a blind fool and cast him into hell (see chapter 1), so the history of his dealings with his people inevitably gets the same treatment. Gnostics mock the Genesis account of the seven-day creation by identifying the days as seven perverse powers with gruesome animal faces. They give them names that deliberately distort well-known biblical names for God:

> The first, Athoth, who is sheep-faced. The second,
> Eloaiou, who is donkey-faced. The third, Astaphaios,
> who is [hyena]-faced. The fourth, Iao, who is serpent-
> faced with seven heads. The fifth is Sabaoth, who is
> dragon-faced. The sixth is Adonin, who is ape-faced.
> The Seventh is Sabbede, who has a luminous fire-face.
> This is the hebdomad (the "sevenness") of the week.[18]

According to another Gnostic text, all the following biblical characters are considered a "laughingstock": Adam, since he was created by this foolish Creator; Abraham, Isaac, and Jacob, since they were named by this same God; David, since he was a friend of this God; Solomon, since, with the vanity of the Creator, he took himself to be Christ; the twelve prophets, since they were actually false prophets appointed by the Creator; Moses, because he was the friend of this impostor God.[19]

When the Gnostics take an interest in biblical history, they do so in order to construct a counterhistory, turning the evil people and nations of biblical history into spiritual heroes. Those who oppose Yahweh, the blind and foolish God, are the true believers. Thus, the Great Seth (Adam and Eve's third son, according to the Bible),[20] who in some forms of Gnosticism is a "Christ" figure, is hailed as the fruit of Sodom and Gomorrah.[21] On the other hand, the inhabitants of Sodom, from which we get the term "sodomy," are a spiritual line called "the great incorruptible, … immovable race,"[22] the "sons of the Great Seth,"[23] or "the generation without a king over it."[24] Another Gnostic text speaks of the "Sodomites" who accept the teaching of the Gnostic Christ-figure, "Shem," son of Noah. These Sodomites have "a pure conscience" and were burned in brimstone and fire "unjustly."[25] Gnostic texts mock the heroes of the Bible as a foolish and cursed race, while hailing the opponents of Yahweh as the true sons of God.

In conclusion, then, we see that the Gnostic texts not only downplay Jesus' birth and history, but they reject the very idea that Jesus was born in a true, physical body. Everything physical is to be mistrusted, since the Old Testament Creator is the true enemy.

HUMANITY

A contemporary German scholar of Gnosticism notes that in Gnosticism, "the humanity of Jesus all but disappears."[26] The only Gnostic text that states the classic biblical affirmation—the Word became flesh—puts a different meaning on the phrase. Though the *Tripartite Tractate* affirms that "the Logos came into being in flesh," it is not referring to a true "incarnation." The "flesh" meant here did not come from the Creator but from "the spiritual Logos." It is a "flesh" conceived outside of time and

space, merely for the sake of being "seen, known and compre-
hended" on earth.[27]

The Gnostic Jesus knows neither pain nor moments of spiritual agony. Jesus is purely spiritual, not interested in or touched
by things essentially human—like excretion. Some Gnostics even
went so far as to state that Jesus never took bathroom breaks
because he had no need of them. You do not need bathroom
breaks if you never eat physical food.[28] It makes sense! As a spirit
being, possessed of gnosis, Jesus is untroubled in his earthly life
by the vagaries and inconveniences of the physical world. The
Gnostic Jesus glides, so to speak, two inches above the earth,
making no real contact with anything physical. This may make
him very spiritual, but any trace of humanity disappears.

This radical freedom can be expressed in two apparently contradictory ways: (1) by withdrawing from all serious contact
with physical life—asceticism, or (2) by deliberately misusing
the elements of human existence in a lifelong orgy—libertinism.
Though these two extremes seem contradictory, the contradiction is only apparent, since both approaches reject the goodness
of human, physical existence.

Gnostics, at the moment of enlightenment, are freed from the
tyranny of the physical, which is why their gospels have no genuine interest in the human Jesus. The Gnostic gospels exist only
because some Gnostics are gifted writers and wrote down what
all Gnostics know intuitively. The Gnostic gospels serve only to
confirm the believer's individual own experience. The Gnostic
gospels, in their form, are somewhat like the biblical book of
Revelation (though obviously not in their content since they reject
the future coming of Christ). This last book of the New Testament
presents itself as revelation of the *risen Jesus from heaven*:

> The revelation of Jesus Christ, which God gave him to
> show to his servants the things that must soon take
> place. He made it known by sending his angel to his
> servant John.[29]

Notice: the book of Revelation does not claim to be a gospel. This is a question of literary genre. It is an "apocalypse" or "revelation." It is not concerned to preserve the earthly teachings and acts of Jesus. The risen Jesus speaks from heaven of things to come in his glorified form, as Lord of history.

All the Gnostic texts present themselves the way Revelation begins. The Jesus who speaks addresses believers from a spiritual realm. The official modern translator of *The Gospel of Truth* recognizes this when he says, "In spite of the title, this work is not a gospel of the same sort as the New Testament gospels: it does not focus upon the words and deeds of Jesus."[30] Even *The Gospel of Thomas* that reproduces words of the earthly Jesus, presents him as "the living Jesus,"[31] (that is, the spiritual, unworldly Jesus) with absolutely no interest in the events of his earthly life or in the historical context of the sayings he reproduces. The deep, secret meaning of *The Gospel of Thomas* is not to be found in the events of the life of Jesus but is hidden in sayings that claim to give nontemporal wisdom for those believers whose goal is to escape the physical world of matter. To sum up what we have found concerning the humanity of Jesus, it is no exaggeration to say that the Jesus of Gnosticism must be as "unhuman" as possible. This is the Gnostic way of expressing radical personal liberation from the Creator and all his works.

THE BIBLICAL JESUS

The biblical Gospels are full of details demonstrating the humanity of Jesus. The God of the biblical Jesus and the God of the gospel writers is God, the good Creator of earthly human existence. Dates and facts are important because the Creator is the Savior who enters time and space to redeem the physical creation. The biblical Gospels fill out in detail this significant event of the historical coming of the Son. The term "gospel," at the time of Jesus, did not mean a list of wise, spiritual sayings. In the ancient world, "gospel" was a term much closer to journalism than to religious speculation. It meant to deliver news of historical events.[32] This should be good news for modern day TV news junkies, who are forever looking for the latest-breaking headline from network news channels. "Gospel" in the Roman empire referred to the proclamation of real events. (See chapter 11 note 71.)

Thus Luke, as a historian, actually tells us he did research among the eyewitnesses in order to write a historically accurate account.[33] Matthew, as we have seen, begins his gospel with a historical genealogy[34] and John opens with the stunning statement: "the [divine] Word *became* flesh."[35] The shortest gospel, Mark begins with the phrase, "The beginning of the gospel of Jesus Christ, the Son of God."[36] We are *not* treated to a list of wise sayings, but to a quote from the Old Testament prophet, Isaiah, speaking about future history. Mark does this to prove that something earthshaking has just happened.[37] After this proof Mark immediately begins to describe the events of the life of Jesus, beginning with the life of John the Baptist.

BIRTH IN SPACE AND TIME

I have had the privilege of watching my wife valiantly and magnificently give birth to our seven children (thank you, honey!), all via natural childbirth. From the safe distance of the spectator end of the bed, I can say that I know what childbirth is like. It would be wrong to suggest that the birth of Jesus was totally "normal," but it is certainly true that anyone passing by that stable in Bethlehem would have heard the sounds of a real labor. This was "natural childbirth," long before Lamaze.

According to the biblical Gospels, Mary was genuinely pregnant. Some older translations put it quaintly, "she was found to be with child."[38] Like every human birth, Mary's water burst and the contractions began, or, as Luke says, "the time came for her to give birth."[39] And give birth she did, to a wet, squawking newborn who needed to be washed and covered in "swaddling cloths."[40] As Mary fed the hungry infant,

Joseph set up a conveniently placed feeding trough with clean hay where Jesus could sleep, so Mary could get some well-earned rest.

We do not know the precise date of this most significant birthday. The later church took over the date (December 25) of the popular pagan festival of Saturnalia, the celebration of the sun, and the winter equinox, and turned the event into Christmas, thus turning feeding troughs into a significant part of Western cultural iconography. However, thanks to the evangelist Luke, who did research on that kind of thing,[41] we do know the precise year.

Joseph and Mary were in Bethlehem because of an imperial order from Caesar Augustus, sometimes known as Octavian, a friend and then enemy of Mark Anthony, of Cleopatra fame. Caesar ordered a census[42] not because he wanted to know the birthday of Jesus—he needed money, and money came through taxes. Having everyone in the kingdom register gave him an accurate estimate for the state budget. Luke tells us it was the *first* census and mentions at least one other.[43] You might forget when the census takers last came to your house, but in those days, you didn't forget, because the census takers did not come to you; you went to them. This particular census was ordered when Publius Sulpicius Quirinius (or Cyrenius) was governor of the massive Roman province of Syria, in whose jurisdiction was the small territory of Palestine. Publius got the name Cyrenius because of a major victory he won for Rome in Cyrene, that is, North Africa. These are all genuine historical figures, attested by records outside of the Bible.

The birthday of Jesus is thus defined in the Gospels with great precision. You might almost speak of an obsession with dates. This birthday is set in relation to the dates of Rome's emperors, governors, and imperial edicts. This was the year 753 of the Roman calendar. That is about as close as you get for dating in the documents of the ancient world.

Unlike the Gnostics, the authors of the biblical Gospels consider history and historical precision to be of great importance.
They want to insert Jesus into the fabric of real history. The apostle Paul helps us understand why. He writes soon after the earthly
life of Jesus, "When the fullness of time had come, God sent forth
his Son, born of woman, born under the law [that is, in a Jewish
home]."[44] Paul here expresses the belief that God, the Creator of
heaven and earth (and thus of history), is active in history and
controls the events of history in order to bring it to a great culmination. The Jesus of the New Testament Gospels lived in history
and saw physical birth as a good thing[45] and considered his own
birth as a significant historical event. So he said to Pilate, "You say
that I am a king. For this purpose I was born and for this purpose
I have come into the world"[46]—whence the famous phrase in the
Apostles' creed: "Suffered under Pontius Pilate."

BACKGROUND: JESUS, SON OF ADAM

It is a source of pride in our family that our ancestors include
such interesting people as Jefferson Davis (first president of the
Confederate Union), John Elliott (first person to translate the Bible
into one of the Native American languages), Fletcher Christian of
Mutiny on the Bounty, and Ernest Shackleton, the famous Antarctic
explorer. One of my uncles was actually named Ernest Shackleton.
John Lennon and I, readers should note, were not related, but we
were good high school friends, sharing a desk, avoiding serious
schoolwork, and, unbeknownst to us, playing nascent Beatle music.

The biblical writers are very proud of Jesus' family history.
They record his family tree not once but twice, tracing his earthly
family back to Abraham in one and to Adam in the other. Why
would the Gospels waste so much space on boring genealogical
lists? What on earth begot the "begats"? Gnostic aversion to
"begetting" explains why.[47] The people who appear in these lists
are real, live, colorful characters—from famous kings like David
and Solomon to foreign women, some with shady backgrounds,

like Tamar and Rahab. These family trees are so Jewish, so Old Testament, so affirming of real history, so affirming of God the good Creator.

Sightseeing is generally fun, but my visit to my children who live in Berlin included a trip to the Sachsenhausen Concentration Camp, just forty-five minutes from the center of town. Fun is not the word. I touched the gallows where prisoners were hanged for insubordination as a public warning to all the others; I walked through the cells where living men had rotted away through disease, malnutrition, and cold; I wandered through a series of white-tiled "clinic" rooms where gruesome experiments were performed on human beings; I observed the ovens where the cadavers were incinerated—all in the name of human progress. How could such sophisticated human beings so hate other human beings—right on the edge of a normal twentieth-century suburban township? The anti-Semitism in Germany was not limited to the Nazis. Certain Bible scholars in the 1920s and 1930s dismissed the Old Testament as primitive and rejected the apostle Paul as someone who sought to re-Judify original Christianity. They preferred an idealized Jesus who looked and sounded much more Greek and Western, or shall we say Aryan? Their Jesus was not the thoroughly Jewish Jesus we meet in the biblical Gospels. The Gnostics were not proto-Nazis, but their view of Jesus, in its rejection of all things Jewish and Old Testament, is profoundly anti-Semitic.

The Old Testament book of Genesis provides a genealogy of a particular family, a lineage that goes from Adam, to Seth, to Abraham, to Isaac, and to Jacob, whose sons finally constitute the twelve tribes of the nation of Israel. Genesis recounts the history of all the ancient nations.[48] The book of Numbers begins with three long chapters of genealogies of the generations of Israel's major families. The gospel writers proudly place Jesus in that same family line.

In addition to their careful genealogies, Matthew and Luke

use other means to emphasize the historicity of Jesus. They tell us of his birth to Jewish parents, in a Jewish town, Bethlehem. Joseph and Mary were conscious of being part of that national family history, and specifically of the royal lineage of the house of David.[49] They were careful to keep the Old Testament laws and customs. In obedience to the Law, eight days after his birth, they took Jesus to Jerusalem to present him to the temple priests.[50] At that moment, in the temple they were hailed by two pious, well-known Jews. One, Simeon, conspicuous in Jerusalem for his outstanding piety and knowledge of Old Testament Scripture, declared the baby Jesus to be the fulfillment of Israel's hope for deliverance. The other, Anna, an eighty-four-year-old widow who had spent most of her life in the temple, fasting and praying, also identified the baby as Israel's redeemer.[51]

Jesus was raised in the town of Nazareth, along with brothers and sisters. Like all male Jews he learned a trade, that of his father Joseph, who was a house builder/carpenter. His parents reflected the kind of Jewish piety they saw in Simeon and Anna. It is said of them that they did "everything according to the Law of the Lord."[52] Individually, Joseph is described as a "righteous man,"[53] and Mary "blessed ... among women."[54] In other words, their lives were deeply embedded in Old Testament piety and practice. This is also the point of the angelic message. The angel Gabriel appeared to Mary and declared about her son, "He will be great and will be called the Son of the Most High. And the Lord God will give to him the throne of his father David."[55] Mary sought to understand her calling to be the mother of Jesus in the light of this Old Testament history and prophecy. She saw the birth of her child as one more example of God's faithfulness to his people, in "helping his servant Israel, remembering to be merciful to Abraham and his descendants forever, even as he said to our fathers."[56]

Biblically pious Jewish parents taught Jesus the Scriptures

and he so matured in wisdom that when he visited the temple at age twelve, he confounded the religious leaders and the official Jerusalem teachers of the Law with his knowledge. Later on, as an adult, Jesus declared that he has not come to destroy the Scriptures but to fulfill them.[57] There is deep continuity between, on the one hand, Jesus' life and teaching and, on the other, his ethnic and national background. In the gospel of John, sometimes called a "spiritual" gospel, Jesus is recognized by some of the Jewish authorities as having come from God,[58] and Jesus himself says to the Samaritan woman, "salvation is from the Jews."[59] In sum, Jesus was raised in a very pious Jewish home by godly parents, and their faith clearly had a deep impact on him.

In his later life as a prophet and teacher, Jesus closely identified with the history of Israel. He saw his own calling as a reflection and fulfillment of the history of Israel. Far from rejecting that history, he made it his own. His vision was to see Gentiles "come from east and west and recline at table with Abraham, Isaac, and Jacob in the kingdom of heaven."[60] He made it known that he worships "the God of Abraham, and the God of Isaac, and the God of Jacob … [the] God … of the living."[61] He declared that "Abraham and Isaac and Jacob and all the prophets [will be] in the kingdom of God."[62] In other words, the biblical patriarchs of the past were integrated into Jesus' major teaching about the kingdom. According to Jesus, Abraham is not a laughingstock, but a prophet who saw the coming of Jesus as the fulfillment of the covenant God gave to him.[63] Jesus said, "Abraham rejoiced that he would see my day. He saw it and was glad."[64] Jesus believed the kingdom he brought was the restored and renewed kingdom of David.[65] David prophesied of Jesus[66] and Isaiah saw his glory.[67]

TRULY HUMAN

As biographies, the Gospels are disappointing. We would like to know how Jesus behaved as a kid,[69] what he looked like, how he spent his free time—if they had free time then. Instead, we get the main lines of his three-year public ministry all over Palestine, which he began at the age of thirty, plus a good portion of his teaching. But the stark fact of the Gospels is the odd concentration on the *events* of the last week of his life, what is called "the Passion." Here we have a lot less teaching and a lot more doing, especially suffering. The humanity of Jesus is never more in evidence. The general focus on events and actions narrows to an almost microscopic focus on the smallest of details, as this long, drawn-out, and murderous week reaches its woeful climax.

Anyone who has watched Mel Gibson's movie, *The Passion of The Christ*, knows what I mean. The flogging seems endless, as Roman floggings in real life must have seemed. The biblical Gospels spend an inordinate amount of time on the passion of Jesus. One German scholar called the biblical Gospels "passion narratives with long introductions." But whatever their shape, they are narratives because history, in its large scope and its small details, is significant to the gospel writers. Specifically, with this emphasis on the final week of the life of Jesus, the gospel writers want to state that the passion gives meaning to all the rest, and that the death of Jesus is the climax of human history. It is a real death of a real human being.

It is true: The Bible does not recount bathroom breaks for Jesus. However, they are there by implication, since Jesus ate and drank with all kinds of people and was even accused of partying too much with the wrong kind of people![69] Though Christianity has not always made the point with excessive zeal, being concerned to show his divinity, the Jesus of the Bible is a truly human, physical man, submitted to the laws of the Creation order. Like his father, Joseph,[70] he plies the same house-building trade. He got tired, sleepy, thirsty, hungry, angry, and sad. He bled real blood, really died, and was buried as a human corpse in a tomb.

CONCLUSION

The two pictures of Jesus could hardly be more dissimilar in their attitudes toward their hero's human history. The Gnostic Jesus denies his humanity and repudiates his family and ethnic history for turning him from his great mission of deliverance out of the physical bondage of the flesh and of creational structures. The biblical Jesus is fully human, as a child submits to his parents, and as an adult assumes the great national hopes of his ethnic past.

CHAPTER 4

THE DIVINITY OF JESUS

I believe in Jesus, messenger of God's Word,
bringer of God's healing, heart of God's compassion,
bright star in the firmament of God's
prophets, mystics and saints.
THE FAITH OF A THOMAS BELIEVER[1]

We believe ... in one Lord Jesus Christ, the only begotten
Son of God ...
God of God, Light of light,
very God of very God, ...
being of one substance with the Father, by whom all things
were made.
THE NICENE CREED

Apreacher arrived at a small rural church on Sunday morning, well in time for the ten o'clock service. Anxiously waiting in front of the ancient, locked chapel, his fears of a no-show disappeared when, at 9:55 a.m., a gruff farmer and two old ladies showed up. On the principle "where two or three are gathered together," he began the proceedings precisely at ten, and went through the whole formal service—responsive reading, recitation of the Creed, and, of course, the offering. The farmer, holding a deep red velvet offering bag in his gnarled hand, passed it to the remaining congregation of two, and then stuck the bag in front of the visiting preacher. Since his sermon that day was on giving, the preacher felt obliged to practice what he was about to preach, so he placed a crisp twenty dollar bill in the bag with as much ostentation as was appropriately possible.

At the end of the service, from the same gnarled hand appeared an envelope containing the preacher's honorarium. The preacher graciously received it and stuffed it into his pocket. Arriving home, he eagerly opened the envelope, and to his great disappointment pulled out—a twenty dollar bill. There was a bright side, however. He had discovered a wonderful illustration for a future sermon: "The more you put in, the more you get out!"

You will get from the two views of Jesus only what is already in them. When we raise the question of the divinity of Jesus, we are back to what each viewpoint teaches about the nature of God. Your view of God determines everything else you do or think. In this chapter, we will to some extent revisit what we observed in chapter 1, namely that Gnosticism and the Bible contain two opposing views of God that work themselves out in two different views of Jesus as divine.

THE DIVINITY OF THE GNOSTIC JESUS

You cannot have a kingdom without a king. The kingdom is important in the Gnostic gospels, but the Gnostics call themselves "kingless." In their kingdom, there are no Indian braves; everybody is a chief. There are no subjects; everybody is a king. This philosophy becomes clear in the Gnostic equivalent of the so-called "confession of Caesarea Philippi," an event recounted in both *The Gospel of Thomas*[2] and the biblical Gospels of Matthew and Mark.[3] This story tells of the disciples' response to Jesus' question, "Who do you say that I am?" In *The Gospel of Thomas*, when Jesus asked Peter to tell him who he is like, Peter replied:

"a righteous angel." When Jesus asked Matthew, he replied, "a wise philosopher." This hardly plumbs the spiritual depths of the person of Jesus. Thomas does understand Jesus, but in a strange and unexpected way.

When Jesus asked Thomas, he replied, "Master, I am incapable of saying what you are like." The reply of Jesus was even more astonishing: "I am not your master." Then Jesus took him to one side and told him three secrets. When Thomas returned, the others asked him what Jesus said. Thomas refused to tell them because he knew that they would stone him. This is a clear reference to the Jewish penalty for blasphemy, for making oneself God. What does this mean?

Jesus would not allow Thomas to call him "master" because Thomas had "drunk from the bubbling stream." He had come to possess the secret gnosis/knowledge of his own divinity. Tau Malachi, the contemporary Gnostic teacher understands the force of this saying. The true believer becomes a "living Yeshua" and owns a personal sense of "Messianic consciousness."[4]

An enigmatic saying in Thomas seems to affirm the same thing. Jesus says, "Where there are three gods, they are gods. Where there are two or one, I am with him."[5] Here *Thomas* seems to remodel a canonical saying in a Gnostic direction. In Matthew the biblical Jesus says, "For where two or three are gathered in my name, there am I among them."[6] In *Thomas*, Jesus is not *with* them in the sense the Bible understands. Rather his presence reminds the disciples that they *are divine*.

The Gnostic *Apocryphon of John* says that man's wisdom makes him "greater than those who had made him, and made him stronger than that of the first ruler [Yahweh]."[7] Paul's statement in 1 Corinthians 2:9–10, "As it is written, What no eye has seen, nor ear heard, nor the heart of man imagined, what God has 'prepared for those who love him'—these things God has revealed to us through the Spirit. For the Spirit searches everything, even the depths of God," is turned against Paul's God. To the Gnostic believer is promised what no "*angel*-eye" has seen and what no "*archon*-ear" has heard.[8] In other words, believers see and hear and know more than the God who foolishly created them.

The Gnostic view of divinity is consistently applied to the person of Jesus. The "unknowable" "Father of the All," is the spiritual power behind all things. If "God" and the believer are one, sharing the same divine substance or nature, so Jesus, though "divine," is no more divine than any true believer.

THE DIVINITY OF THE BIBLICAL JESUS

Jesus' message about the kingdom has more to it than meets the eye. As we noted, Jesus speaks of the "mystery of the kingdom."[9] The mystery concerns both the present form of the kingdom, which is veiled during the ministry of Jesus, and also the enigmatic person of Jesus the King. To understand Jesus we must place him within Old Testament expectations. God promises, "Behold, the days are coming, says the LORD, that I will raise to David a Branch of righteousness. A king shall reign and prosper … He will be called 'The Lord our Righteousness.'"[10]

Those who knew Jesus in the flesh sensed, from time to time, that there was more to him than his superior teaching. After his resurrection, they eventually hail him as equal with and in the form of God.[11] He is "the Word" who "was God,"[12] the Creator through whom all things were made.[13] He is described as "the only God, who is at the Father's side."[14] Because of this, those who knew him apply to Christ Old Testament texts that originally spoke of God. The early Christians believed that with the coming of Jesus, they were experiencing what the Old Testament prophesied as the most incredible good news, literally "gospel": "Get you up to a high mountain, O Zion, herald of good news; … say to the cities of Judah, 'Behold your God!'"[15] God the transcendent Creator of heaven and earth had come, in Jesus, to save what he had made.

Some recent treatments of Jesus affirm that this view of Jesus and his divinity was a fabrication, created by the church in the fourth century. Many people now believe that Jesus was purely human. However, the evidence of the New Testament is over-whelming, making such affirmations completely untenable. That Jesus was first considered divine only in the fourth century is nonsense! In the second and third centuries, all the leading Christians believed in the divinity of Jesus. Even when we go further back, into the first century, we have clear evidence that the church considered Jesus to be divine. Paul wrote the earliest books of the New Testament. He was studying in the Jerusalem rabbinic school during the public ministry of Jesus and became a Christian a couple of years after the death and resurrection of Jesus.[16] This contemporary of Jesus, an intellectual genius and converted rabbi, affirms everywhere that Jesus was divine.[17]

That, of course, was the witness of the all the other writings of the first-century apostles. The Gospels are more than confes-sions. Though written later than Paul's letters in some cases, they self-consciously attempt to preserve the unique context of the human, earthly life of Jesus. In other words, they do not simply read into the historical events their later post-resurrection faith. They conscientiously describe the good and the bad. Nothing is airbrushed. The disciples are dumb. They fail to understand. They all abandon Jesus when it gets tough. In this context of sur-prising honesty, great effort is given to describe the period of Christ's earthly humiliation, which was a time of veiling, of suf-fering leading to death.

The goal of Jesus' life is to save the world through death on a cross. Nothing, not even the revelation of his true nature, must hinder that goal. During his earthly life, his divinity is, therefore, necessarily ambiguous and suggestive. "Veiled in flesh," as the Christmas carol *Hark the Herald Angels Sing* says, the divinity of Jesus nevertheless peeks through at key moments, catching everyone by surprise. Jesus is genuinely human. He does not walk two inches above the ground—but he does walk on water. The unthinkable finally convinces his close associates—this very human Jesus was actually God the Creator in a human body.

One of these surprising moments occurs in the biblical version of the event referred to in *Thomas*, which we discussed above. There are some formal comparisons, but the meaning is quite distinct. Matthew's account reads as follows:

> Now when Jesus came into the district of Caesarea Philippi, he asked his disciples, "Who do people say that the Son of Man is?" And they said, "Some say John the Baptist, others say Elijah, and others Jeremiah or one the prophets." He said to them, "But who do you say that I am?" Simon Peter replied, "You are the Christ, the Son of the living God." And Jesus answered him, "Blessed are you, Simon Bar-Jonah! For flesh and blood has not revealed this to you, but my Father who is in heaven."[18]

Unlike *Thomas*, there was no infighting among the apostles. The difference was between them and the "people," those who observed Jesus from afar. However, even the opinions of the public were quite different from those offered by the disciples in the Gnostic *Gospel of Thomas*. The people at least saw in Jesus not a figure from pagan religion but a major prophet of Old Testament history.

The true revelation of who Jesus is—"the Christ, the Son of the living God"—is both biblical, for *the Christ* is the long-awaited Messiah, and disturbingly radical, for the title *Son of the living God* is without precedence in the whole of the Bible.[19] The revelation is so radical that though it comes through the mouth of Peter it actually comes directly from God himself in heaven. Jesus is marked off as different from all other human beings as having a qualitatively different relationship to God.

In *Thomas*, true believers could not even call Jesus "master." In the biblical accounts, the disciples were afraid in the presence of Jesus, since they found themselves in the presence of God himself. When Jesus met them walking on the sea, they fell back in awe and were scared silly, just like the Old Testament prophets when meeting with God.[20] They heard the divine voice at the baptism, and also at the transfiguration, ordering them to obey Jesus as "my beloved Son."[21] At these moments we sense a great distance between Jesus and his followers. The creature stands in awe of the Creator.

The confession of Jesus as divine is thus not a later invention of power-hungry bishops to bolster their authority. It is an essential element of Christian faith from the beginning. Jesus from time to time during his earthly life reveals amazing things about himself. He constantly refers to God exclusively as "my Father" rather than "our Father."[22] The gospel of John explains that this was the reason the Jews were seeking to kill, because "he was even calling God his own Father, making himself equal with God."[23]

Jesus also speaks about his divine preexistence, of the glory he had with the Father before the world was.[24] In the middle of his ministry he makes this startling claim: "All things have been handed over to me by my Father, and no one knows who the Son is except the Father, or who the Father is except the Son and anyone to whom the Son chooses to reveal him."[25] In another gospel, before his death, he says a similar thing, identifying himself with the Father and the Spirit in the mystery of the Trinity: "But when the Helper comes, whom I will send to you from the Father, the Spirit of truth, who proceeds from the Father, he will bear witness about me."[26] Here Jesus links himself in a unique way with God the Father and God the Spirit. Having made this claim during his life, it is not surprising that, after the resurrection, he commands his disciples to baptize in the name of the Father, the Son and the Holy Spirit.[27]

It is in the context of Jesus' claims to be uniquely related to the divine Trinity that the gospel accounts of his virgin birth make sense. Such astonishing claims to divinity as Jesus

expressed during his earthly ministry oblige us to take seriously
the gospel accounts of his birth. If the divine Word did become
flesh, as the apostles declare,[28] that event must have been a
miraculous, unique occurrence. The Gospels claim such uniqueness, though with surprising understatement. "Now the birth of
Jesus Christ took place in this way. When his mother Mary had
been betrothed to Joseph, before they came together she was
found to be with child from the Holy Spirit."[29]

The gospel record is unambiguous in its affirmation of a
divine Jesus—unless you are content to dismiss all this as the
pure invention of gullible followers. If you take the Bible at
its face value, however, you discover the disquieting declaration that God became flesh. The gospel of John, one of the
towering pillars of New Testament faith, begins with this
claim. It ends with the confession of the historical Thomas, a
confession that roundly contradicts the Gnostic *Thomas* (for
whom Jesus is not his disciple's "master" but his equal). The
biblical Thomas, falling before Jesus in worship, is not "mas-
terless" but submits to the lordship of one greater than he. On
his knees before the risen Jesus, he cries out, "My Lord and
my God!"[30]

The biblical Jesus, while truly human, is also mysteriously
divine. The Bible means by divinity the personal, transcendent
Creator God, who, in his nature, is separate from the creation.
For creatures to be divine is strictly unthinkable. The incredible
claim of the New Testament is that in Jesus God is present in the
creation in human flesh through the miracle of the incarnation.
Such divinity we creatures will never know. Jesus is unique.
While the humanity of Jesus emphasizes his identification with
us, his divinity marks him out as mysteriously and disturbingly
different.

The Gnostic Jesus is divine only as all Gnostics are. In fact, he
is their twin. The biblical Jesus is unique, the only human being
that is also divine. The definition of Jesus' divinity determines
the kind of spiritual life Jesus teaches.

CHAPTER 5

JESUS AND SPIRITUALITY

*I've had too many experiences over the past fifteen years
to remain stuck in the old definitions of "truth."*
SHIRLEY MACLAINE[1]

*And when the Spirit of truth comes, he will convict the world concerning sin
and righteousness and judgment: He will guide you into all the truth, ... He
will glorify me, for he will take what is mine and declare it to you.*
JOHN 16:8–14

I n the short history of America, we have witnessed two great
spiritual revivals, or, as we used to call them, "awakenings."
The First Great Awakening occurred between the 1730s and
1770s and was associated with the great Protestant preachers
Jonathan Edwards and George Whitfield. The Second Great
Awakening took place during the 1820s and 1830s under the
influence of the mass evangelists Charles Finney and Theodore
Weld. While they varied in setting, theology, and impact, these
first two "awakenings" were decidedly Christian. The *biblical*
Jesus was at the center of their spirituality.

THE THIRD GREAT AWAKENING

Social observers wonder if we are not now in the midst of a third

Great Awakening.[2] We have come through a long period of secular humanism and religious skepticism and are now becoming ever more spiritual, but we have never been more confused about the nature of that spirituality.[3] Unlike the first two revivals, this third awakening is of a decidedly nonbiblical spiritual orientation. In it, Jesus is only one of many interesting gurus.

"Orientation" is the right word if, as someone said, "orientation" is knowing where the East is! Many spiritual seekers since the sixties have sought spirituality and religious identity in *Eastern* religions. Chances are you've met someone who is Episcopalian, does yoga, and meditates on the *Tibetan Book of the Dead*. Or you've met a Jew who believes his true bar mitzvah happened through Hindu meditation. In 2002, it was estimated that forty million Americans embraced the New Age movement.[4] Although I recognize that the term "New Age" is somewhat dated, I use it occasionally, because it is a commonly understood term that serves as a general description of the new spirituality. Most people would understand what you mean and probably agree, if you asked them if some form of New Age is "the prominent spiritual viewpoint of America."[5] Between fifteen and twenty million Americans practice yoga, a technique that serves as a wide gateway into Eastern religion. *The Celestine Prophecy*, a "new spirituality" novel, sold eight million copies. *The Da Vinci Code*, another novel expressing the "new spirituality," has gone far beyond that to become the best-selling adult fiction book of all time, according to one Web site evaluation. *TV Guide* recently included four New Age figures in its top-ten list of spiritual thinkers, and, of course, the spiritual influence of seemingly innocuous movies such as *The Lion King* and *Star Wars* is incalculable.

This "third awakening" clearly includes the rediscovery of ancient Gnostic spirituality. It also includes a "new" view of Jesus that "liberates" him from the narrow confines of the biblical Gospels.

The kind of spirituality Jesus taught has thus become a burning issue in our time. Was Jesus a unique teacher or one of many? Did Jesus practice Gnostic or biblical spirituality? "Both" does not seem to be an acceptable answer in terms of what we have examined to this point. The two systems of Gnosticism and biblical Christianity are mutually opposed. This is also true of the spirituality Jesus taught and practiced.

GNOSTIC SPIRITUALITY

PRAYER

When you think of spirituality in the West, particularly in the narrow sense of "spiritual disciplines," you immediately think of prayer. This is not the case in the Gnostic texts. The Jesus of *Thomas* never taught his disciples to pray. Indeed, he programmatically commands them *not to pray* lest they be "condemned."[6] We are alerted that something different is going on in Gnostic spirituality relative to the biblical record.

To be accurate, there are a few references to prayer in the scrolls that should be noted. One Gnostic text proposes "praying in secret,"[7] as Jesus taught in Matthew, though this secret praying has a Gnostic twist. Praying "to your Father who is in secret" is understood as communing with the God you find within. Your inner self is the secret chamber. "That which is within them all [that is, all true Gnostics]," says the Jesus of *Philip*, "is the Fullness [that is, divinity]."[8] In this kind of praying, it would be accurate to say, "My prayers go no farther than the ceiling." They are not meant to. When you *go within*, as Shirley MacLaine used to say, "prayer" is radically redefined.

Two Gnostic texts contain the word "prayer" in their titles. *The Prayer of the Apostle Paul* contains an echo of the Lord's Prayer. In this prayer, the Gnostic apostle, using in part the language of 1 Corinthians[9] and in part that of Jesus,[10] asks, "My Redeemer ... grant what no angel-eye has [seen] and no archon-ear <has> heard and what [has not] entered into the human heart

... which came to be after the image of the psychic God ... for yours is the power [and] the glory and the blessing and the [greatness] for ever and ever."[11]† Notice a few things in this prayer. The Redeemer God, to whom the prayer is addressed, is not "our Father who is heaven." That God of the Bible is the "psychic God," the blind and ignorant God who created matter. The "angels" and "archons" (rulers) are the evil cherubim and divine beings that surround this false God. Also, what is requested is not daily bread or help with temptation but knowledge of the unknowable divine Spirit behind all things. It is a prayer for mystical illumination for knowledge that comes from behind and beyond the biblical God of Creation. This is recognized by the modern translator, who sees a "striking resemblance not only to prayers in the Corpus Hermeticum (a non-Christian form of Gnosticism) but also to invocations found in magical texts."[12] A third-century AD Gnostic theologian, Justinus, also indicates how we should take this reference to Paul's words. It is the *present* experience of the knowledge of the self in cosmic unity with the divine that fulfills the words of Paul. "Drinking of the upper waters" of spiritual ecstasy is claimed to be the same as seeing "what eye has not seen and ear has not heard and has not occurred to the human mind."[13] Such "seeing" is then proposed as a present spiritual reality.

The other text with "prayer" in the title extends just over a half page. Called *The Prayer of Thanksgiving*, it begins "O undisturbed name, honored with the name God." The "prayer" gives thanks for what the translators call "deifying knowledge": "Thou hast *made us divine* through Thy knowledge."[14] The translators note that in the Nag Hammadi collection, this prayer text comes immediately after the *Discourse on the Eighth and Ninth*, which is a sort of manual describing the technique

---

† In the Gnostic texts I cite, square brackets indicate a lacuna (hole) in the parchment; pointed brackets indicate modern corrections to changes or omissions by the original scribe.

for the attainment of mystical experiences. The translators tie the "deifying knowledge" to what has been attained via mystical trance in the previous book.[15]

Gnostic specialist, Elaine Pagels, says, "They [the Gnostics] argued that one's own experience offers the ultimate criterion for truth." Gnosticism, she says, has nothing to do "with belief but with 'dimensions of experience' and 'religious imagination.'"[16] If that is what is meant by prayer, then it is quite different from what we meet in the biblical Gospels.

In the entire collection of Gnostic texts, prayer is mentioned only a handful of times—with a Gnostic twist that eviscerates from prayer its traditional nature. What the Gnostic really proposes is not prayer but inner mystical experience, communion with and meditation upon the higher inner self.

IRRATIONAL

Meditation unhooks the mind from its normal functions. The Gnostic Jesus reveals this to James, who must seek to be "full of the Spirit," but be "lacking in reason."[17] The Spirit takes the believer beyond reason and the illusion of physical reality, beyond the farthest reaches of the created cosmos, into communion with the alien, unknowable Father.[18] This can be described in Gnostic terminology as the "mind being separated from the body of darkness ... the putrid root,"[19] a mind that has "no dealings with the body."[20] It is liberated to experience the Light.[21] As we shall see below, at this level, the Gnostic Jesus sounds very much like a mystical teacher from the East. Swami Vivekananda, the well-known disciple of the great Hindu saint, Ramakrishna, in his description of the goal of yoga, says, "we get beyond the senses, our minds become superconscious, we get beyond the intellect ... where reasoning cannot reach."[22] In his authoritative work, *Divine Bliss*, Swami Sivananda states, "we must consciously destroy the mind," and another Hindu guru, Osho Raineesh, speaks of "killing the mind." The mind is "that which separates you from God."[23] At this level, whether in Hinduism or Gnosticism, the whole notion of "communion with God" as understood in the "Christian" tradition, is radically redefined. In another Gnostic text, Jesus speaks of a "living book" with magical letters "written by the Unity," that is, "the Father." These are not your typical letters as found in the Bible. They are not "consonants or vowels," that would be part of a logical form of expression as people normally use letters. Rather, in this "living book," each individual letter is mysteriously a complete thought, in and of itself, which one discerns by spiritual intuition.[24] This "living book" is "the word of the Father."[25] Clearly the notion of words, letters, and books is here redefined in the direction of extreme mysticism or what is sometimes called in occultic literature "spirit writing."

When my wife and I visited New Zealand, we attended a Maori festival and got into conversation with a very intense woodcarver who said he had no time for all the touristy activity going on around him. We spent some time plying him with questions about his craft, which led him to express the spiritual nature of the communication in his art. He had received little, if any, formal education and was not much interested in reading and writing. We asked him how he knew the ancient traditions of Maori lore. He told us that he and his fellow craftsmen would meet through the night and communicate *without words* in order to know what to put into their artistic work. A similar practice of deep communication without words seems to have been a part of Gnostic spirituality, as the following would indicate.

SPIRITUAL TECHNIQUES

In the Gnostic *Apocalypse of Peter* when Jesus revealed truth to Peter, Peter was in a trance, from which he emerged when the discourse ends.[26] In the ancient Gnostic texts, spirituality is an out-of-body, nonrational experience. The present Gnostic bishop of Los Angeles, commenting on the Gnostic *Gospel of the Egyptians*, makes this clear:

> The invocations and prayers of thanksgiving are
> addressed to Jesus by his particular mystic name,
> Iesseus-Mazareus-Iessedekeus. There can be little
> doubt that these prayers are indeed the result of
> vivid ecstatic experiences and that the string of mys-
> tic letters ... are in the nature of glossolalia—that is,
> of ecstatic utterances expressed in sounds that do not
> reflect any earthly language.[27]

In six of the Nag Hammadi texts you find this strange repetition of apparently nonsense words.[28] Here is one example:
"Zoxathazo a oo ee ooo eeeoooo ee oooooooooo ooooo uuuuuu
oooooooooooooooo Zozazoth."[29] What is going on? Oddly
enough, these "words" seem to be at the heart of the Gnostic
appeal, both ancient and modern. Gnosticism delivers immediate
and tangible spiritual life through what a modern scholar of
Transpersonal Psychology calls "technologies of the sacred."[30]
Transpersonal Psychology is an academic discipline that studies
and promotes paranormal practice. It offers a whole series of
techniques for creating mystical experiences found throughout
human history in all the non-Christian religions of the world.[31]
These include breathwork, drugs (especially LSD), drumming,
chanting, mantras, mystical initiations, yoga, and mind-numbing
meditation. All these time-tried techniques are "essential to
shamanism,"[32] to quote a leading transpersonal psychologist,
allowing the individual to be in touch with the spiritual realities
of the world beyond.[33] In this use of spiritual technologies,
Gnosticism is no exception.

"Extreme mysticism" well describes what one finds in some
of the manuals of spirituality that are part of the Nag Hammadi
library. In the oddly named *Discourse on the Eighth and the Ninth*,
a type of Gnostic Christ reveals to the seeker the way to bliss. At
death, the soul escapes from the body and ascends through
seven cosmic spheres to arrive at the eighth and ninth domains
of spiritual repose. Such an experience serves as a model for
earthly spirituality. The journey of the soul after death can be

anticipated before death through spiritual disciplines. Denying the reality of the physical body, the soul seeks in the present a mystical passing through seven degrees to reach, if only momentarily, the Gnostic nirvana to gaze upon the Light of the All.

In the so-called *Naassene Sermon*, recently brought to public attention,[34] the Jesus of these Gnostic worshippers of the Serpent of Eden—[*naas* is "serpent" in Hebrew]—teaches in vivid manner the classic notion of the ascent of the soul. As Jesus emerges from the Jordan he causes the river to flow in the opposite direction. According to the spiritual, symbolic meaning, the river that flows downward flows into matter and decay, while the river that flows upward returns to its divine source. The river flowing downward produces "a generation of men." When "the river flows upwards ... a generation of gods takes place."[35] The lost connection to the All is rediscovered, or, as it is stated in Hindu tradition, one "becomes permanently established in God consciousness."[36]

The kingdom of God is a trancelike state that can be described, as it would be in Buddhism, as "nothingness." "That which is ... nothing," reads a Gnostic text on spirituality, "and which consists of nothing, inasmuch as it is indivisible—a point—will become through its own reflective power an incomprehensible magnitude. This ... is the kingdom of heaven."[37]

I hope you are not lost by now. Some of the language in the Gnostic writing seems abstract and difficult—and is intentionally so! These sacred technologies seek to bring the Gnostic believer to a state in which the mind is disconnected from the body, so as to find a focus on nonbodily, spiritual "realities." To prepare yourself for such an experience, you banish false notions of yourself from your mind. You separate yourself "from the somatic darkness ... from psychic chaos in mind and the femininity of desire." Further, you "reprove the dead creation" within yourself as well as "the divine cosmoCreator of the perceptible world."[38] Then finally you can employ techniques of trance, such as the nonsense phrases mentioned above. At the apex of this ascent, you are promised a beatific vision, a *mystical union*. The human initiate claims to know "a stillness of silence within me" and "hear[s] the blessedness whereby I kn[o]w myself as <I am>."[39] This is *gnosis*.

SERPENT WORSHIPPERS

The descriptions of these obscure spiritual practices are indeed intentionally confusing. Gnostics want to keep outsiders in the dark. Though they invite seekers to enter, the secret can only be found by serious, deeply spiritual initiation. The seemingly harmless *Gospel of Thomas* describes itself as "the secret sayings of the living Jesus," and Jesus exhorts, "Let him who seeks continue seeking until he finds. When he finds ... he will rule over the All."[40] The book ends with the prospect of the transformation of Mary into "a ... male ... living spirit."[41] It would appear that the book as a whole is a means of mystic initiation which culminates in a promise of cosmic union by shedding gender distinction. What does all this mean, and how is it achieved?

It is rare and illuminating to discover a practicing Gnostic who has penetrated beyond the veil of obscure language to experience firsthand the reality of Gnostic initiation. One such insider, Mark Gaffney, an ex-Roman Catholic and a brilliant thinker, has been won over to the Gnostic Jesus and describes with great clarity the experience this Jesus brings.[42]

Gaffney believes that the real Jesus initiated his disciples into the esoteric worship of the Serpent. The Gnostic Naassenes emphasize with great clarity what all Gnostics believe: that the true voice of Jesus was first heard in the Genesis Serpent, who promised to Adam and Eve an experience of death-defying soul transformation. Against the lies of Yahweh, the serpent of Eden brought true wisdom to the original couple. His message of life revealed to Adam and Eve that they possessed true spiritual life within themselves and that if they would only realize it and unleash that inner spiritual power, they could save the world.

How does one unleash innate spiritual power? Here is where Gaffney's account is most helpful and specific. He describes a five-day workshop called "Life, Death and Transitions," led by the Swiss psychiatrist, Elisabeth Kübler-Ross, an expert on "near-death experiences." One evening Kübler-Ross recounted how "she had quite literally gone out of herself in a blessed experience of cosmic consciousness." Gaffney, who implies having had the same kind of experience, believes that "Gnostic Christians had direct knowledge of higher spiritual states like the one experienced by Kübler-Ross."[43] Another contemporary Gnostic, the above-mentioned bishop of the Ecclesia Gnostica states categorically, "There can be little doubt that the Gnostics employed effective methods for the cultivation of transcendental states of consciousness."[44] But where does the serpent come in?

A sculptured alabaster bowl, dating from the third or fourth century AD depicts the Naassenes in a circle, in a collective moment of transport, worshipping, in the center, a winged serpent. Gaffney makes a case for understanding the Gnostic serpent spirituality in terms of the Hindu yoga tradition of "kundalini energy." This energy, believed to be coiled at the base of the spine, lies dormant until aroused by techniques of concentrated meditation. The serpent energy is said to ascend from the base of the spine through the other six "chakra" points, leading to the point of "maximum focus and concentration" where one experiences the "indivisible point," above the head, where all distinctions are compressed into a "singularity," or "the void." Here, personal identity and the identity of God are fused.

You must be wondering how such obscure practices could interest anyone. You may think this material concerns past history or faraway places. As I was writing these lines, my copy of *Newsweek* arrived. On the front cover was a most illuminating picture. Behind the title, "The New Science of Mind and Body," is a photograph of the face of a woman in a mystical trance. On the top of her head, in a kind of bubble, is the image of the *Vitruvian Man*, Leonardo da Vinci's study of the proportions of the human frame.[45] For many this drawing has come to represent human perfection, so the symbolism is most interesting. In mystical trance we find our true, perfect selves.

Here is a clear, contemporary statement of such spirituality from the Gnostic bishop Stephan Hoeller: "The essence of the human being is not merely created by God but *is* God."[46] The *Newsweek* article emphasized the importance of meditation and yoga for mental, physical, and spiritual health and showed how Eastern and Gnostic thinking have invaded our Western world. Hoeller himself associates yoga with Gnosticism: "Alchemy [spiritual transformation] was the Yoga of the Gnostics."[47] The implication is that yoga will bring about for us a similar transformation.

THE GOAL OF SPIRITUALITY

"As early as the first century," claims Gaffney, Gnostic "Christians" "were practicing a fully developed system of kundalini yoga very similar to what is described in the Vedas and practiced in India today."[48] Though he may be wrong about the date, Gaffney is not wrong about the nature of Gnostic practice, for the goal of Gnostic spirituality is *gnosis*, knowing the self as an expression of "the All," which is indeed found in the religions of the East.[49] The goal is to escape from "multiplicity" into "Unity," which is another name for the divine. True believers "purify themselves from multiplicity into Unity." This process is a visionary ascent to God through various levels (seven,[50] thirteen[51]), by which matter, darkness, and death are destroyed.[52] The Gnostic Jesus practices this technique and achieves supreme union with the divine while still part of this world.[53] Then he teaches the technique to his disciples. "When I came," says Jesus, "I opened up the way. I taught them the passage through which will pass the elect and solitary ones."[54] Like other forms of non-Christian spirituality, the Gnostic experience joins the opposites, rising beyond them to total unity.

You may not have heard of such techniques or experiences, but they are common to many religious traditions. Joining the opposites is found in most Eastern religions. Gaffney shows how close this spirituality is to Hinduism. For instance, the ancient scriptures of India are called the Vedas, and the root of veda is "vid" meaning "to know," as in "gnosis."[55] The knowledge gained through kundalini yoga meditation is the same as that proposed by Buddhism and Taoism.[56]

The Gospel of Philip describes light and darkness, life and death, left and right as "inseparable ... brothers,"[57] so that good is not really good, evil is not really evil, life is not really life, nor death really death. While these elements dissolve into one another, the true Gnostic rises above them into the indissoluble, eternal world.[58] Death comes from multiplicity. So, for example, according to the teaching of Jesus to Philip, it was only when Eve was separated from Adam that death came into being. When Adam refinds his complete, androgynous (that is, both male and female) self, then death will no longer exist.[59] The Jesus of *Thomas* describes this as retaking one's place at the "beginning" and thus defeating death.[60] It is the prerequisite for "entering the kingdom of heaven."[61] Simply put, the "kingdom" is a mystical, out-of-body experience.

The Gnostic Jesus declares the possibility of entrance into a "kingdom" of spiritual liberation, beyond the opposites of good and evil, male and female, where the concepts of sin and guilt and creational structures have been transcended. This Jesus is still alive and well, and, in the seventies, "appeared" to Helen Schucman, an atheistic, New York Jewish psychologist. Schucman wrote down what Jesus said to her, published it as *A Course in Miracles*, which became a New Age best seller. In this communication, Jesus says to the reader, "Do not make the pathetic error of clinging to the old rugged cross.... Your only calling here is to devote yourself with active willingness to the denial of guilt in all its forms."[62] This is the same message the old Gnostic Jesus brings. In *The Gospel of Mary*, Peter asks Jesus, "What is the sin of the world?" and Jesus answers, "There is no sin."[63]

In this spirituality, there is no place for prayer to a personal Lord and no place for the confession of sin or guilt. The Gnostic Jesus proposes a powerful trancelike experience of self-redemption by which one communes with the spiritual energies within the self and through the process comes to the knowledge that the higher self is god.

THE SPIRITUALITY OF THE BIBLICAL JESUS

The two accounts of Jesus, the Gnostic and the biblical, have two totally different perspectives on spirituality. For the biblical Jesus, spirituality is tied to the notion of the coming of the kingdom at a point of time in history. Spirituality is not an individual experience, disconnected from what Jesus is accomplishing on earth. The specific, definable, historical events of Jesus' life have both physical and spiritual implications. Jesus' life and ministry, his death and resurrection, and the coming of the Spirit are all tied together and influence the believer's *experience* of the kingdom. Though there is no place for the irrational, the message of the kingdom is not in words only but also in enabling power—as the apostle Paul says about the coming of the gospel: "Our gospel came to you not only in word, but also in power and in the Holy Spirit and with full conviction."[64] Jesus brings the gospel of the kingdom in the power of the Spirit. This understanding of the Spirit determines Jesus' teaching and practice of spirituality.

JESUS AND PRAYER

Confusion about the nature of prayer abounds in our time.

- Christians practice yoga and the Jesus of the Bible is co-opted for a kind of mystical spirituality never found in his teaching.

- The *Office of Prayer Research* of the spiritual movement known as *Unity* called for "learning more about the power of prayer" at the Barcelona meeting of *The Parliament of the World's Religions* in June, 2004.[65]
- Sri Chinmoy, Hindu guru in charge of the Meditation Room at the United Nations, at the opening ceremonies of the same *Parliament* in Barcelona, "prays for the oneness of all the religions" during his "Opening Meditation."[66]

In these examples, "prayer" is not being used the way the Jesus of the Gospels used the term. Since most religions of the world confuse the Creator and the creature, they cannot really "pray" in the biblical sense of the term, because they do not hallow or set apart God's name, as Jesus taught us. Some, like Buddhism, deny the very existence of a Creator, and so cannot use the biblical term "prayer" for the spirituality they pursue.[67]

Even a superficial examination of prayer in the Bible shows that it is understood as meaningful and specific requests to a personal God—not as a shopping list, of course, but as an expression of deeply personal communion. Prayer in this sense is central to the spirituality of Jesus. He constantly practiced it himself,[68] and in the Lord's Prayer, taught it to his disciples.[69] Interestingly, the second thing he taught his disciples to pray was for the *coming* of God's kingdom: "Our Father who is in heaven … your kingdom come." But we get ahead of ourselves. I simply want to show the place of the kingdom in Jesus' praying and hence in his spirituality.

The first thing for which his disciples must pray is, "May your name be hallowed." Notice the logic of the prayer: first, the name of the one addressed is evoked: "Our Father who is in heaven." Then there is the hallowing of the name of the one addressed.

In insisting that we address our prayer to the "Father who is in heaven," Jesus wants us to honor the theistic, personal character of biblical spirituality. By "theistic" I mean recognizing God as a different, personal, uncreated being, separate from all other created personal beings. This is the God of the biblical Jesus, as we documented in chapter 2. Prayer, says Jesus, must reflect this essential fact of biblical spirituality. We are not meditating on our inner selves. We are addressing the personal Creator of the cosmos who exists and who is different than we are.

That is why, after the address, the first *request*, "May your name be hallowed," concerns the *holiness* of God's name. If the name of God as "the Father in heaven" clearly implies that he is the "transcendent Lord, Creator of heaven and earth," then to hallow or sanctify that name is to recognize the character of God as majestically higher than us.

In the Bible, "to sanctify" or "to make holy" essentially means "to set apart in a special place or for a special task." That is why, in Scripture, things are distinguished and have their own functions and identities. God and the world are distinguished; we must set God apart in his own celestial place. Within the created order, God made things to be distinguished, such as males and females, humans and animals, animals and plants, things true or false, to name just a few. Beyond these created distinctions and with the entrance of sin into the world, the Bible requires the further rigor of distinguishing between holy and unholy, good and evil, righteousness and unrighteousness, Christ and Satan, and so on. Thus, in the spirituality taught by the biblical Jesus, there is no "joining the opposites." To do so would actually be an unholy act. Specifically, claiming that we are divine, merging ourselves as creatures with the being of God as Creator fails to hallow and therefore sullies the specific name and character of God. At this point the Jesus of Gnosticism and the Jesus of the Bible could not be more profoundly opposed on this much-debated subject of the nature of spirituality.

JESUS AND PAGAN "PRAYER"

The Spirit of God, who energizes the human heart, is sometimes called the "power of God."[70] But this notion of spiritual power can never be employed to justify mind-denying mystical trance. Christian living must commend itself "by purity, knowledge, patience, kindness, by the Holy Spirit, by genuine love, by truthful speech, and by the power of God."[71] In other words, morality, truthful intelligibility, acts of kindness and love are not eliminated in the spiritual quest, they are energized and deepened by the Spirit's work.

Jesus understood the difference between "theistic" praying and pagan mantras. "And when you pray," says Jesus, "do not heap up empty phrases as the Gentiles do, for they think that they will be heard for their many words."[72]

The Greek verb used here means "use many (meaningless) words, babble, to use vain repetitions, to say the same words over and over again."[73] Jesus clearly knew pagans, possibly from having worked in the building trade in Sepphoris, a major Greco-Roman town in Gentile Galilee close to where Jesus lived and ministered. His description of mindless repetition to produce trancelike experiences fits the techniques of pagan spirituality examined above. It is most instructive that Jesus of the biblical Gospels does not integrate these "technologies of the sacred" into his own spiritual methodology. Rather, he specifically denies their genuine spiritual validity. He rejects them as manipulative and ineffectual. Later Jesus commands his disciples to "watch and pray that you may not enter into temptation."[74] "Watch" means stay awake, to stay in control of one's faculties, and not be carried away in some dreamlike sleep. In the place of ecstasy-producing techniques, Jesus proposes biblical praying, that is, as we noted, *meaningful speech to the personal God.*

This is theistic spirituality—spirituality that recognizes a fundamental difference between the creature praying and the Creator hearing and answering. This is why the Lord's Prayer, as noted above, begins, "Our Father who is in heaven." The humble tax collector coming to the synagogue to pray understands this. Not even lifting up his eyes to heaven, he says, "God, be merciful to me, a sinner!" This is the attitude in prayer Jesus demands of *every* disciple. This is why we must pray to the Father, "Forgive us our debts, as we also have forgiven our debtors."[75] This praying recognizes the transcendent Lord, our unworthiness, and the needy neighbor.

Theistic prayer for other people (supplication) is also quite a different activity than mystical meditation, which is focused entirely upon the self. Praying with other people in mind is an essentially selfless activity, with no thought of one's own personal ecstatic state. One thinks only of the needs of others and God's will. Jesus even prays for the seemingly insignificant kids whose doting parents bring them to him.[76] This kind of prayer necessarily includes the desire to forgive other people as one prays.[77] Jesus even requires of his disciples that they pray for those who abuse and persecute them.[78]

Theistic praying of the kind that Jesus taught demands faith.[79] Faith implies personal deference and respect in the presence of the personal God of the Bible. Stephan Hoeller, the Gnostic bishop, speaks of faith as "a primitive mental condition ... that wants to go on enjoying the security and confidence of a world still presided over by powerful, responsible, kindly parents."[80] The biblical Jesus would reply "Truly, I say to you, whoever does not receive the kingdom of God like a child shall not enter it."[81]

Jesus' God, the Father and Creator, cannot be manipulated with spiritual techniques that produce gnosis (knowledge) for those who believe themselves spiritually mature. As Jesus says, the pagans think they will be heard by constant repetition. In other words, their mantras seek to produce results. Their techniques make it happen, or so they think.

My wife rarely nags me. If I do not respond to her request to take out the garbage the first time, the garbage will sit there until next year! Nagging is manipulative and usually ends in failure because we are dealing with the mystery of individual human beings. In personal relationships, and especially in our relationship with God, there is mystery, a space that can only be filled by the trust that is ready to wait and see. In biblical piety we walk by faith and one day will "know-see." Thus faith is essential in expressing our state of dependence as human creatures. Faith and "gnosis" can thus be compared as two kinds of spirituality. Faith reaches out beyond the self whereas "gnosis" goes within. Faith respects the otherness and majesty of God; "gnosis" makes one the same as God. Faith requires revelation and gladly submits to God's Word; "gnosis" is self-revelation with no need of the Bible.

JESUS AND THE SPIRIT

This Lord's Prayer includes the role and work of the Spirit. When Jesus teaches us to pray, "May your kingdom come," we must remember that the Spirit is involved in this prayer because he both comes when the kingdom comes and is the means whereby one enters into the kingdom. Furthermore, Jesus teaches us to pray for the gift of the Spirit: "If you then, who are evil, know how to give good gifts to your children, how much more will the heavenly Father give the Holy Spirit to those who ask him!"[82]

If the Spirit is part of Christian prayer, and thus Christian spirituality, we have here mingled both the rational and the suprarational. We use our minds when we pray because we communicate meaningful requests for specific, even down-to-earth things, like daily bread, protection from evil, prayer for enemies and those who persecute you.[83] At the same time, the Spirit adds his stamp of approval and the deepening of our spiritual awareness. Thus, not just our minds but our hearts are moved by the life-giving character of truth; as the apostle Paul says, "For the kingdom of God does not consist in talk but in power."[84] Jesus says it first, "Whoever believes in me, as the Scripture has said, 'Out of his heart will flow rivers of living water.'" And the apostle

John adds, "Now this he said about the Spirit, whom those who believed in him were to receive, for as yet the Spirit had not been given, because Jesus was not yet glorified."[85]

The word "spiritual" starts with the word "spirit." The spirituality offered by the biblical Jesus depends on the power of the Holy Spirit. In order to understand that kind of spirituality, we must first connect the work of the Holy Spirit with Jesus' ministry and kingdom.

Before the beginning of his public ministry, Jesus is baptized by John, who declares that his own baptism is only with water, an outward sign of the future kingdom. Jesus' baptism, says John, will be *with the Holy Spirit*, the seal of the kingdom that has arrived.[86] At this baptism, Jesus receives the Spirit and is publicly declared to be God's unique Son. The two things happen together: (1) The Spirit comes on Jesus, and (2) At that moment he is divinely identified as God's Messiah/King who announces the kingdom.

This explosive event, orchestrated by God, begins the time of the fulfillment of God's plan to save his people and bless the nations. This is why the Spirit is called "the gift my Father promised."[87] The Spirit is involved in all that happens to Jesus. The Holy Spirit causes Mary to be pregnant with Jesus, descends on him at his baptism, and leads him into the desert to be tempted by the Devil.[88] By the power of the Holy Spirit, Jesus inaugurates his kingdom and defeats the Devil and evil in the wilderness. Jesus emerges "in the power of the Spirit to Galilee"[89] to announce the good news of the kingdom: "The time is fulfilled, and the kingdom of God is at hand; repent and believe in the gospel."[90]

These are all aspects of the earthshaking event of God's intervention in history to bring about salvation. Jesus' first synagogue sermon associates the Spirit and the kingdom. The Old Testament reading for that day just happened to be from Isaiah. They ask Jesus to read it, and this is what he read:

The Spirit of the Lord is upon me, because he has
anointed me to proclaim good news to the poor. He has
sent me to proclaim liberty to the captives and recover-
ing of sight to the blind, to set at liberty those who are
oppressed, to proclaim the year of the Lord's favor.[91]

Then, after rolling up the scroll, Jesus declared to everyone's
surprise, "Today this Scripture has been fulfilled in your hearing."[92] In other words, by the power of the Spirit, Jesus had
begun to realize the conditions of liberation inherent within the
notion of the kingdom. Thus Jesus healed the sick, raised the
dead, and calmed the storm. His Spirit-empowered ministry
began to destroy the power and oppression of evil, and
inevitably came into direct conflict with evil spirits. Jesus saw
this confrontation as programmatic: "If it is by the Spirit of God
that I cast out demons, then the kingdom of God has come upon
you."[93] Remember, this saying of Jesus is not about people discovering that they are divine. It is announcing the arrival of
God's reign from the outside, defeating the evil powers through
the ministry of his beloved, Spirit-led Son. Jesus' acts of liberation celebrated the arrival of the kingdom, but he himself still
saw its full manifestation as a future event. He prophesied a time
when "the kingdom of God [will] come with power."[94]
Specifically, the new creation/future kingdom comes with the
resurrection of the flesh and the transformation of the universe,
as the apostle Paul declares. Jesus at his resurrection was
declared "the Son of God *in power*[95] according to the Spirit of
holiness *by his resurrection from the dead*."[96]

The Spirit by whose power creation first came into being[97] is
also the powerful agent of the rebirth of creation. By faith we
now taste the down payment of new birth, but we await its full
manifestation in the new birth of our physical flesh, that is, the
resurrection of the body.

In the present the Spirit is given both as the revealer of this
final word of truth[98] and the effective mediator of it to believers.

Biblical revelation is not merely true information from God. The Spirit of God makes God immediate and personal to the spirits of individual believers. By the Spirit, God seeks personal communion with the sons of Adam and daughters of Eve. According to Jesus, entering this kingdom of God is entering into communion with God, on his new terms, on the basis of his objective work. It is thus the work of the Spirit: "Unless one is born of water and the Spirit, he cannot enter the kingdom of God."[99] One enters the final kingdom by God's grace, by personal faith, and by the life-changing mediation of the Spirit, who is also personal.

These acts of divine, creative power are not symbolic ways of describing ecstatic mystical experiences. They are events in the objective work of the personal, triune God of Creation and redemption, applied by the Spirit with transforming power to the life of the believer.

Biblical spirituality must and does take all of this into account—the objective and the subjective, the informative and the transformative. For this reason the spirituality Jesus taught can never be reduced to out-of-body states of personal mysticism. It is always the physical infused by the Spirit, liberated from the power of sin, to serve God the Creator, to give him thanks and bring him glory,[100] whether now in our earthly bodies—"your will be done on earth"—or, in the future, in our transformed bodies. That is why Jesus teaches his disciples to pray, not to meditate.

To sum up, the Gnostic Jesus rejects prayer and encourages mystical experiences that fuse the human with the divine. The biblical Jesus teaches a piety of prayer that respects the Creator/creature distinction and encourages a personal relationship with the personal Lord of the Universe. The Jesus of the Bible proposes no spiritual technologies that produce altered states of consciousness in which we might come to think of ourselves as divine. He reveals the personal Father and Creator who is known in the simplicity of prayer and in a relationship of personal faith.

I once had to address 1,700 college students. To get their attention I shouted into the mike, "SEX!" In my defense, that was the subject of my lecture—Paul's treatment of sexuality in Romans, chapter one—and it did get their attention. And now that I have yours, it is important to know that sexuality was an essential element of Gnostic spirituality, and that the biblical Jesus had much to say on the topic as well. Such will be the subject of the next chapter.

CHAPTER 6

JESUS AND SEXUALITY

What you saw was not about sex, it was about spirituality. The Hieros Gamos ritual is not a perversion. It's a deeply sacrosanct ceremony.
THE DA VINCI CODE[1]

And God said to them, "Be fruitful and multiply and fill the earth...."
GENESIS 1:28

Behold, children are a heritage from the Lord, the fruit of the womb a reward.
PSALM 127:3

an Brown got it right. For the Gnostic Jesus, sexuality and spirituality are soul brothers, joined at the hip, so to speak. This, however, is also true for the biblical Jesus—as it should be. A spiritual view of the world includes everything in the world. But notice: Different views of spirituality will produce different views of sexuality (Peter Jones, *God of Sex*, Victor, 2006). One is not progressive and edgy, the other staid and reactionary. Both flow out of two mutually contradictory worldviews, both as old as the hills.

THE GNOSTIC JESUS

A couple in my church loaned me a copy of *The Da Vinci Code,* thinking I might be interested in reading it. Little did I know at the time that I would one day write an analysis of it. I settled down on a long airplane trip to read it, and I was intrigued by Brown's description of a reality I had lived many years ago. The following passage rang so true to my own experience: "Teabing felt a joyous sense of homecoming when he saw the misty hills of Kent.... England was less than an hour from Paris [by plane], and yet a world away. This morning the damp, spring green of his homeland looked particularly welcoming."[2]

When I was teaching in France, I experienced that same phenomenon. Every other year, I would drive my wife and our seven children in a five-seater(!) sedan on a straight-shot, twenty-four hour marathon from Marseille to my childhood home in Liverpool to visit my parents. I can remember as if it were yesterday the mixed sense of utter exhaustion, excitement (as the children began to wake up), fulfillment, and tranquility as we drove—on the left side, which was finally the *right* side!— along the tree-lined roads of Kent in southern England, observing the early morning mist give way to the soft rays of the sun on what was surely going to be a rare, wonderful, sunny English summer's day.

Brown uses his descriptive skills to recount perhaps the most powerful scene in his story, which takes place in wind-swept Normandy. The heroine, Sophie Neveu, accidentally discovers her naked grandfather, Jacques Saunière, engaged in a secret sex ritual in the basement of his old country house, as a circle of well-heeled, elitist worshippers rock back and forth, chanting. The men are dressed in black, the women in white; all are wearing masks. Later the hero and expert in symbology, Robert Langdon, explains to Sophie that the ritual of *Hieros Gamos*, "Holy Marriage," was "not about sex, but about spirituality ... not a perversion [but] ... a deeply sacrosanct ceremony ... nothing to do with eroticism ... [but] an act through which male and female experienced God."[3]

Brown pushes us to consider a Jesus who practiced free sex and who made it more than a delicious rebellion against a church labeled as antisex. His book paints free sex as a holy, spiritual and ecstatic duty. What better excuse could anyone want for indulging the passions?

Much of Brown's material about "free sex" and "Holy Marriage" comes from the teaching of the Gnostic Jesus. And here, truth is stranger than this fiction. The Gnostics are deeply conflicted about sex, even more than some early church fathers who tended to see sex as sin. For the Gnostic, sex is both evil and deeply infused with powerful spirituality.

The Evil Woman

It was not the early church that demeaned women. It was Gnosticism. Many Gnostic texts put down the woman in no uncertain terms. Take this one, for example: "Flee from the insanity and fetters of femaleness and embrace instead the salvation of men."[4] I have not found a statement like this within the mainstream of Christianity in its two thousand years of history.[5]

According to the Gnostic Jesus, as we noted above, physical, heterosexual intercourse is evil because it carries on the work of Ialdaboath, the evil and blind Creator. The Gnostic texts develop this subject at length. The Chief Archon, the "cat-faced" Yahweh, creates sexual intercourse to embroil the first pair in matter.[6] Thus the soul became entrapped in "a contemptible body."[7] Women and sexual desire render escape from the material body more difficult. The Gnostic Jesus teaches that heterosexual sex, childbirth, and motherhood are evil, a result of the Fall. Conceiving wombs and milk-giving breasts are rejected,[8] as are physical mothers in general.[9] The sex act, in whatever form practiced can be used only by unmarried, solitary people for spiritual rituals that produce enlightenment—not babies! Stephan Hoeller, the contemporary Gnostic, states, "It is more important to be a woman than to be a mother."[10] As we shall see, however, even being a woman in Gnosticism is not very important. The Gnostic Christ comes to remind people of their heavenly origin and, by implication, to warn them of the trap of gender-specific sexuality.[11] He orders his disciples to "abandon bestiality,"[12] "to destroy [the] works of femaleness,"[13] and pronounces a curse on "you who love intimacy with womankind and polluted intercourse with it."[14]

This ancient refusal of marriage and childbirth has suddenly become thoroughly modern. We should have known. In the great contemporary rush to practice Gnostic forms of *spirituality*, the Gnostic worldview will be applied to everything and to sexuality in particular. That androgyny, homosexuality, and the refusal of child-bearing and marriage have taken such a hold in our contemporary culture is linked to the rise of Gnostic spirituality. A generation ago, Americans would not have imagined the need for books with titles like *Marriage Under Fire*,[15] or that states would pass a Defense of Marriage Act or the existence of a political movement such as Alliance for Marriage, whose goal is to defend traditional marriage via the adoption of a Constitutional amendment. But the present cultural acceptance of abortion, homosexuality, and the discussion of the nature of marriage is related not so much to new theories of democracy and civil rights as to the great shifts taking place at the deep level of spirituality.

Hieros Gamos—The Lure of "Holy" Sex

In ancient Gnosticism, though *physical* sex is evil, *spiritual* sex is dynamite. Physical sex is slavery; spiritual sex the gateway to liberation. The *Hieros Gamos* (holy marriage or the bridal chamber) is the ultimate mystery. For the Gnostic Jesus, there is nothing higher. Jesus in *The Gospel of Philip* mentions a number of sacraments—*Baptism*, for beginners, is called "the Holy Place"; *Redemption* is the "Holy of Holy," but the *Bridal Chamber* is identified as "the Holy of the Holies."[16] If the Bridal Chamber were a purely symbolic notion, a mere word picture or image of the soul's union with the divine, the place of sexuality would be easier to understand, but sexuality in Gnosticism is more complicated.

Physical sexual activity is formally denied. Jesus declares that the "mystery of marriage" is for the one who is "above desire."[17] Robert Langdon, one of the leading characters in *The Da Vinci Code*, borrows directly from such thinking when he says that *Hieros Gamos* sex was "not about sex ... nothing to do with eroticism ... but about spirituality."[18] According to the Gnostic *Gospel of Philip*, only the "solitary" ones enter the bridal chamber. Jesus further reveals that spiritual beings are engendered by the word, not by sexual intercourse. This is all very asexual. There is, however, physical contact. Since the word issues from the mouth, true Gnostics, "conceive and give birth ... by a kiss."[19] Mary Magdelene is described as "the one who was called his [Jesus'] companion,"[20] whom Jesus kisses "on her [mouth]."[21] Such intimacy provokes offense in the other disciples.[22] Perhaps the problem is not simply seeing a woman raised above them, but the physical relationship that intimate male-female kissing tends to create.

However, Gnosticism insists that the bridal chamber is not for animals, slaves, or "defiled women" (probably married women) but for spiritually superior "free men and virgins."[23] "Marriage" to "virgins," whatever that means, is justified by noting that Adam was born of two virgins, "the Spirit and the virgin earth," and Christ was also born of a virgin.[24] Then the Jesus of *Philip* speaks of the "children of the bridal chamber" as spiritual fruit or offspring of these free men and virgins. This product is not a bouncing, bonny baby but a "perfect [spiritual] child"[25] or "immortal foetus."[26]

The actual experience of the bridal chamber is not divulged. *Philip's* Jesus contrasts human sexual intercourse with the higher intercourse of spirit with spirit,[27] the "marriage of defilement" with "the undefiled marriage, a true mystery ... [which] belongs not to desire but to the will."[28] The nonsexual character of the bridal chamber seems to be maintained.

The Gnostic gospel that makes so much of the bridal chamber also speaks ambiguously of the importance of nakedness. "It is those who ... unclothe themselves ... who are not naked."[29]

Since this bridal chamber is the place where Eden is reenacted, where "the woman is [re-?]united to her husband,"[30] clothing is a sign of the Fall, and nakedness part of the restoration. Those who enter "must cast off their clothes,"[31] and are "clothed in the perfect light."[32] How close are we to the terminology of Wiccan rites which describe the naked participants in spiritual exercises as "sky-clad"?

Some scholars dismiss as exaggerated the accounts of the church father, Epiphanius, in his exposé of the Gnostic sects.[33] Epiphanius tells of being forced to participate in such rituals as a youth, so he speaks from experience. In his work, *The Medicine Chest*, he recounts the practice of Gnostic groups who offered prayers to God "naked, as a way of finding 'openness to God.'"[34]

The Naassene alabaster bowl mentioned earlier perhaps adds weight to Epiphanius's questioned testimony. According to the modern-day Gnostic Gaffney, this bowl, or chalice, from the third or fourth century AD "ranks as one of our most important treasures from the ancient past."[35] It constitutes what some think is the origin of the Holy Grail, the chalice that contains the true teaching of original, esoteric Christianity.[36] In the center of the bowl is the winged serpent. Forming a complete circle, heads at the top, feet towards the serpent, are the Gnostic worshippers, males and females, all totally naked.[37]

To say the very least, the material on the bridal chamber and what transpired there is full of innuendo and ambiguity. Putting a group of men and "virgins" *au naturel* in the same room, engaged in deep spiritual intercourse is, to say the least, highly eroticized behavior. We know other Gnostic groups that gave in to carnal temptation and justified their sexual excesses in all kinds of ingenious ways.[38]

Whether Gnostic practice of sexuality took the self-denying (ascetic) or the self-indulging (libertine) form, the result is the same—the undermining of "normative" sexuality for the promotion of esoteric spirituality. This is the great goal of *Hieros Gamos*.

ANDROGYNY

Hieros Gamos is not just a poetic image. Communal "fellowship" in the nude was practiced as the highest form of Gnostic worship. In other words, some form of sexual stimulation, whether physical, mental, or spiritual, was used to promote the goal of mystical transport and the attainment of "gnosis."[39] According to *The Exegesis on the Soul*, the bridal chamber is for the virgin, androgynous soul who awaits spiritual union with her "brother," "the true bridegroom," and they become "a single life, inseparable from each other."[40] According to Mircea Eliade, a leading expert in the History of Religions, this is what is called "ritual androgyny," that is, the deliberate creation of the religious sense of being both male and female in one person.[41]

Such experiences correspond to classic shamanistic rituals. In all kinds of esoteric religious groups throughout history one finds "asexual priest-shamans ... true hermaphrodites," who have a priestly function, according to Eliade, precisely because "they combine in their own person the feminine element (earth) and the masculine element (sky). We here have" says Eliade, "ritual androgyny, a well-known archaic formula for the ... *conjunction oppositorum* [the joining of the opposites]."[42]

"When Eve separated from Adam, the original androgynous unity was broken. The purpose of Christ's coming is to reunite 'Adam' and 'Eve.'"[43] There was no death when Eve was still in Adam. Adam is therefore called a "hermaphrodite,"[44] that is, both male and female. Thus the human soul is described as "androgynous."[45] Death came when Eve was separated from Adam.[46] It is also said that death follows sexual reproduction.[47] The ultimate goal is to return to the state of androgyny where one is both male and female. The Gnostic Jesus commends making "the male and the female one and the same, so that the male not be male nor the female female."[48] Death will be defeated when Adam attains his former androgynous self.[49]

In *The Gospel of Thomas* Salome declares to Jesus that she is his

disciple. Jesus replies that since he is from the Undivided, his
disciples will be "undivided ... filled with light, but if ... divided
[they] will be filled with darkness."[50] In the next saying, Jesus
identifies this teaching as "my mysteries."[51] Inevitably, the final
saying, which brings these "secret sayings ... of the living Jesus"
to a conclusion, has Mary "become a male." This is repeated in
The Gospel of Mary who praises the Savior because "he has prepared us [and] made us into men."[52]

Such androgynous spirituality has a close association with
various pagan practices. Hippolytus witnessed it and documented the fact that the Naassenes he knew openly attended the
pagan worship ceremonies of the Goddess. There they sought
spiritually what the pagan priests realized physically, namely
androgyny through castration.[53] In this regard, Gnostic spirituality also parallels Hindu spirituality, since both recommend a
fusion of sexuality and spirituality.[54] In Tantric or Kundalini
Yoga, androgyny is also the goal, when the two contrary principles of Shiva and Shakti are joined. Eliade explains how, "when
Shakti, who sleeps in the shape of a serpent (*kundalini*), at the
base of his body, is awakened by certain yogic techniques, she
moves ... by way of the *chakras* up to the top of the skull, where
Shiva dwells and unites with him."[55] The yogin, through powerful techniques of sexual-spiritual meditation, is thus transformed
"into a kind of 'androgyne.'"[56]

Another modern Gnostic takes Gaffney's analysis of Gnostic
spiritual sexuality even further. June Singer, in her book, appropriately entitled *Androgyny*, shows exactly how this Eastern
fusion of sexuality and spirituality produces the androgynous
Hieros Gamos. With reference to the Hindu Vedic scriptures, she
shows how Kundalini yoga succeeds in "internalizing sexual
potency ... when *prana* [sexual energy] is drawn inward, instead
of being discharged outward, [which then] becomes available to
infuse one's own cosmic consciousness ... Individuals come to
unity within themselves."[57] One comes to know "the conjunction

in one's own being, of male and female," and of "being one's own lover."[58]

One does not need the opposite sex, except for initial stimu-lation—as the Naassene alabaster bowl suggests. Thus the essence of the androgynous joining of the opposites in *Hieros Gamos* turns out to be an experience of "self-fertilization"[59] to achieve "union within the self,"[60] creating not physical children but a spiritual child.[61]

The Gnostic Jesus teaches spiritual-sexual techniques of arousal, by which the disciple reaches states of mystical fusion with the All. In this state of out-of-body bliss, all distinctions, including gender distinctions, lose their power. Once reached, the state of ritual androgyny then serves to underline the funda-mental Gnostic conviction that redemption is liberation from all earthly and biological constraints. Sex serves spirituality, prov-ing that the true self is uncreated, as old as God.

The Montgomery County public school system just approved a curriculum based on the recommendations of the Citizens' Advisory Committee on Family Life and Human Development in which tenth-graders are taught that gender identity is "a person's internal sense of knowing whether he or she is male or female."[62] In light of the rise of Gnosticism in our day, we must ask how much public policy is driven, consciously, and very often unconsciously, by this "new" androgynous view of both spirituality and sexuality.

The programmatic statement of the influential Jungian psy-chologist and Gnostic convert, June Singer, in 1977 at the height of the movement of sexual liberation flowing from the sixties, would suggest a positive answer to our question: "A new sexual theory is in order.... We have at hand ... all the ingredients we will need ... to fuse the opposites within us. We must look toward a whole way of being ... no longer as exclusively 'mas-culine' or 'feminine' but rather as whole beings in whom the opposite qualities are ever-present."[63] She makes this proposal

for the future of sexuality in full awareness of its worldview ram-
ifications: "What lies in store as we move towards the longed-for
conjunction of the opposites [is the question] ... can the human
psyche realize its own creative potential through building its
own cosmology and supplying it with its own gods?"[64]

The least one can say about the Gnostic Jesus' teaching on
sexuality is that it has powerful contemporary appeal. The real
question, though, is if it agrees with the facts of history.

THE BIBLICAL JESUS AND SEX

As the steam from the Gnostic bathhouse disperses, we begin to
see a different, sharper view of human sexuality on the pages of
the biblical Gospels. Here we find in Jesus' teaching and life not
one glimpse of sexual ambiguity, not one hint of scurrilous scan-
dal, not one suggestion of sex-inspired spiritual bliss. On the
contrary, we see a down-home earthy simplicity that our sex-
obsessed pornographic culture probably finds utterly boring.
Like all the areas we have examined so far, sexuality in the
canonical Jesus' life and ministry is both thoroughly consistent
with biblical spirituality and diametrically opposed to the version we saw in the Gnostic Jesus. We are faced one more time
with a clear choice—a real, live baby or "an immortal, spiritual
foetus."

The biblical Jesus teaches the goodness and exclusiveness of
heterosexuality, the significance of monogamous lifelong marriage, and the blessing of children. All this, once more, flows
from his view of God. These are earthly reflections of the goodness of God the Creator. For Jesus, they are part of the
life-structures provided by the Creator for the well-being of the
cosmos. God the good Creator distributes these earthly gifts
indiscriminately.

BABIES GALORE

Though the circumstances of the birth of Jesus are miraculous and unique, there is great interest in the *baby* Jesus. While

there are no birth narratives in the Gnostic texts, two of the four biblical Gospels devote long opening sections to the birth of two babies—John the Baptist and Jesus. The Gnostic exhortation to "flee maternity" has no place here. Pregnant mothers are front and center in the biblical story of Jesus—part therefore of biblical spirituality. As my wife says, the first home of God incarnate is the womb of a woman.[65] Later, Jesus will anticipate his future return in glory by comparing it to the joy of childbirth: "When a woman is giving birth, she has sorrow because her hour has come, but when she has delivered the baby, she no longer remembers the anguish, for joy that a child has been born into the world."[66]

Once born, the biblical Jesus was raised in a middle-class two-parent family and, as a child, submitted to their parental authority. According to today's standards, the world's most revolutionary figure had very little chance to make it to mature adulthood, having been subjected to a repressive childhood, marked by "obedience."[67] In spite of this structure of obedience, Jesus had his own mind and questioned Mary's wisdom. Even as a child of twelve, he understood that the will of the heavenly Father was superior to that of earthly fathers, but his commitment to and respect of his parents never wavered. This Jesus would never say about his mother what the Jesus of *Thomas* says about his: "My mother [gave me falsehood], but [my] true [Mother] gave me life."[68] On the contrary, Jesus showed great concern and care for Mary right up to his dying day when he placed her safekeeping in the hands of the Beloved Disciple.[69]

While real physical children *never* appeared in the Gnostic texts, the biblical Jesus sought them out. He made a programmatic statement for a "children's ministry" to those wishing to keep them away: "Let the children come to me, and do not hinder them."[70] He gave both time and genuine affection to children, taking them in his arms and praying for them.[71] He was concerned about their well-being and provided for their needs.[72]

In his teaching on prayer, he compared human parents to God the Father, and commended good parenting as something that comes naturally to normal, though sinful, human beings: "If you then, who are evil, know how to give good gifts to your children, how much more will your Father who is in heaven give good things to those who ask him!"[73]

MOTHERS, FATHERS, AND MARRIAGE

Jesus' passing comments on the importance of children and on the normal and expected behavior of selfless parenting presuppose the normativity of the two-parent heterosexual family. However, we do not need to depend only on Jesus' assumptions in this area, for he gives us specific teaching, based on scriptural principles.

Divorce is always a sad and unfortunate thing. Marriages begin with great expectations. The bride is beautiful; the bridegroom early; and the whole event is surrounded by well-wishing friends. Few occasions are more joyful. But marriage is tough and since we are fallible, selfish human beings, divorce is nearly as common as marriage. It was also a problem at the time of Jesus. Seizing this much-debated subject, his opponents tried to trap Jesus into disagreeing with what the Hebrew Scriptures taught on the matter. In his answer, Jesus does not innovate. He establishes his argument on the essential affirmations of previous scriptural principle, in particular, on the original and normative situation of humanity prior to the Fall. Thus he answers: "Have you not read that he who created them from the beginning made them male and female?"[74] The phrases "from the beginning" and "he who created" recall the statement with which the Bible and biblical theism begins, "In the beginning, God created the heavens and the earth,"[75] and also builds upon the further statement, "So God created man in his own image, in the image of God he created him; male and female he created them."[76] All of this created activity is pronounced "very good."[77]

Heterosexual distinctions are part of God's original and good purpose for humanity "from the beginning." From this fundamental distinction emerges the covenantal structure of marriage. Jesus then cites verbatim the biblical text that lays down God's original intention for marriage: "Therefore a man shall leave his father and his mother and hold fast to his wife, and they shall become one flesh."[78] Can we find a clearer endorsement of the biblical understanding of marriage? Instead of undermining physical marriage as "bestiality," Jesus elevates it as God's good intention for humankind.

A profound change is operated here—the male and the female disengage from their filial ties to mother and father in order to form a union that will repeat the same parenting process. In their union, they too will become "mother and father," and carry out the role which in the Old Testament is the guarantor of the well-being of society.[79] There is no hint that Jesus seeks to undermine this normative arrangement, even when he talks about "hating one's wife."[80] He attends a marriage and provides an ample supply of adult libation as a sign of his approval.[81] Most of his disciples were married and later in their own ministry did not feel obliged to abandon their wives but actually took their wives with them.[82]

Thanks to jet lag, I wrote part of this chapter at 4:00 a.m. in an eighteenth-century farmhouse in central France where my wife and I, our seven children, their spouses, and a growing crop of grandchildren met for our first family reunion. I have played some great rounds of golf, eaten some unforgettable meals, had wonderfully romantic experiences with my wife, but one of the greatest pleasures of my life is being the father of this tribe. Deep down I feel like this brings pleasure to the biblical Jesus too.

WAS JESUS MARRIED?

Part of the success of The Da Vinci Code is the unusual affirmation that Jesus was married to Mary Magdelene, with whom he had a child. According to this novel, the term marriage is a little strong.

Jesus had sexual relations with Mary in order to gain the spiritual bliss of sexual orgasm. The baby may well have been a mistake. However, according to the story, after his crucifixion, Mary was spirited away to the South of France were she raised the child, giving birth to a bloodline that eventually became the Merovingian kings of France. Such is one version of the so-called Holy Grail. This helps the story but somewhat stretches the Gnostic view of sexuality!

There is no human, *moral* reason why the biblical Jesus could not have married, since he himself endorsed this God-given institution. Jesus did teach that certain situations called for celibacy,[83] in particular, specific and extraordinary prophetic ministries that entailed danger and persecution.[84] This was not unusual at the time of Jesus. The prophet John the Baptist, as far as we know, was not married; members of the Jewish sect of Qumran were self-consciously celibate because they believed they were living in extraordinary times; the apostle Paul was not married either, for the same reason.[85]

Apart from the later Grail legends (the earliest of which go back to the third or fourth century), and the Gnostic *Gospel of Philip*, which dates from the middle of the third century, no texts affirm that Jesus was married. Actually, even *Philip* does not say Jesus was married to Mary, only that she was his "companion." This fits with Brown's description of Mary as Jesus' sexual partner. Since *Philip* rejects physical marriage, even this noncanonical text fails to give evidence of Jesus' *marital* state. If Jesus were married, one would expect Paul to have argued for his right to marriage by appealing not only to other apostles who traveled with their wives, but supremely to Jesus' travels with his "wife." There is no such mention.[86] The idea might sell lots of books, but as a fact of history it fails miserably.

Why did Jesus not marry? Doubtless he saw his calling as a prophet destined to go to Jerusalem and die, hardly appropriate conditions for the raising of a family, and Jesus was aware of this woeful calling at a relatively early age. Beyond that, Jesus' great goal was to be the Bridegroom of the church, the family of the future kingdom, in which membership does not depend on bloodlines. Also, in his unique role as Son of God, both God and man, marriage for him was not in the plan of redemption.

Jesus' teaching on marriage contains both a major affirmation and a deep qualification. His major affirmation is to honor marriage as a good gift granted by the benevolent Creator. His deep qualification is that something better is on the way. So, on earth, marriage is not for everyone, and celibacy is a valid option. Jesus teaches that physical sex is great, but it is not the last word. No better text shows this than the exchange between Jesus and another group of opponents who try to trick him into saying absurdities. This group, the Sadducees, did not believe in the resurrection, and so they try to make the very idea of resurrection ridiculous.

> There came to him some Sadducees, those who deny that there is a resurrection, and they asked him a question, saying, "Teacher, Moses wrote for us that if a man's brother dies, having a wife but no children, the man must take the widow and raise up offspring for his brother. Now there were seven brothers. The first took a wife, and died without children. And the second and the third took her, and likewise all seven left no children and died. Afterward the woman also died. In the resurrection, therefore, whose wife will the woman be? For the seven had her as wife." And Jesus said to them, "The sons of this age marry and are given in marriage, but those who are considered worthy to attain to that age and to the resurrection from the dead neither marry nor are given in marriage, for they cannot die anymore, because they are equal to angels and are sons of God, being sons of the resurrection."[87]

The opponents hoped to show by this example that resurrection was absurd. Once you admitted to believing in resurrection, they maintained, you would be faced with a situation of one wife and seven husbands. Many cultures have defended one husband and seven wives, but the opposite arrangement was for first-century Judaism absurd indeed.

Jesus does an amazing end-run around these first-century materialists, as he often did. He shows their lack of faith in God's transforming power. Jesus places marriage in its rightful context, as a promise of things to come. With the phrase, "the sons of this age marry and are given in marriage," Jesus normalizes marriage for the present age. It is God's created structure for this world. God says to the first pair in Genesis 1:28, "Be fruitful and multiply and fill the earth." Such is the MO for life on this earth. Sexuality is not for the promotion of ecstatic spiritual trances but for the pursuit of the creation mandate, human fellowship and enjoyment, and personal significance. Like eating, such a view of sex does not mean it cannot be exhilarating and deeply satisfying. I have to eat to stay alive, but I personally prefer staying alive on French cuisine than on hamburgers and fries. But Jesus knew that creation was only God's first work. God's second great work is the transformation of the physical heavens and the earth through the power of the resurrection into something of even greater splendor.

Since the "sons of the resurrection cannot die anymore," argues Jesus, they therefore "neither marry nor are given in marriage." In other words, in the transformed, immortal state, physical reproduction is no longer necessary. Marriage as we know it will come to an end. The new heavens and earth no longer need offspring-producing sex. In this coming time, marriage itself finds its fulfillment in the bringing together of Christ and his people in the marriage supper of the Lamb. This is the true *Hieros Gamos*, the bridal chamber of the glorified cosmos where righteousness dwells, and where creatures find eternal and uninhibited communion with their Maker and Redeemer.[88]

For the Gnostic Jesus, physical marriage is an example of beastiality. It is the work of the evil god of creation and must be repudiated. The only present valid reality is "spiritual marriage." For the biblical Jesus, this—worldy physical marriage brings honor and glory to God the Creator as a fundamental element of biblical spirituality. Spiritual marriage is for heaven, bringing final glory to God, the Redeemer and Consummator.

CHAPTER 7

THE MORALS OF JESUS

I am the prostitute and the venerable one.
I am the wife and the virgin
THE THUNDER, PERFECT MIND 6:17–18

But it is easier for heaven and earth to pass away than
for one dot of the Law to become void.
LUKE 16:17

George Soros: The 'God' Who Carries Around Some Dangerous Demons." This was the intriguing heading to an article about the billionaire George Soros who has, since childhood, considered himself "some kind of god."[1] With the vast amounts of money at his disposal, Soros can make "the once unthinkable acceptable." Soros describes himself as an "amoral" financial speculator whose financial dealings have, in fact, left millions in poverty. He admits, "In my personal capacity I am not a philanthropic person. I am very much self-centered." He also states, "I do not accept the rules imposed by others," and he reserves the right to decide when "normal rules" do not apply.

When do the rules apply? Who says? All human beings are faced with the question of morals, a question that causes us to rise higher than mere beasts. It seems to be a question we cannot avoid. Even people who deny a moral universe can easily be found morally indignant at the "unfairness of it all" when cheated out of a financial deal by a scheming partner or denied a parking spot by an unscrupulous motorist at the very moment when one is late for an important appointment.

THE GNOSTIC JESUS

The Jesus of *The Gospel of Mary* makes a programmatic ethical statement: "Do not lay down any rules beyond what I appointed for you and do not give a law like the lawgiver lest you be constrained by it."[2] This is called "the gospel of the kingdom." In the Nag Hammadi texts one expression occurs over and over to define the ideal ethical state—"without a king."[3] The Gnostics know themselves to be "without a king."

Contemporary Americans would not use that term but surely know what it means. For the original patriots, getting rid of my fellow-countryman, King George III, must have felt so good! Gnostics understood the ecstasy of that freedom when they got rid of God, the ultimate King. One modern Gnostic, Professor Harold Bloom of Yale University, raised on the Jewish Torah, suddenly realized at his conversion to Gnosticism, with a patent sense of relief, that he was "uncreated, as old as God."[4] He came to share the old Gnostic understanding of true belief as the rejection of any external authority. The Gnostics admit no king, no lord, and no lawgiving god. They are self-defining. They "stand alone" (from the Greek, *monachos*, which eventually gave us the word "monk"). They are untrammeled by any external, created structure or divine law. Thus the essence of their humanity is unabridged freedom.

The Gospel of Mary's Jesus repudiates the validity of Old Testament law and promotes a do-it-yourself law defined by individual spiritual intuitions. To understand the "rules" that the Gnostic Jesus lays down, we can look at those he gives to Thomas. When Thomas called him "master," Jesus effectively commanded him not to call him "master." Because Thomas had drunk from the "bubbling spring" of spiritual enlightenment that Jesus provided, Thomas was his own "master."[5] Or, as Jesus says to his followers in *The Gospel of Philip*, "You saw the Spirit, you became Spirit. You saw the Christ, you became Christ. You saw [the Father], you shall become Father."[6] What is affirmed here is total divinization. The believer becomes a fully functioning member of the divine "Trinity." The implications are obvious—God is a lawgiver; a believer is "god"; a believer is his own lawgiver. These statements also imply that the notion of "law" as a generally accepted standard of behavior has been emptied of any meaningful content. That's "the rest of the story." The first part of the story starts a long way back.

THE GNOSTIC NON-FALL

In the Gnostic explanation of origins, the Fall is not the result of human disobedience to the law of God, the Creator. The Gnostic texts contain no such notions as "trespasses, sin, or disobedience." The Fall is not an ethical event. It is the fall of spirit into matter over which human beings had no control. The *creation of matter* is the root of evil, so Yahweh (who created matter) is really the source of all evil.

Matter suffocates spirit. Humans are imprisoned in the bonds of earthly, physical life, a situation of blindness described by Hinduism as *maya*, illusion. Humanity's problem is not sin but sleep, not iniquity but delusional intoxication with the material world, and ignorance of the true human nature.[7] The ancient Gnostic texts explain how matter came to exist. The goddess Sophia, a divine emanation of the Father of the All, independently and inquisitively desired foreknowledge.[8] Her "thought" germinated within her, and she gave birth to an aborted fetus, Ialdaboath (Yahweh, the Creator).[9] Ialdaboath, freeing himself from his well-intentioned mother, formed other "archons," or rulers, and together they created the material cosmos.

Don't let this language confuse you. The strange and mythical imagery is the Gnostic attempt to keep their notion of the true God totally separate and untouched by responsibility for the physical creation. The myth continues. To undo her honest mistake, the goddess Sophia sends the serpent to "seduce Adam and Eve into breaking Ialdaboath's command,"[10] in order to break the Creator's hold upon them. By their rebellion, they realize true human liberation. The Serpent/Satan is thus the first appearance of the Gnostic Christ. This identification is specifically and explicitly made in the Gnostic *Testimony of Truth*.[11] In Gnostic terms, the Serpent reincarnates in Jesus, and Jesus' wisdom is a retelling of the Serpent's wisdom.

With this radical move, the Gnostics turn the biblical notion of good and evil upside down. Here "Ialdaboath's command" or law is associated from the beginning with evil. The Torah is transformed into a book of soul-destroying lies. Keeping "God's law" is life-threatening error, which is diametrically opposed to the health of the soul. In this version of Genesis, the Serpent, whom the Bible says was the wisest, or most cunning, of all the creatures,[12] has become not just clever but good. God, the wise and good Creator, has become not just a fool but the personification of the Devil.

If the human problem is not ultimately a moral one,[13] then the solution cannot be a moral one either. This is why Gnosticism is called *Gnos*ticism. *Gnosis* means knowledge and in the Gnostic system, salvation comes from the experience of a certain kind of knowledge. This vivid spiritual experience allows us to rediscover the knowledge that our original nature was godlike. In this experience, ignorance and intoxication with matter are once and for all destroyed.

What happens to morals in this liberating experience? You will perhaps remember that at the moment of suprarational trance, all contradictions and opposites are transcended. This is the famous *conjunction oppositorum*—the joining of the opposites. All the distinctions that define our earthly existence—Creator-creature, Christ-Satan, male-female, animal-human, truth-falsehood, right-wrong—all evaporate in the hot sun of the human-divine encounter. Did I say "right and wrong"? The distinction between right and wrong is also transcended when an individual discovers "gnosis." Obviously, this has huge implications for the ethical life of the Gnostic believer, who is no longer constrained by the right/wrong definitions of the foolish God, Yahweh. An ethical system requires distinctions—not this behavior but that—while mature "Christian" Gnostic believers pass beyond such simplistic ways of thinking, and are free to put the world back together according to their own individual spiritual judgments.

This is not just ancient history. New Hampshire homosexual Bishop V. Gene Robinson who left his wife and two young daughters in 1986 and moved in with another man said during Planned Parenthood's fifth annual prayer breakfast: "The world is not black and white … We need to teach people about nuance, about holding things in tension, that this can be true and that can be true, and somewhere between is the right answer. It's a very adult way of living, you know…. What an unimaginative God it would be if God only put one meaning in any verse of Scripture."[14]

When a believer becomes one with the divine, his life becomes identical with the life of God. Indeed, the two are forever completely fused. The Gnostic Sophia is defined by contradiction. She deconstructs all earthly rational categories in a monistic joining of the opposites. She presents herself with great frankness, in a series of self-contradictory couplets:

> For the first and the last am I.
> I am the adored and the despised one.
> I am the prostitute and the venerable one.
> I am the wife and the virgin.
> I am the mother and the daughter.

> I myself am the stillness that is beyond
> understanding and the conception
> whose thoughts are numerous.

I am the voice, the sound of which is myriad
    and the word (logos), whose
    appearance is manifold.

I am shame and fearlessness.
I am without shame; I am ashamed.

    I am without mind and I am wise.
    For I myself am the Greek's wisdom and the
        barbarian's knowledge.
    I myself am the judgment of the Greeks and the
        barbarians.
    I am the one whose likeness is great in Egypt.
    [Isis]

I am the one who is called life and whom you
    call death.
I am the one who is called law and whom
    you have called lawless ...
I, I myself am godless, and it is I whose God
    is manifold.

    I am the immutable essence and the one who has
        no immutable essence.
    I am the joining and the dissolution.

I, I myself am without sin and the root of sin
    originates from me.

    It is I who is called truth and lawlessness.[15]

Sophia, who rises beyond the dualities, becomes the model
for all Gnostic believers. They, too, being divine like Sophia,
live in the self-created "space" between "law" and the "law-
less," between "sin and sinlessness," as they transcend the
polarities of earthly existence by the experience of gnosis and
from then on live as gods. This is the deep reasoning behind the
statements of the Gnostic Jesus allowing his followers to live
any way they choose, either breaking all the rules for personal

freedom or living as isolated, self-denying hermits, completely disassociated from the world.

For such divine beings, the very idea of judgment is unthinkable. If there is a notion of judgment in Gnosticism, it is reserved for Yahweh/Ialdaboath and his evil angels, as we saw in chapter 1. The Creator and his legalistic legions are cast into Tartarus, the classical term for hell.[16]

The "ethics of the kingdom" in this understanding of the moral order is quite different from what we find in the ethical teaching of the Jesus in the biblical Gospels.

THE BIBLICAL JESUS

In the canonical gospels the biblical Jesus also makes a programmatic, though thunderously different, ethical statement. It comes as Jesus begins his public ministry and announces the arrival of the kingdom.[17] At this moment he lays down the law of the kingdom, often called "the Sermon on the Mount."[18] Throughout his life and ministry, the biblical Jesus maintains the moral and structural polarities (good and evil, male and female, etc.) inherent in a divinely created universe, which was the pride of his national heritage. Yahweh, the Lawgiver, reminds Israel of their great privilege: "And what great nation is there, that has statutes and rules so righteous as all this law that I set before you today?"[19] Jesus does not repudiate this law. Embedded in the opening section of his first sermon we read, "Do not think that I have come to abolish the Law or the Prophets; I have not come to abolish them but to fulfill them. For truly, I say to you, until heaven and earth pass away, not an iota, not a dot, will pass from the Law until all is accomplished."[20] Keeping God's law is *the* requirement for entering the kingdom, as Jesus declares in the verses that follow: "Unless your righteousness exceeds that of the scribes and Pharisees, you will never enter the kingdom of heaven."[21] Jesus specifically quotes and requires obedience to specific items in the Ten

Commandments—Honor your father and your mother;[22] do not murder; do not commit adultery; do not steal; do not bear false witness; do not defraud.[23]

For Jesus the specific laws are summed up in the two great commandments to love God and to love the neighbor. Keeping them, one may enter the kingdom.[24] As we read on in the sermon, we see that the law of the Old Testament is not only maintained, but even intensified. Jesus, as the Second Moses and the new Lawgiver, stands in the place of Moses to indicate the ethical goal to which the law of Moses pointed. The phrase, "You have heard that it was said to the people long ago [by Moses] … but I say unto you," introduces Jesus' ethical teaching, where the command of Moses is made more stringent and more specific. Murder is defined as hatred in one's soul; adultery is committed by a lustful thought; the comfort of "legal" divorce becomes evidence rather of the hardness of men's hearts; the stringent veracity of a formal oath becomes the standard for everyday speech; legal revenge is replaced by proactive help of the adversary; justified hate of the enemy must be supplanted by love of the enemy.[25] The incredible ethical demands made by the biblical Jesus are summed up in the final command of the Sermon: "You therefore must be [ethically] perfect, as your heavenly Father is perfect."[26] "Scribes and Pharisees," as amazing as they supposedly are, are not the ethical standard. God himself is the rule by which all are judged. This Jesus is not Sophia, who recommends that we join the opposites and jettison all ethical standards. This Jesus is the very voice of the Creator God of the Bible,[27] the Lawgiver of Israel who, though transcending our creaturely condition, yet stands behind his ethical demands.

When Jesus said he came to fulfill the law, he was not kidding. This legislator of the new law of the final kingdom is the one who embodies in his own actions these new and impossible demands. Jesus is not only the model of behavior standing behind the so-called "love chapter" of 1 Corinthians 13, he is the one who, before anyone else, fulfills the new law he promulgates on the mountainside in Galilee. In other words, he meets his own moral demands. He is not just the "Word of God"; he is the "law of God" personified.

JESUS AND TEMPTATION

Kings and presidents sometimes abuse their authority, claiming to be above the law. If any human might have made such a claim, it was Jesus. However, he was not only "born under the law," as the apostle Paul says, but was tempted to break that law and fought hard to "learn obedience." As a true human being in a moral universe defined by God the Creator, Jesus, like Adam and Eve, and like us, was faced with a test of his commitment to the law of God.

We sometimes fail to see the importance of painful events in our lives—those moments that face us with moral choices; moments that force us to answer questions about who we are as human beings. Choices made in the space of a few seconds, in the heat of desire, or in moments of moral weakness can determine the way we orient our lives for years to come. We sometimes call our failures the foolishness of youth, though some of us, alas, are eternal adolescents! A wise person—at any age—knows what is happening, knows human weakness, and takes preventive action immediately.

I shall never forget the reaction of my fifteen-year-old son when pornographic images first popped up on his computer screen. As for most young men, the images fascinated him, and he gave in. But his next, unusually wise reaction was to come to us, his parents, and confess his weakness and ask us to remove the computer from his room. That is how you deal with temptation, however old you are. Call it the "Joseph technique"—run a mile away, right away.[28]

One of the most stunning moral examples we have was when Jesus faced temptation. The fact that he was tempted, and the way he handled that temptation demonstrated both the reality of his created humanity and his understanding of morals. This "King of the Jews" was not himself "without a king," as the Gnostics bragged. This biblical Jesus consciously lived in obedience before God, the king and Creator of the universe.[29] He did not play around with demonic temptation, but before he could run away, he needed to stand and fight, dealing blows to the evil one in our place.

The "temptation of Jesus," as recorded in the Gospels, was one of the most crucial moments in his life.[30] It occurred at the beginning of his public ministry, just after Jesus had been baptized. In submitting himself to the waters of judgment Jesus showed, in symbolic form, his commitment to follow God's will to death. At the baptism, the heavenly Father declared to Jesus that he is the beloved, obedient son. The human Jesus must have felt elated, but pride often comes before a fall, and that obedience must be tested again in less than ideal conditions. The Spirit led Jesus into the wilderness to be tempted by the Devil.[31]

The Devil *tempts* and God *tests*, though the Greek verb is the same. The Devil wants us to fall, while God wants us to succeed. We must see that temptation involves both these sides of the experience. So the Devil did his best to cause Jesus to deviate from his divine calling. God, on the other hand, puts the resolve of his "beloved son" to the test in order to confirm his son's determination to do the will of his Father. The first Adam met temptation in ideal conditions of Edenic bliss. The Old Testament children of Israel met their temptation in the wilderness, led by the Spirit. Both Adam and Israel failed. But the second Adam, the true Israelite, faced temptation alone in the brutal conditions of the cursed wilderness—and succeeded. Moral probation of his Son was part of the divine plan. Thus "the Spirit drove Jesus into the wilderness."[32]

The accounts are not fairy tales or charades. They are not symbolic myths. These experiences happened in a real moment in the life of real human beings, and were charged with deep significance. Jesus' temptation, though brief, has eternal implications—even more than those of Adam or Israel—not only for Jesus himself, but also for the history of the world. Jesus' response is most instructive.

Jesus endured three clever, diabolical temptations that either allude to or misquote Scripture. Cleverly, the Devil did not quote *Playboy* or the Hindu *Bagavad Gita*. He quoted the Bible. How subtle can you get? Here are the three temptations:

1. *"If you are the Son of God, command these stones to become loaves of bread."*

The original temptation of Adam and Eve had to do with eating.[33] Here Jesus was tempted to short-circuit the testing process by cutting short his fasting with a miracle. In spite of the urge to eat, Jesus refused. We, who have been raised to snack when the least little hunger-pain grumbles in the lower regions, can hardly imagine such a scene. But Jesus knew that God had a purpose in this deprivation, to teach him utter dependence upon God. But before he ran, he reminded the Devil with a one-liner of why he was running. Jesus answered, also from Scripture: "It is written, 'Man shall not live by bread alone, but by every word that comes from the mouth of God.'"[34] The temptation was a prolonged affair. There would be two more before Jesus could "run."

2. *"Then the devil took him to the holy city and set him on the pinnacle of the temple and said to him, 'If you are the Son of God, throw yourself down, for it is written, "He will command his angels concerning you," and "On their hands they will bear you up, lest you strike your foot against a stone."'"*[35]

The second was a temptation to put God's goodness to the test. Just as the Serpent suggested to Adam and Eve that God could not be trusted in his stated purpose for them,[36] now the Devil was suggesting that Jesus threaten suicide to be sure of God's concern for him. Even though Jesus, as a human being, would doubtless have enjoyed seeing in some miraculous way a demonstration of God's fatherly protection and care, especially in such a threatening situation, his reply of faith and obedience was remarkable: "It is written, 'You shall not put the Lord your God to the test.'"[37]

3. *"The devil took him to a very high mountain and showed him all the kingdoms of the world and their glory, and he said to him, 'All these I will give you, if you will fall down and worship me.'"*

There is good reason to think that the original temptation of the Serpent was to get Adam and Eve to take things into their own hands, hurry along God's plan to end the temptation, and thus bring about a transformed universe.[38] This was certainly the suggestion the Devil made to Jesus. The Devil was desperate, having failed in his appeal to Jesus' human needs of food and reassurance. Now he appealed to Jesus' sense of mission. He promised to provide a quick way to realize God's intention to redeem the world, though without dealing with the problem of evil through suffering and atoning death.

Jesus would have nothing to do with the Devil's plan, nor would he give him the place of sovereign Lord, ruler of the universe. So he replied, "Be gone, Satan! For it is written, 'You shall worship the Lord your God and him only shall you serve.'" Actually, with this third reply, it was the Devil who ran, realizing how futile his attempts had been. The gospel says: "When the Devil had finished all this tempting, he left him until an opportune time."[39]

We have said that Jesus' temptation proved both his genuine humanity and his commitment to a biblical view of ethics and thus to Holy Scripture. Surrounded as we are with gurus who tell us to look within, to find within our own soul the desires of our heart and the norms of personal behavior, we are astonished at Jesus. His soul was deeper than any other, yet he showed us a model of humble, human obedience. He followed the piety of the Psalmist David who said programmatically at the beginning of the book of Psalms, "Blessed is the man [whose] delight is in the law of the Lord." A pastor/teacher of the sixteenth century, John Calvin, commenting on this psalm, says, "The Psalmist ... teach[es] us that God is only rightly served when his law is obeyed. It is not left to every man to frame a system of religion according to his own judgment, but the standard of godliness is to be taken from the Word of God."[40]

If ever someone could have framed his own "system of religion according to his own judgment," it surely was Jesus. He of all people could have answered the Devil from the depths of his own wisdom. He, of all people, could have "gone within." Yet he did not. He goes without. He *quotes the Bible!* At the moment of great physical weakness and immense spiritual importance, Jesus quoted Old Testament Scripture, which he deeply understood. Did you realize that Jesus' three answers are quotations of three Bible texts from a section of Deuteronomy, chapters 6—8, whose very theme is to explain why Israel had to pass through the testing in the wilderness before reaching the Promised Land? "The Lord your God led you all the way in the desert ... to humble you and to test you to know what was in your heart, whether or not you would keep his commandment."[41]

This is the Jesus who is God's law, but also who lives under that law. He meets all God's standards for true righteousness, providing perfect obedience that stands up against the most ardent temptation. After the resurrection his disciples will understand and develop the significance of this truth. They see him as the one who is "tested in all ways like us,"[42] "learning obedience by suffering,"[43] doing all this as a human substitute in our place. They see him as a man "made like his brothers in every way,"[44] who himself suffered when he was tempted [and] is able to help those who are being tempted.[45] The Jesus of the Bible is a real man who knows and understands the human lot, who "bears our griefs and carries our sorrows,"[46] and thus "can sympathize with our weaknesses."[47]

The incessant demand for righteousness that we mentioned

earlier is mixed with the realistic awareness of the omnipres-
ence of human sin. In preparation for the coming of Jesus, John
the Baptist calls on the people to confess their sins.[48] Jesus
declares that we are all "law-breakers,"[49] that sin enslaves us,[50]
that the Spirit's role is to "convict the world of sin,"[51] that at the
final judgment he will "declare to ... workers of lawlessness ...
'I never knew you; depart from me,'"[52] and that sinners will die
in their sins.[53] Such an insistence on the moral character of
human life and of life in the kingdom gives rise to a predomi-
nant place in the preaching of Jesus for the notion of judgment.
The God of Jesus is a righteous judge who one day will judge
the nations and establish righteousness in the entire cosmos.[54]
The dualities that structure this present life are maintained in
the world to come. The future form of the kingdom has positive
and negative consequences. Thus, in Jesus' preaching of the
coming kingdom, there is the theme of the inevitability of judgment. Jesus predicts a judgment day of final separation,
between "sheep" and "goats," between those on the right hand
and those on the left.[55]

Positively, Jesus promises to drink the new wine of festive
celebration with his disciples in the coming kingdom of God.[56]
These disciples come from all the nations of the earth,[57] and
include unlikely sinners like the thief on the cross.[58] To the original unbelieving twelve, Jesus promises, "Truly, I say to you, in
the new world, when the Son of Man will sit on his glorious
throne, you who have followed me will also sit on twelve
thrones, judging the twelve tribes of Israel."[59] To all who are his
disciples Jesus, the King, will say, "Come, you who are blessed
by my Father, inherit the kingdom prepared for you from the
foundation of the world."[60]

On the other hand, those who thought they would get in by
reason of status, self-worthiness, or birth, the so-called sons of
the kingdom, will be "thrown into the outer darkness. In that
place there will be weeping and gnashing of teeth."[61] To them

and all those like them, Jesus the judge will say, "Depart from me, you cursed, into the eternal fire prepared for the devil and his angels."[62]

The Jesus of Gnosticism provides techniques and thinking that relativize good and evil, allow one to rise above the simple polarities of "good" and "evil," and thereby eliminate the "false" problems of sin and guilt. According to the Jesus of the Bible, the human predicament and fate is a moral one, so the solution must be a moral one too. There *is* a solution, as the following chapter will show. In a word, the Jesus of the Gospels presents himself not just as the moral teacher, but also as the one who forgives sins.[63] That is what his name Jesus means, as the angel says to Mary, "You shall call his name Jesus, for he will save his people from their sins."[64] When John the Baptist sees Jesus, the one thing he cries out, of all the things he could have said, is, "Behold, the Lamb of God, who takes away the sin of the world!"[65]

While Gnosticism has no category of forgiveness, forgiveness leaps from virtually every page in the biblical Gospels; and always, it is tied to the death of Jesus. Inevitably, the Gnostic and biblical Gospels will see the significance of the death of Jesus in very different ways.

CHAPTER 8

THE DEATH OF JESUS

One who experiences Messianic consciousness ... knows oneself as an immortal Spirit, is a bornless and deathless Spirit.... With this knowledge death is no longer death."
—TAU MALACHI[1]

The people dwelling in darkness have seen a great light, and for those dwelling in the region and shadow of death, on them a light has dawned.
MATTHEW 4:16

My wife knew a set of twins in high school. At first, she couldn't tell them apart very well, but then her brother began to date one of them. Before long, she recognized Jenny from Janie easily, even at a distance. At first, and especially from a distance, the Gnostic Jesus and the biblical Jesus may look alike. But the closer we examine them, the less they look alike.[2] As we zoom in carefully, we begin to wonder if they are even brothers, let alone twins. With what we have seen so far, it will not surprise us to discover that the Gnostic Jesus has a completely different view of death than that espoused by the biblical Jesus.

DEATH FOR THE GNOSTIC JESUS

Eastern gurus have become a common sight in the West. Their flowing robes and long gray hair and beards, their expensive limos, adoring disciples, and impressive real estate, which serves as a cult center—all this gives them the odd, suspicious aura of con men. Some most certainly are, but we probably don't see the sincere and serious ones who remain quietly in their simple cells or remote monasteries, devoted to hours of deep meditation. Their goal is to become so unattached to temporal things that the passage from life to death is peaceful and natural—nearly imperceptible. One Buddhist guru, deep in meditation, died but remained in his meditative posture for two days, and no one realized he was dead. For his disciples, this was the ideal death. Death has become a natural and logical sequel to a certain kind of lifelong quest. It is merely "a stage in the cycle of life wherein an organism undergoes transformation [so] what is there to fear?"[3]

When you dig a little deeper, you find that Gnosticism has a similar view of death.

The kingdom is an essential notion in the teaching of both the Gnostic Jesus and the biblical Jesus, as noted above. In Gnosticism, the kingdom represents a state of spiritual, mystical ecstasy, the place where one has escaped the clutches of physical existence. For the Gnostic Jesus, entrance into the kingdom is gained by means of a change of understanding about the self, a self liberated from misleading notions of gender, family, history, morality, physicality, even death itself. Thus the two ideas, kingdom and death, are deeply connected.

The Gnostic texts give a fairly consistent picture of Jesus' view of death—his own and death in general—though there are problems. Individual Gnostic gospels come at the subject in different ways; their language and meaning are not always clear; and most of all, unlike in the biblical Gospels, the subject of death is not often discussed.

The Secret Book of James claims to be a special revelation of Jesus to James and Peter, not to all the Twelve. This could be a somewhat convoluted version of the gospel account of the transfiguration,

minus the apostle John, Moses, and Elijah.[4] Jesus encourages
these two disciples to be full of the Spirit but empty of reason,[5]
and it is certainly true that this book contains passages that, perhaps deliberately, defy rational comprehension. The teaching on
death, however, seems quite clear. True disciples who are "equal
to Jesus,"[6] are exhorted to "scorn death"[7] and "the kingdom of
death."[8] This "kingdom" is the product of the false God, the
Creator of the flesh.[9] The Gnostic Jesus teaches that death is our
friend that liberates spiritual beings from the limits of our evil
flesh. Thus Jesus declares that "none of those who fear death will
be saved."[10] We must not fear death, but embrace it because, as
the end of fleshly existence, it functions as the gateway to true
spiritual life. True believers can thus embrace death as the final
moment of spiritual deliverance.

In *The Gospel of Truth* this same Gnostic view of the physical
world provides the background for everything else. Way back in
the mists of existence, according to the Gnostic myth of origins,
"ignorance" appeared from nowhere. "Ignorance" gave rise to
"error" which became powerful, and foolishly created physical
matter.[11] Jesus Christ came from the true Father and reveals to
the Gnostics that they are not from this world of ignorant, error-
prone matter, but in their essential being, they share the divine
perfection of the true Father.[12]

This is the same kind of teaching one finds in *The Tripartate
Tractate* where Christ is granted some form of bodily existence,
even incarnation, and hence undergoes suffering and death.[13]
But it is all to show the superiority of spirituality over the illusion of physical existence. However, on the cross, Jesus reveals
that physical life is merely "perishable rags," and that truth is
"imperishable" since it comes from the true Father and has nothing to do with created reality.[14] In fact, on the cross, Jesus reveals
that death cannot touch the immortal and divine soul of the
Gnostic believer. Like God, Gnostics cannot die. The ancient
Greeks called this the "immortality of the soul."

Such a view of Jesus' death is nevertheless unusual. The more consistent expressions go all the way and deny entirely Christ's physical reality. In *The First Apocalypse of James*, Jesus reassures James: "Do not be concerned for me ... never have I suffered in any way."[15] This fact is explained in another text which argues that the one who died on the cross was not Christ but Simon or other unknown men who were struck with reeds, who bore the cross, on whose head was placed the crown of thorns, etc., while Christ laughed at their ignorance.[16] The *Apocalypse of Peter* makes the same point.

> The Savior said to me [Peter]: "He whom you saw on the tree, glad and laughing, this is the living Jesus. But this one into whose hands and feet they drive the nails is his fleshly part, which is the substitute being put to shame, the one who came into being in his likeness."[17]

Christ is sitting on the branch of a tree (possibly the cross) looking down, laughing at the ignorance of those who are actually killing someone else. In this text, the irony and ignorance are even greater. The one whom they crucify is "the first-born [of creation], and the home of demons ... of Elohim, of the cross which is under the Law."[18] Here the physical creation by the hand of Elohim has become the home of demons.

The above treatments give two slightly differing accounts of Christ's death. In the first, Christ suffers and dies on the cross to reveal that physical life is worthless and that eternal, bodiless existence is the desirable state for which true believers are destined. In the second, it has become inconceivable that Christ, the true messenger from the Father of the All, could actually take on human flesh in any way. Thus the incarnation is only apparent. Christ only *appears* to have physical flesh. In this case, the crucifixion must have involved a human substitute. Christ only appears to have died.

A third approach, which is perhaps the most typical of the

Gnostic texts, is to avoid the subject altogether. Only seven of the fifty-two texts deal with the death of Christ, and even those seven hardly give the subject a serious treatment, and for good reason. If, from the earliest days, the Gnostics or their precursors were known as those who denied that Jesus Christ had come in the flesh,[19] then what happened to the flesh would hardly constitute a serious subject of theological debate.

In *The Gospel of Thomas*, often considered the most "biblical" of the Gnostic gospels, there is equally no discussion about the crucifixion and physical death of Jesus. Jesus is introduced from the beginning as "the living Jesus," a Jesus who has no physical relationship with things around him. The disciples ask Jesus about the "repose of the dead" and the arrival of the "new world," and Jesus replies that they have "already taken place."[20] Such "realized eschatology" or "spiritualization of the future" is typical of Gnosticism, for which there is no significant future consummation or final judgment. All one can say is that death here has been totally spiritualized. Thus Jesus can describe the physical world as "a corpse,"[21] a living thing that is already dead.

You find in *Thomas* the classic statement about destroying and rebuilding "this house,"[22] which in the Bible gives rise to much teaching on the death of Christ and his relationship to the temple, all reappearing in his trial. In *Thomas* there is not one word of comment, just the enigmatic statement, "I shall destroy this house, and no one will be able to rebuild it."

It is nevertheless true to say that, in a certain sense, this gospel is *all* about death, or, at least, about avoiding death. It begins with the promise: "Whosoever finds the interpretation of these sayings will not experience death."[23] Jesus implies that his disciples will avoid the experience of death by attaining to some kind of mystical knowledge hidden in his words. Avoiding death is tied to Jesus. Near the end of the gospel, Jesus makes the statement, "The one who lives from the Living One [Jesus himself] will not see death."[24] In both these sayings, though "death" is evoked, the reality of physical death has been spiritualized out of existence. Jesus, who in this gospel calls himself "the Living One," does not face physical death. He merely assures his followers that, in the experience of mystical transport, death disappears. Such teaching is a Christianized form of the pagan mystery religions where mystical initiation into the powers of the god or goddess delivers one from the fear of death into a state of immortality.

In *Thomas*, like other Gnostic texts, physical life is seen as the product of a blind and foolish Creator. If physical life has no real existence, then neither does physical death. Both are products of illusion and spiritual blindness, and their true nature must be ascertained through mystical insight or gnosis. The Gnostic Jesus chooses to overcome death by denying its objective existence.

Jesus teaches that genuinely spiritual human beings understand that they cannot die. They were originally a part of God, but fell into the false reality of physical matter. They awake from ignorance and sleep by rediscovering the truth about themselves: They belong to another world, "the kingdom of the Father," and are untouched by suffering and death.

As in Buddhism, Gnostic meditation on the spiritual eliminates the illusory effects of the physical. Meditation, which is becoming more popular by the hour in contemporary culture, is based on the notion that suffering and death exist only when you falsely choose to believe them real. Like the "Jesus" of *A Course in Miracles*, who teaches that the only sin is to believe that there *is* sin, the Gnostic Jesus teaches that death exists only in unenlightened minds.

It should not surprise us that the Gnostic texts do not deal with the subject of death in general, or Jesus' death in particular. Why talk about something that has no existence? A Gnostic would certainly never make a movie like Mel Gibson's *The Passion of The Christ!*

DEATH FOR THE BIBLICAL JESUS

I mention Gibson's movie once more because it evokes the fundamental difference between the death of Jesus in Gnosticism and his death in the biblical Gospels. Without going entirely Gnostic, many people today are perturbed by the biblical view of the death of Christ. The *New York Times* review of the ABC film, *Judas*, a sort of anti-passion movie, calls *Judas* a "balm to those who felt that Mr. Gibson gloried in the violence of the crucifixion at the expense of Jesus' message of love and forgiveness."[25] Kenneth Turan of the *Los Angeles Times* declares that Gibson's *The Passion* "fosters a one-dimensional view of Jesus, reducing his entire life and world-transforming teachings to His sufferings, to the notion that He was exclusively someone who was willing to absorb unspeakable punishment for our sins."[26]

Gibson concentrates on the final hours of the earthly life of Jesus and does not try to represent the Gospels in their entirety. But the gospel writers also concentrate on the Passion Week. They see "Jesus' message of love and forgiveness" as fundamentally tied to and ultimately expressed in his passion. Jesus' death was "world-transforming." We remember the German theologian Martin Kahler's definition of the Gospels as "passion narratives with long introductions." This is no exaggeration. The short gospel of Mark, with sixteen chapters, already tells us in the first six verses of the third chapter that the Pharisees were watching Jesus and were conspiring with the political authorities how they might kill him.[27] In the much longer gospel of Luke (twenty-four chapters), Jesus begins his final journey to Jerusalem and the cross as early as the end of chapter nine.[28] In other words, almost two thirds of this gospel are devoted to the events of the passion. In John (twenty-one chapters), Jesus says in chapter eight, *"now you seek to kill me,"*[29] and from chapter thirteen on, Jesus and his disciples are in the upper room, just hours from the events of the crucifixion. The preponderance of the passion is undeniable and we are led to ask, *why?*

Two statements from notable figures in the Christian movement set the parameters of the answer.

- The pre-Christian prophet and cousin of Jesus, John the
  Baptist

John gives us *the earliest contemporary understanding* of the
death of Jesus. As Jesus comes to him for baptism at the very
beginning of his ministry, John declares, "Behold, the Lamb of
God, who takes away the sin of the world."[30] The work of the
Messiah is conceived in essentially sacrificial terms.

- One of the earliest converts, the apostle Paul

Paul gives us *the earliest written Christian confession* of the
death of Jesus, coming from the thirties of the first century.[31] Paul
cites a Christian creed, written in a different style from his own,
which he explicitly said he *received*.[32] He quotes this creed as
essential, as of "first importance," for the content of the Christian
gospel, "without which there is no Gospel."[33] The first line of this
creed declares: "Christ died for our sins according to the
Scriptures."[34] Again, the Messiah's essential work is tied to his
atoning death.

In other words, both John before the cross and Paul immediately after it affirm a major, atoning moral significance to the
death of Jesus. Does this agree with what Jesus himself taught?

As noted above, Jesus' central teaching was about the
kingdom, which he understood in terms of the fulfillment of
Old Testament prophecies. The prophets comfort Israel with
the hope that, after the exile in Babylon, God will restore the
kingdom of Israel:

> They shall come and sing aloud on the height of Zion,
> and they shall be radiant over the goodness of the Lord,
> over the grain, the wine, and the oil, and over the
> young of the flock and the herd; their life shall be like a
> watered garden, and they shall languish no more.[35]

This will be a restored "kingdom" because there will be a

king: "They shall serve the Lord their God and David their king, whom I will raise up for them."[36]

This idyllic future is contrasted to the reality of the present disaster. God, through his prophet, states why the exile took place, "I have hidden my face from this city because of all their evil."[37] Israel is guilty, says the Lord, "because your guilt is great, because your sins are flagrant, I have done these things to you."[38]

Because the restoration of the kingdom must take account of sin, God's promise of blessing includes the following: "I will cleanse them from all the guilt of their sin against me, and I will forgive all the guilt of their sin and rebellion against me."[39] This cleansing will come about because God "will cause a righteous Branch to spring up for David, and he shall execute justice and righteousness in the land."[40] The kingdom will be reestablished because the Lord "will forgive their iniquity, and ... will remember their sin no more,"[41] so that "you shall be my people, and I will be your God."[42]

Jesus' teaching about his own death fits this Old Testament context. It is often preceded by the little Greek word *dei* which means "it is necessary" or "it must take place." This little word has a big meaning. It signals the fulfillment of scriptural prophecy.[43] After the confession of Peter, the gospel account states, "From that time Jesus began to show his disciples that he *must* go to Jerusalem and suffer many things from the elders and chief priests and scribes, and be killed, and on the third day be raised."[44] It is clear that the "must" has to do with Scripture because later, in the garden of Gethsemane when this prophecy of Jesus is about to become a reality as the soldiers come to take him, Jesus says, "Have you come out as against a robber, with swords and clubs to capture me? Day after day I was with you in the temple teaching, and you did not seize me. But let the Scriptures be fulfilled."[45] "Go ahead," says Jesus, "arrest me, in fulfillment of Scripture."

Since Jesus saw his whole ministry as a fulfillment of Scripture,[46] it is obvious that this would also include his death. Of his forthcoming death he declares (again using the little word *dei*, "must"), "For I tell you that this Scripture *must* be fulfilled in me: 'And he was numbered with the transgressors.' For what is written about me has its fulfillment."[47] Jesus cites from Isaiah.[53] He actually sees Isaiah writing *about him* in the famous text describing the death of the Servant. The Servant of the Lord in Isaiah is God's Anointed One, who leads a second and final Exodus of God's people back to their land to reestablish the kingdom. But in order for this to happen, the leader must bear the sins of the people. Thanks to Handel's *Messiah*, many of the words in this Old Testament prophecy are familiar, but that does not make them any less significant. Here is what is said about the death of the Servant:

> He was wounded for our transgressions; he was
> crushed for our iniquities; … the Lord has laid on him
> the iniquity of us all…. Yet it was the will of the Lord
> to crush him; … his soul makes an offering for sin …
> he bore the sin of many, and makes intercession for
> the transgressors.[48]

The Gospels consistently understand the death of Jesus in this light. The whole agonizing event of the crucifixion, in its smallest details, is conceived as the *necessary* fulfillment of Scripture.[49] Jesus thirsts according to the Scriptures;[50] the soldiers cast lots for his clothes according to the Scriptures;[51] they thrust a spear in his side according to the Scriptures;[52] Jesus' bones are not broken according to the Scriptures.[53]

There is nothing of this in Dan Brown's *The Da Vinci Code*, but, more to the point, there is nothing of this in any of the Gnostic gospels. The Hebrew Scriptures are either totally ignored or turned on their head to say what they clearly do not mean to say. In the biblical Gospels, as in the case of the Servant figure of the prophecy of Isaiah,[54] the death of Jesus as an atoning sacrifice for sinners, fulfills the conditions for the coming of the kingdom and provides the means by which believers can be pardoned. As the King, as God's "Righteous" branch of David, Jesus brings to the kingdom its required righteousness. This is why Jesus, in his last Passover meal, takes the cup of wine and says to his disciples, who represent the new kingdom people of God, "Drink of it, all of you, for this is my blood of the covenant, which is poured out for many for the forgiveness of sins."[55] This reference to "many" recalls the word about the death of the Servant who "bore the sin of *many*, and makes intercession for the transgressors."[56]

In summary, Jesus, at the beginning of his ministry, after having defeated the Evil One in the wilderness, announces in Galilee the coming of the kingdom. The kingdom comes because Jesus the King has come and defeated the Devil, but as yet only in principle. Toward the end of his ministry we learn that there is more. The original temptations return with even greater force. Close to the end, Peter, who had just declared who Jesus really was by revelation from the Father in heaven,[57] suddenly (three verses later) repeats the diabolical suggestion that Jesus not go to the cross, and Jesus turns on him with a sudden burst of terrifying anger, "Get out of my sight, Satan."[58] On the cross the chief priests and their entourage, like Satan in the wilderness, mockingly urge Jesus to save himself.[59] In this way, the reality of the beginning in the wilderness is deeply connected to what happens at the end.

After prophesying his own death "according to the Scriptures,"[60] Jesus then immediately prophesies a coming of the kingdom "in power."[61] This powerful coming of the kingdom describes his final and definitive defeat of the Evil One at the cross, and his resurrection on the third day, but that—the resurrectional nature of the kingdom—must be the subject of the next chapter. Jesus in his victory over death and sin has become the cornerstone of the coming kingdom, as he himself says, "Have you never read in the Scriptures: "The stone that the builders rejected has become the cornerstone; this was the Lord's doing, and it is marvelous in our eyes?"[62]

CHAPTER 9

THE RESURRECTION OF JESUS

I shall destroy [this] house, and no one will be able to rebuild it.[1]
THE GOSPEL OF THOMAS 71

*Jesus answered them, "Destroy this temple,
and in three days I will raise it up."*
JOHN 2:19

To my great surprise, I found myself seated in the personal office of the retired chairman of the Religious Studies Department of the University of Wellington in New Zealand. Wellington curves around a magnificent bay and is the home of the production team of the movie series *The Lord of the Rings*. My wife had come prepared to find all the sites of this epic movie. In preparation for *my* trip, I had read the work of Lloyd Geering, a Presbyterian minister and theologian of the church "down under," who had created the Department of Religious Studies in Wellington and was its first chairman. During his long career, Geering, now in his eighties, received numerous national and international honors, including "Companion of the British Empire." His recent, profoundly anti-Christian books, promoted by "The Jesus Seminar," reject the God of the Bible and call for an end to Christianity as we have known it.

In preparation for the coming of the planetary society, Geering proposes redating history, starting with GE 1 ("global era 1," the equivalent of AD 2000). This would eliminate not only any trace of the British Empire but even the memory of Christianity. Perhaps Geering will one day be honored posthumously with "Companion of the Planetary Empire."

As I sat in Geering's old office, the guest of his successor, I thought over what I had read of Geering's early career in the 1950s and 1960s. A brilliant Christian theologian, Geering decided he could no longer affirm the *physical* resurrection of Jesus. Examined by the church authorities, Geering argued that he was not opposed to the resurrection of Jesus as a "spiritual" event, but had problems with interpreting it in merely physical terms. The argument seemed justified to many and Geering was able to avoid ecclesiastical censure. As a matter of fact, "spiritual" rather than "physical" resurrection is very much at home in the Gnostic scrolls. Is it a difference without significance?

Ministers I met in Australia and New Zealand say that the Presbyterian Church of New Zealand, from that moment on, went into a decline from which it has never recovered. Geering's theological development finally denied not only the physical resurrection, but, like the Gnostic Jesus, the very existence of the God who, the Scripture declares, raised Jesus from the dead.

The resurrection of Jesus is the turning point of human history, and represents the great watershed of theology. Like no other historical event, it captures the enormity of the crisis of death, where our worst fears and our highest aspirations meet. The one who understands the truth about Jesus' death and resurrection—whatever that truth is, Gnostic or biblical— has understood everything about the cosmos. On no other subject are the Gnostic Jesus and the biblical Jesus more starkly contrasted.

RESURRECTION ACCORDING TO THE GNOSTIC JESUS

As we noted, the Gnostic texts teach what Lloyd Geering came to believe, namely that Jesus' resurrection was a purely "spiritual" event. What do the Gnostics mean by the term?

One of the shortest of the fifty-two Nag Hammadi texts (only three pages long), is called *The Treatise on the Resurrection*. The anonymous author, who writes to his pupil, Rheginos, seems to make orthodox statements, affirming that Christ existed in the flesh and, as the Son of Man, possessed both humanity and divinity.[2] He uses a form of the Pauline terminology to state that "the imperishable descends upon the perishable" and that the Savior "swallowed the visible by the invisible." The Jesus of this treatise encourages believers that they have "suffered with him, ... arose with him, and ... went to heaven with him."[3] Though at first blush orthodox, the teaching of this *Treatise* in typical Gnostic manner rejects the physical creation entirely. There is no divine creation of the physical, which is defined as a little piece of the Pleroma or Fullness, which accidentally "broke loose ... and became [the] world."[4] The physical world is a mistake or, as the text says, "an illusion."[5] To rectify this "fall into matter," the unknown author of the *Treatise* recommends a return to the spiritual reality from which it came.

Here is the classic Gnostic notion of redemption. Gnostics posit a world that starts with the spiritual state of the divine and immortal soul, which falls into the physical and must then return to its original spiritual state—the movement is threefold: *spiritual, physical, spiritual*. The difference from New Testament thinking could not be more stark. The apostle Paul explicitly states, "But it is not the spiritual that is first but the natural [or physical], and then the spiritual."[6] Here the movement for the cosmos is twofold: *physical, then spiritual*. God creates the physical "from nothing," and one day will transform it through the spiritual power of the resurrection.

Returning to *The Treatise on the Resurrection*, there is no future hope of a physical resurrection for the believer since the author sees the resurrection as a past, *spiritual* event. We meet this view briefly in *The Gospel of Thomas*, so the notion of a past, spiritual resurrection is clearly part of the Gnostic system. The disciples ask Jesus when the "new world" will come. The Jesus of *Thomas* answers, "What you look forward to has already come."[7] In his introduction to *The Treatise on the Resurrection*, the official modern translator observes that the Gnostic author's view is similar to the teaching Paul combats when he reprimands the "Christian" teachers Hymenaeus and Philetus for propounding that "the resurrection (of believers) has already occurred."[8] As later full-blown Gnosticism goes, this view, denounced by Paul, is, in a certain sense, moderate. A modern expert on Gnosticism, Princeton's Elaine Pagels, argues that the Gnostic view is an acceptable variant of the New Testament teaching on the resurrection.[9] But such is not the approach of someone who saw the risen Lord. For the apostle Paul, the Gnostic way is not simply another acceptable way. It is the "antithesis" of the true way.[10] He calls it "gangrene,"[11] "wickedness,"[12] and "sin."[13] Whom should we believe? Pagels or Paul? Doubtless the brilliant Paul could see where such a "moderate" view would eventually lead—to a full-blown Gnostic rejection of the physical world as evil and of the Creator as a fool. To that kind of Gnosticism we now turn.

The remaining fifty-one Nag Hammadi texts show us the logical end of the approach advocated in the *Treatise*. Ironically, they show us what the Gnostics thought of the resurrection by failing to mention it! Apart from the discussion in the *Treatise*, resurrection is not raised in serious theological discussion. There is no event to be described; no empty tomb; no earthshaking transformation of the flesh to be witnessed; no miraculous appearances of Jesus that shake the disciples to the core of their being. The Gnostic Jesus is always what he was—a spirit being.

With the eyes of gnosis, Gnostic disciples see beyond the external physical plane to behold spiritual truth.

The physical resurrection is pointless for two reasons—first, the physical body is worthless to start with, and deserves to rot in the ground; second, the Gnostics believed that Christ did not die on the cross. Someone else did. They certainly didn't care about the body of his worthless substitute.

When the Gnostic texts do speak of the physical resurrection, it is in a dismissive fashion. For example, the Jesus of *Thomas* makes a statement about "this house," which recalls the words of the biblical Jesus who predicts his own bodily resurrection, referring to his body as the temple. In *Thomas* Jesus says, "I shall destroy [this] house, and no one will be able to rebuild it."[14] If the Jesus of *Thomas*, in speaking of "this [destroyed] house," is alluding to his physical body, then he is clearly rejecting the very notion of physical resurrection when he states categorically, "No one will be able to rebuild it."

This latter interpretation would fit with what we find in *The Gospel of Philip*. Here Jesus teaches that in past aeons the precious soul fell into a "contemptible body."[15] Another Gnostic text, *The Book of Thomas the Contender*, makes the same point more graphically. Jesus says to his "brother," Judas Thomas, "[the] body is bestial ... [and] will perish."[16] The Jesus of *Philip* implies that the true believer must get rid of this contemptible physical thing which is the body. Resurrection is the last thing on his mind. Death is welcomed as a way of escape and a minor inconvenience. According to *Philip*, we should not say that Jesus "died first then rose," but rather that Jesus "rose up first and then died."[17]

This confusing language suggests that Jesus' resurrection is not a physical event. If Jesus could rise before his physical body died, his "resurrection" occurred before his death. This Gnostic Jesus teaches, in the same passage, that those who hope for the resurrection of their flesh are making a big mistake. Only those who leave their bodies behind, who now see themselves as "naked," will enter the true kingdom of God, for "flesh and blood shall not be able to inherit the kingdom of God."[18] *Philip* makes it clear that true believers will never inherit flesh and blood, but must learn to "unclothe" themselves now, by disavowing the flesh, in order to enter the kingdom. Becoming pure soul, returning to the original pre-created state of spiritual, nonbodily existence, "this," says the Gnostic *Exegesis of the Soul*, "is the resurrection that is from the dead."[19]

This then is what the system of Gnosticism means by the three stages of redemption, mentioned above: first the spiritual, then the physical, then the spiritual again. This circular version of existence is graphically portrayed in a Gnostic symbol you may have seen, the "ouroboros," a snake in the form of a circle with its tail in its mouth. The soul, as a piece of the divine spiritual essence, has always existed. Through error, it falls into the clutches of the evil Creator of physical matter. By gaining gnosis and spiritual enlightenment about its inner divine nature, it experiences a mystical resurrection that creates a moment of spiritual ecstasy and enlightenment. The soul then sees through the illusion of the body and matter as real and understands itself to be immortal. The fear of death is vanquished. Through gnosis, "new birth" or "resurrection" occurs. At the moment of physical death, the soul fully escapes the prison house of the body and returns to its original, disembodied spiritual state.

I used the term "system." The Gnostic worldview contains a systematic consistency and implacable logic. Gnosticism in its many forms is now becoming the spiritual choice of many, so it is important to see the implications of its worldview. Where you begin determines where you end up. Here we see how important is our definition of God, which is why I began this book with Jesus' view of God. Gnosticism and the New Testament present two conflicting views of God. If God is what the Gnostics describe him to be—a cosmic spirit beyond and within all things—then resurrection *cannot* be bodily. Any mention of "resurrection" or "new birth" is borrowed from another system, the biblical one, and reinterpreted to mean something quite different.

For the Gnostics, resurrection means the "spiritual" rediscovery of one's higher, inner self as a piece of God. The Gnostic bishop, Stephan Hoeller, confirms this, and also shows the closeness of Gnosticism to Eastern religions, when he says, "The Gnostics share with the Hindus ... the notion that the divine essence is present deep within human nature."[20] Such knowledge removes the sting or fear of death. Death, as final release from the body, becomes the Gnostic's friend. This is what Gnosticism means by resurrection—the destruction of the body for the liberation of the spirit.

THE BIBLICAL RESURRECTION

In the novel *A Prayer for Owen Meany*, the narrator says, "Easter is the main event; if you do not believe in the resurrection, you're not a believer."[21] Biblical faith cannot include variants that eliminate the "main event," thus destroying its foundation. The apostle Paul was "intolerant" of the teaching of Hymenaeus and Philetus in the church at Ephesus and of other unnamed false teachers in Corinth who were teaching about the resurrection.[22] Paul is not overreacting, jealous of people who disagreed with him in some minor detail.[23] The differences are not mere "difficulties," or a "failure to grasp ... connections," as some scholars maintain.[24] For Paul, the *physical* resurrection of Jesus[25] is the essence of biblical religion. Without it, there is no Christian faith. If the resurrection did not happen in the way the original apostles say it did, then instead of being preachers of good news, they become "purveyors of lies."[26] Paul calls the Gnostic view of resurrection "wickedness"[27] and "sin."[28] His language seems over the top and politically incorrect. Having studied Paul, I believe that his language emerges from his jealous passion for the person and the honor of God. Does this seem remote? Paul calls this "spiritual" view of resurrection, "ignorance of God," the result of something like a "drunken stupor."[29] This is what we miss in the modern debate over the nature of the resurrection—the person of God. We saw that the Gnostic view of the resurrection flowed out of their view of God. Here Paul says that their "ignorance," as it relates to God the Creator, is "inexcusable."[30] His thinking is anticipated in the pre-Christian Jewish book, *Wisdom of Solomon*, which states:

> What born fools all men were who lived in ignorance
> of God, who from the good things before their eyes
> could not learn to know him who really is and failed
> to recognize the Artificier, though they observed his
> works.[31]

Paul believes that everyone knows God the Creator, but that human beings "suppress the truth"[32] and are "blinded by the god of this world."[33] This is doubtless what he means by "drunken stupor." They are thus "without God and without hope in the world."[34] This rejection and willful blindness concerning God the Creator is what is "taught by demons and deceiving spirits"[35] in the church at Ephesus. The false view of the resurrection as it was taught in Ephesus flows out of the prior denial of God the good Creator.

Such denial can come in many forms. In the Ephesian church where the "proto-Gnostic" false teachers reject bodily resurrection, they also deny God the good Creator by "forbid[ding] people to marry and order[ing] them to abstain from certain foods, *which God created*."[36] At first, their desire for celibacy and a sensible diet does not seem radical or demonic, but Paul exposes their real motivation, which is the rejection of God the Creator—hence their view of resurrection.

In responding to them, Paul gives both a resounding affirmation of creation, "Everything God created is good,"[37] and a warning, "Turn away from godless chatter and the opposing ideas of what is falsely called knowledge"—literally, *gnosis*.[38] This is why we can call this error "proto-*Gnostic*." It is not the full-blown Gnosticism of the second and third centuries, but takes a major step along the path.

If God created fleshly bodies and pronounced them "good" at the beginning, then his final work of new creation will include the resurrection and the transformation of what was created good at the first. In the biblical system, if resurrection has taken place, the garden tomb in Jerusalem cannot contain Jesus' rotting corpse.

This is why Paul insists on a different chronology from the pagan and Gnostic one. For him the biblical order is: first the *physical,* then the *spiritual*.[39] He is affirming the goodness and the necessity of the first creation—the *physical*—before the second re-creative act of God, transforming and infusing the original physical with the *spiritual*, the future life of the new creation.[40]

Jesus employs the same logic. The person of God, Creator of heaven and earth, determines for him the nature of resurrection in general, and of his resurrection in particular. Of course, as we addressed the question of the resurrection of Jesus, we began with the apostles' witness to this earthshaking event. Before he died, Jesus could not speak about the resurrection in the same way that he could after he rose, or in the way that the apostles could later speak of it, as Spirit-inspired witnesses. While he was ministering, the resurrection was still future. However, it would be wrong to think that he did not teach about it at all. His earthly teaching on the subject is of great interest.

Jews who didn't believe in the resurrection were known as Sadducees, and Jesus tells them, "You are wrong, because you know neither the Scriptures nor the power of God."[41] According to Jesus, their failure to view the resurrection correctly stems from their ignorance of God and his life-giving power as Creator, revealed in the Old Testament Scriptures. The view of the

Sadducees was not identical to that of the later false teachers in Corinth and Ephesus. However, in this exchange we see that Jesus' view of resurrection is based on a correct knowledge of the character of the God of Scripture.

Words and phrases are important. Just like Paul, Jesus uses the phrase, "resurrection of the dead."[42] Paul, according to Luke, uses the same phrase on Mars Hill, to the mockery of the Athenian skeptics.[43] Presumably, had he evoked a more "spiritual" notion, like "resurrection of the soul," or "liberation of the spirit," the Greek intellectuals of the day would have listened to him with more respect. This expression, as used by Jesus and Paul, though consistently translated "resurrection of the dead," literally means "resurrection of dead persons." The term "dead" in the Greek phrase is a masculine plural. It thus resists the Gnostic notion of the soul escaping from the mortal body which it leaves behind in the grave. For the Bible, it is dead people— body and soul—who are made to "stand up again," brought back to life in resurrection bodies. When God resurrects there is no remainder. Thus the tomb of Jesus *had* to be empty.

Jesus predicts not only his death but also his resurrection, which is an essential part of his *message*, though it does not take up a large part of his *teaching*. Resurrection is what he *does* (really what God does to him). It is an experience, like death, that he undergoes for the purposes of redemption.

The verb Jesus often uses for resurrection means literally "stand up again." In the Old Testament it is often employed to describe the Lord engaging in determined action. The Lord reassures the psalmist, "Because the poor are plundered, because the needy groan, *I will now arise*."[44] The imagery suggests the Lord is seated on his heavenly throne, then stands up to intervene, as in the past, on behalf of the afflicted. So David pleads with the Lord, "Take hold of shield and buckler and *rise* for my help!"[45] The verb is applied to human beings, rising from sleep,[46] or from death. David's enemies say of him, "A deadly thing is poured out on

THE RESURRECTION OF JESUS

him; he will not rise again from where he lies."[47] David is as good as dead and will remain that way. But David renews his faith in the Lord and affirms, "But you, O Lord, be gracious to me, and *raise me up*, that I may repay them!"[48] Though David here probably means that he will recover from his sick bed to fight again, there is little doubt that he also believed in physical resurrection from the dead. Such a prospect is an almost unthinkable possibility, and in his more "realistic" moments, the psalmist asks, "Do you show your wonders to the dead? Do those who are dead *rise up* and praise you?"[49] While to human view, resurrection is impossible, yet in faith he declares, "I have set the Lord always before me; ... Therefore my heart is glad, and my whole being rejoices; my flesh also dwells secure. For you will not abandon my soul to Sheol, or let your holy one see corruption."[50]

The apostle Peter applies this text to Jesus, described as "David's greater Son." He does so in the first post-resurrection sermon ever preached, in Jerusalem, on the Day of Pentecost, seven weeks after the crucifixion of Jesus, in the same city, to prove from Scripture why the tomb of Jesus, just a mile away, was empty.[51] Job has the same faith: "And after my skin has been thus destroyed, yet in my flesh I shall see God."[52] The prophet Isaiah, after predicting the death of the Servant, states, "After his soul makes an offering for sin, he shall see his offspring; he shall prolong his days."[53]

This is the scriptural background of all that Jesus says about resurrection. What we noted about the little word "must" applies not only to his death, but also to Jesus' resurrection. About the risen Jesus, when he appears to the two disciples on the road to Emmaus, Luke says that "he opened their minds to understand the Scriptures, and said to them, 'Thus it is *written*, that the Christ *must* suffer and on the third day rise from the dead.'"[54] This is what the earliest post-Easter Christian creed also affirms: "that he was raised on the third day according to the *Scriptures*."[55]

We see that Jesus (and the church following him) draws his

understanding and expectations of his own resurrection from the Old Testament. God, the good Creator of Genesis, promises to glorify one day in the act of resurrection what he created as good, but which sin had marred by death. The divine promise focused on the coming Davidic King, the representative "son" of God.

Resurrection is not an add-on or a secondary theme. It is not a legend or an isolated miracle. It is the heart and soul of the message of Jesus concerning the kingdom. Why do I tie kingdom to resurrection? Immediately after predicting his resurrection,[56] Jesus makes an important declaration: "Truly [lit. Amen], I say to you, there are some standing here who will not die until they have seen the kingdom of God come with power."[57] The next event in the gospel of Mark recounts how Jesus takes three disciples up into a mountain and is "transfigured" or transformed before them. Specifically, "his clothes became radiant, intensely white, as no one on earth could bleach them." Many have wondered what this transfiguring or material transformation meant. It is clearly still the fleshly Jesus, and yet it is Jesus in a halo of dazzling glory. The closest comparable event is the blinding appearance of the risen Lord, shining brighter than the sun. It is the glorious manifestation that Paul witnessed on the road to Damascus.[58]

The transfiguration is an anticipation of the resurrection of Jesus, which will take place a short time later, granted to those who would be the foundation of the church.[59] There are four reasons for thinking this:

1. In this very text, Jesus had just predicted his resurrection.[60]
2. As they descend from the mountain, Jesus instructs his disciples "to tell no one what they had seen, until the Son of Man had *risen from the dead*."[61]
3. Immediately, the disciples wonder what this *rising from the dead* might mean.[62]

4. Jesus describes the transfiguration as "the kingdom of God come with power,"[63] which is the way the apostle Paul describes the resurrection of Jesus. He speaks of Christ, the eternal Son, "declared to be the Son of God *in power*[64] according to the Spirit of holiness *by his resurrection from the dead.*"[65]

Why make such a fuss of this connection between Jesus' kingdom teaching and the resurrection? Quite simply because Jesus' understanding of the kingdom of God includes the glorious, powerful transformation of the physical universe. God the Creator of the physical universe will also transform it. The God who dresses the lilies and clothes the grass will make all things new. God's kingdom coming in power is his miraculous resurrection of the material flesh of Jesus as a down payment of the transformation of the cosmos.

In the Old Testament, the phrase "in power" often refers to God's power that intervenes to change the fortunes of his people.[66] Referring to the deliverance from Egypt, the psalmist declares, "It was you who split open the sea *by your power.*"[67] During his ministry, Jesus brings in the kingdom by a demonstration of power of the Spirit over evil spirits,[68] but the definitive and final form of the kingdom is when God, by his power, resurrects the universe, starting with the physical body of Jesus. This is the "power of God" that the Sadducees did not know because they rejected from the outset the possibility of resurrection. This is why Jesus associates the transfiguration with the coming kingdom in power. It gives a glimpse of the nature of the resurrection body and the future cosmos. At the transfiguration, the disciples see the real Jesus, but it is Jesus gloriously transfigured. The same is true at the resurrection. While the glorified body of Jesus is liberated from its earthly restraints, the Jesus who effortlessly passed through closed doors is still recognizable as Jesus.[69] This is how the Bible sees the coming kingdom. It is not a this-worldly community of gentle people applying the radical ethic of the Sermon on the Mount. The coming kingdom begins with the defeat of death. The mortal is clothed with immortality; the perishable puts on the imperishable; the *dead* are raised.[70] God who established the original kingdom of living, physical beings by an act of unspeakable power (i.e., the Creation) will, by that same creative power, bring in his eternal kingdom.[71] This is "the gospel of the kingdom."[72] The good caterpillar of the original creation, even though marred by sin, becomes by resurrection power the dazzlingly beautiful butterfly of the new creation. The kingdom Jesus announces is the new heavens and the new earth. The poor in spirit *will* receive the kingdom of heaven; the meek *will* inherit a transformed earth.[73]

In Conclusion

With the question of the resurrection, we arrive at the end of this long but necessary exercise. We have attempted to lay out, side by side, the two possible pictures of Jesus, both of which can be found in texts that go back to ancient times. Perhaps until now we have been able to study the comparison with intellectual curiosity, but remain neutral in our attitude. The resurrection, however, forces a decision on us as mortal beings, destined to die. We reach a genuine watershed where the difference between the two accounts of Jesus calls for a decision.

For the Gnostic, the resurrection is a nonevent. Death is a pleasant, necessary bridge that takes both Jesus and the believer back beyond the physical and returns them to the original non-created spiritual reality that has always existed.

The deciding element in New Testament faith is the fact that Jesus' bloodied and disfigured corpse came back to life in a form more glorious than in his previous earthly existence. In the biblical Gospels, the power of death is vanquished by the death of Jesus as a righteous "offering for sin," which makes possible the restoration of physical flesh in a new and trans-formed state. Resurrection is not a return to a prior disembodied spiritual existence. It is a "new creation" that never before existed. In the event of resurrection, everything Jesus taught about humanity, about the physical world, about himself, and about God is vindicated.

In the following two chapters, I would like to present the necessity of your choice and then I would ask your permission to explain mine.

CHAPTER 10

YOUR CHOICE

The Vision of Christ that thou dost see
Is my vision's greatest enemy.
Both read the Bible day and night,
But thou read black where I read white.
—WILLIAM BLAKE[1]

We have looked carefully at two pictures of Jesus. Both have roots in ancient times and both still have enormous power and appeal in the twenty-first century, even at the level of popular entertainment. The biblical Jesus has provided material for a successful movie, *The Passion of The Christ*.[2] The Gnostic Jesus has served as a model for one of the most successful novels of all time, *The Da Vinci Code*, and its movie version.

Ever since his birth more than two millennia ago, Jesus has posed an enigma, causing culture after culture to answer the demands of his person and message. Each generation faces the evidence anew, and all of us must make the most important choice of our lives—which Jesus will we accept? Some of you reading this book have not yet made your choice. Others have chosen, but are reevaluating that choice in light of what seems to be new evidence, such as newly discovered Gnostic scrolls and the new versions of church history. Before you got married, you looked hard at your prospective spouse. Before you bought your house, you examined the termite inspection. Even before buying a pound of butter, you wondered whether you could find a better price at the market down the street. So in making the most important decision of your life—the decision about Jesus—it is important to do your research. We need to clear the decks and get rid of sloppy and misleading arguments so the options are clear.

In this chapter I want to examine:

1. the claim that the Gnostic and the biblical pictures of Jesus are *two versions of the same story*;
2. the modern claim to neutrality;
3. how, behind the explicit or implicit claims of neutrality, lie deeply religious motivations;
4. why the "two versions" approach to Christianity is impossible, since *Gnosticism is a non-Christian religion*; and
5. why you need to weigh your own choice in the light of the massive religious conflict going on around us at the beginning of the third millennium.

I will be referring to the main writers and thinkers who are making Gnosticism popular. Perhaps I should have provided you with a cast of characters! It doesn't matter if you don't remember the names, but please remember their thinking, because you will hear their ideas in the movie theater, on TV, in the news media, and perhaps even in your church. I hope that when you have finished the chapter, you will find it easier to recognize each Jesus when you meet him, and to make a sound choice between them.

Two Versions of the Same Story

"Can't we all just get along?" was Rodney King's plaintive cry after his severe beating by police and their subsequent acquittal that resulted in rioting in Los Angeles. His question has come to express our cultural desire for tolerance and might well be applied to the Jesus controversy. Can't the two Jesuses just get along? Jena Malone stars in the movie *Saved!*, which mocks Christianity for its hypocrisy and narrow-minded idiocy—some of it deserved—and suggests that Jews, homosexuals, Christians, and moral rebels are all part of a happy spiritual family. Malone thinks the movie "has a very Christian message about love and acceptance ... the basic teachings of Jesus Christ." She goes on: "I feel this movie is very much pro-faith, in the sense of having the courage to find your own belief system."[3]

LARGER AND LEFT

Malone is among many who are coming to see "faith" as a "pick and choose" solution, which allows them to keep the name "Christian" and still borrow good ideas from all religions. This contemporary view of faith is well-served by the ancient Gnostic texts, which many scholars now propose as a variant form of early Christianity. They believe this variant form has a rightful place in the "large tent" of an inclusive church. To do this, the church fathers, who opposed the Gnostic texts when they were first written, are seen as nearsighted and narrow, having deprived the church of the complete view of Jesus. James Robinson, the director of the translation project of the Gnostic texts, believes they contain genuine teaching from Jesus that, when mixed with elements from the Bible, fills out the biblical picture to give us the full-orbed Jesus we need for our global era.[4] For Robinson, the Gnostics represent a form of "left-wing Christianity"[5]—left-wing, but *Christian* nevertheless.

WIDER AND UNFAMILIAR

Another Gnostic specialist, Elaine Pagels, sees Gnosticism as "a wider view of Christianity."[6] I studied with her at Harvard in the late sixties and recognized her to be a brilliant young woman. She was in the inner circle of scholars who had access to the Gnostic texts before they were made publicly available. Her book, *The Gnostic Gospels*, published when she was thirty-five, was an immediate best seller.[7] Almost singlehandedly, it brought the Nag Hammadi texts out of the ivy-leafed towers and into the public square. Writing with "the instincts of a novelist," as one reviewer said, she succeeded in making the ancient Gnostic heretics "likeable." She offered Gnosticism as an alternate but valid expression of early Christianity. As an "objective historian," Pagels rehabilitated the Gnostic "Christians" by portraying them as forgotten heroes of an old class war between the politically motivated orthodox bishops and their hapless spiritual victims. Pagels sees the Gnostic gospels as complementary to the canonical ones rather than as antithetical, heretical rivals, as the church fathers "myopically"[8] wrote and taught. Says Pagels:

> [T]he discovery of Thomas's gospel shows us that other early Christians held quite different understandings of "the gospel." ... what Christians have disparagingly called Gnostic and heretical sometimes turn out to be forms of Christian teaching that are merely unfamiliar to us.[9]

DEEPER AND OPEN TO ALL

Victor de Waal, a former Dean of Canterbury Cathedral, is a regular visitor to a New Age center located in the town of Dent in England. "I don't see it as an alternative; I see it as deepening one's faith," the former dean explained. He went on to argue that his dabbling in the New Age was in no way inconsistent with his Christian commitments, because the "spirituality" he now practiced is "not committed to a particular tradition," but open to all.[10] According to these thinkers, Gnosticism offers us today a Jesus for the 21st century whose appeal is larger, wider, and deeper than that of the biblical Jesus.

THE CLAIM TO NEUTRALITY

Human beings have agendas. As soon as you open your mouth to speak, you have some sense of what you want to say in the context of a belief system. If you speak out of no context whatsoever, you will end up in a mental hospital. Imagine the dialogue of a movie that has no plot or development, no thesis, no drama. We do not speak randomly. When it comes to speaking about Jesus, those who favor the *biblical* Jesus usually recognize and admit their faith commitment. Such "believers" are often accused of religious bias. Those promoting the Gnostic Jesus, however, usually claim to be neutral historians—objective observers of religious history. But scholars also have a religious grid through which they analyze history. Like other human beings, they stand in a particular place and view the world from a limited perspective. All interpretations must be checked by corroborating, independent evidence before any claim to historical reliability and objectivity can be made.

Sometimes our biases are so ingrained that we are unaware of them. Michael Baigent, Richard Leigh, and Henry Lincoln also say that they neutrally are open to all religions. These gifted authors wrote a book called *Holy Blood, Holy Grail*,[11] which presents a popular and modern version of the Gnostic Jesus. Claiming to be objective historians, they deny having *any* "prejudices or preconceptions, ... [or any] vested interest of any kind." They say they are being "sympathetic to the core of validity in most of the world's major faiths," while being "indifferent to the dogma and the theology that make up their superstructures."[12] With blinding naiveté, they have set *themselves* up as judges of what is "core" and what is "indifferent superstructure," and *their* definitions determine the choice of a Gnostic Jesus.

Elaine Pagels, the "objective" historian of the early church, declares that "the winners write history." Such a notion draws out our emotions. "Let's get the villains out," is the response of those raised on victimhood and personal rights. Proposing Gnosticism as an acceptable variety of Christianity, the reconstruction fits well with our postmodern mindset. A canonical Bible, a patriarchal God, a hierarchical, gender-distinguishing church, an accusatory law, and a final judgment—all these are unacceptable elements of a dysfunctional worldview whose time is over. The objective historian, above the fray, shows us the biases of power hungry bishops intent on establishing control over the growing Christian movement.[13] Pagels's appeal to inclusiveness in the name of tolerance and the public good strikes a harmonious chord in our ears. However, her approach is not as full, fair, and tolerant as it first appears. It is misleading, because while defending the Gnostic view of Jesus as a valid Christian variant, under the guise of a "neutral" historian, she like many others, holds to a particular understanding of religious truth.

DEEPLY RELIGIOUS MOTIVATIONS

Many scholars who admire the Gnostic Jesus are known for their "prior commitment to a radical liberal viewpoint."[14] Professor Gilles Quispel, a Dutch scholar whose name has long been associated with the academic study of the Nag Hammadi texts has more than an academic interest in the subject. He was Carl Jung's close associate, and saw Gnostic belief as analogous to the best in "depth psychology."[15] Fellow Jungian and Gnostic convert June Singer dedicates her book, *The Gnostic Book of Hours*[16] to Quispel not only for his scholarship, but because his *"inner wisdom* provided the thread that led me through the labyrinthine ways of gnosis."[17] When Singer speaks of Quispel's "inner wisdom" she is referring to a deep religious commitment, prior to all scholarly and scientific arguments, which fits with her own religious view of the universe.

Other scholarly proponents of the Gnostic Jesus formed "The Jesus Seminar" to popularize Gnosticism by publishing easily accessible books. They include the Seminar's founder, Robert Funk, and a well-known writer, Marcus Borg. These men did not originally possess such a liberal religious viewpoint. After rebelling against a childhood background of Christian fundamentalism, they have both adopted some form of nontheistic, Gnostic spirituality.[18]

The translator of the Gnostic texts, James Robinson, was also a firm Christian believer at one time. In fact, he was a Calvinistic Presbyterian minister who made an early exit from orthodoxy. He replaced the biblical spirituality of his youth with a fascination for the Gnostic Jesus as a "holy man," comparable to Buddha, Krishna, or the other great mystics of the world's religions.[19] The Gnostic Bishop Stephan Hoeller mentions Robinson's attendance at the Los Angeles Ecclesia Gnostica[20]—which is a long way from the First Presbyterian Church of Hattiesburg, Mississippi, where Robinson began.

Elaine Pagels tries hard to peel away the blind prejudices of our past ways of understanding Jesus. However, like the poor, our prejudices are always with us, and Pagels explains what has influenced her. She was once an "evangelical Christian," though that turned out to be merely a youthful phase. She attended a delightful tea at the Zen Center in San Francisco with the Roshi Richard Baker and Brother David Steindl-Rast, suggesting her openness to the new spirituality of religious syncretism that these men represent. After suffering bereavement, she found a spiritual home in the Church of the Heavenly Rest in New York, where she was able to reject the notion that being a Christian was "synonymous with accepting a set of beliefs" such as the Apostles' Creed. She is interested in the blending of Christianity and Buddhism.[21] Pagels has collaborated with the Association for Transpersonal Psychology, a discipline devoted to the study and promotion of esoteric, paranormal spirituality and healing.[22] These religious experiences, as well as clear statements in her books, present a limpid picture of her theological prejudices. She believes that religions are essentially the same, that theological conflicts are about power not truth, and that the answer lies in bringing all the religious traditions together. We see that she is far from being a neutral observer of history. She does precisely what she accuses the early church fathers of doing—promoting her view of faith.

In the case of Pagels, the "truth" of her nonscientific, deeply-held religious assumptions colors everything she writes as a historian.

All these proponents of the Gnostic Jesus believe that Christianity is merely one form of the faith held by all the world's major religions, what is called syncretism (all religions are one). Thus the differences between the Gnostic and the biblical Jesus are downplayed. However, holding the Gnostic and the biblical Jesus together as valid variants is not ultimately open-ness and inclusiveness but a sophisticated though unmistakable expression of a particular, syncretistic religious view of the nature of the world. For these two Jesuses cannot ultimately be reconciled, so one view ultimately wins.

If you want to make an informed choice about Jesus, you must remember that no one, not even scholars, comes to Jesus with a religious blank slate. We all come with religious and spiritual commitments that determine the way we look at the historical evidence. The least we can do is to acknowledge them.

By keeping the Gnostic Jesus in the Christian camp, those who were raised on the Bible can still claim a place within the church, even if they are disenchanted with the Bible's essential message. If such scholars can show that the Gnostic Jesus had followers dating back into the mists of early Christian history, then they, modern Gnostic "Christians," cannot be accused of simply changing the Christian gospel to suit the times. They claim to be a valid Christian alternative, an ancient option that should be accepted in today's pluralistic church. Elaine Pagels, in her book, *The Gnostic Gospels*, which sought to rehabilitate Gnosticism as a genuine expression of early Christianity, is a clear example. Pagels states, "To the impoverishment of Christian tradition, Gnosticism, which offered alternatives to what became the main thrust of Christian orthodoxy, was forced out."[23]

It is little wonder that Christians who come into contact with such thinking are so confused. It is burdensome to keep mentioning *The Da Vinci Code*, but the book does an exceptionally good job of muddying the Christian waters, so that even some reasonably sane and solid Christians have a hard time seeing clearly. Even my own daughter, raised in a home where the Bible is read every night and Gnosticism is a part of the daily dinnertime conversation, after reading Brown's novel, said, "I knew most of what he says isn't right, but I'd have a hard time explaining to my friends exactly why."

If she is confused, then how many average Christians, with even less understanding of the issues, can sense that something isn't right, but can't quite identify the problem? The confusion must be dispelled. Gnosticism is *not* a form of Christianity, but actually a form of religious paganism that cannot be successfully proposed as an authentic variant of the Christian gospel. This is not a very politically-correct statement, but I am not the only one to say it.

GNOSTICISM: A NON-CHRISTIAN RELIGION

A cuckoo bird lays its eggs in another bird's nest. The unsuspecting parents feed the baby cuckoo until it grows so big it takes over the nest and kicks the other birds out. Gnosticism is the cuckoo's egg in the Christian nest. Duncan Greenlees is a modern Gnostic, and makes no claims to being Christian. He describes the relationship of Gnosticism to Christianity during the early centuries:

> Gnosticism is a system of direct knowledge of God ...
> in the early centuries of this era, amid a growing
> Christianity, it took on the form of the Christian faith,
> while rejecting most of its specific beliefs. Its wording
> is therefore largely Christian, while its spirit is that of
> the latest paganism of the West.[24]

Do you get his point? With no obvious axe to grind, this modern-day self-consciously non-Christian Gnostic affirms that Gnosticism is in no sense a genuine form of original Christianity.

The two most renowned experts on Gnosticism are two German scholars—Hans Jonas[25] and Kurt Rudolf.[26] Neither sees Gnosticism as Christian. For Jonas, Gnosticism is an example of "revived Eastern thought" brought to the West by Alexander the Great.[27] When Oriental mysticism invaded the pragmatic West after Alexander's conquests, it brought a new dynamic of occult spirituality, creating a "prevalence for half a millennium of the Gnosis conception of religion,"[28] supremely expressed in the so-called "mystery cults."[29] We noted above that certain "Christian" Gnostics attended these cults.

Similarly, for Rudolf, Gnosticism is an independent world religion, not a narrowly limited Christian heresy. He argues that one of the "most important results" of German History of Religions scholarship of the twentieth century was to produce the "proof that the Gnostic movement was originally *a non-Christian phenomenon* [italics mine]."[30]

Rudolf describes Gnosticism as "a parasite prosper[ing] on the soil of a host religion."[31] Remember the cuckoo? Rudolf admits that the "link with Christian ideas ... greatly helped [Gnosticism's] expansion." But he goes on to say that the mix "contained a deadly germ to which sooner or later it was to succumb in competition with the official Christian church." In other words, in spite of what a number of pro-Gnostic modern scholars allege, history shows that the two systems proved to be fatally and philosophically incompatible. The church fathers were not "myopic heresy hunters," as James Robinson constantly affirms,[32] or power-hungry patriarchs, deliberately suppressing what they knew deep-down to be true.[33] This now is the belief of millions having read in *The Da Vinci Code* a more popularized version of this view of history:

> It was all about power ... the modern Bible was
> compiled by men who possessed a political agenda

> ... to solidify their own power base ... Constantine
> and his male successors successfully converted the
> world from matriarchal paganism to patriarchal
> Christianity by waging a campaign of propaganda
> that demonized the sacred feminine, obliterating the
> goddess from modern religion for ever.[34]

This has an immediate effect in the popular culture. When Chris Matthews and Jane Fonda discuss religion on *Hardball*, they sanctimoniously "reveal" to their viewership what all those "in the know" now know that early Christianity became "patri-archal" and left the feminist Jesus out of the Bible.[35]

However, when you compare the two theological systems of Gnosticism and the Bible, the church fathers appear as lucid the-ologians who identified the interloper and eventually kicked the Gnostic cuckoo out of the ecclesiastical nest—for reasons of intellectual consistency and truth, not power.

As a matter of fact, the Gnostic cuckoo survived and built its own nest, with considerable help from a religious mystic by the name of Mani (born in AD 216 in present-day Iraq). Another German expert in Gnosticism, Christof Markschies, Professor of Historical Theology at the University of Heidelburg, argues that Gnosticism was able to grow comfortably in the pagan nest of Manichaeism, an ancient religious synthesis that included Buddhism and Zoroastrianism. "From being [for a time] a Christian heresy it finally becomes a separate religion, claiming to be the religion that transcended all previous religions."[36] Markschies says this about Gnosticism's Christian phase. "The attempt by [early] Christian theologians to explain Christianity by systems of 'gnosis' led away from Christianity."[37] In other words, "gnosis" in its essence was alien to the gospel, which cer-tain speculative Christian thinkings tried to adapt to Christianity but finally failed.

In an anecdote, Pagels virtually admits the same. When she had tea with Roshi, head of the Zen Center of San Francisco, she recounts that as she explained *The Gospel of Thomas* at length to Roshi (a.k.a. Richard Baker), he finally laughed and said to Pagels, "Had I known *The Gospel of Thomas*, I wouldn't have had to become a Buddhist."[38] In other words, Gnosticism and Buddhism are essentially interchangeable—but neither is Christian.

A modern Gnostic, Mark Gaffney affirms, without exaggeration, that the Gnostic paradigm contains notions that are "utterly subversive to orthodox Christianity [and will] stand [that] tradition on its head."[39] A tradition on its head can't get very far. Another modern Gnostic, June Singer, honestly states:

> The whole of the Gnostic mythology ... reads everything in a direction opposite from orthodox theology. What is true in a limited worldview [the biblical worldview, according to Singer] is false in an unlimited worldview [the Gnostic]. What is true in a closed system is false in an open system. And vice versa.[40]

For Singer the relationship is not one of "different perspectives" but of "truth and falsehood"; that is, of mutually irreconcilable notions. She opts for the "truth" of the open Gnostic system. When Pagels argues that Gnosticism merely "widens" Christianity, this is what the ancient Gnostics attempted—and failed. Fuzzy terms like "width" and "depth" are only feasible if you refuse to admit the vast theological gulf between biblical faith and Gnosticism that non-Christian Gnostics have no difficulty recognizing. Even Pagels admits a whole series of major contradictions that blow the systems apart, not widen them—that the "living Jesus" of *The Gospel of Thomas* could equally be a "living Buddha"; that Hinduism and Buddhism doubtless influenced Gnosticism;[41] that the God of orthodox Judaism and Christianity, as the Creator, distinct from the creation, is different from Gnosticism where "the self and the divine are identical";[42] that the Jesus of *The Gospel of Thomas* speaks of "illusion and enlightenment, not of sin and repentance."[43] This is not widening. We are faced with two irreconcilable religious belief systems that have a few nonessential terms in common.

THE BIRD CAN'T FLY!

Pagels may claim that Gnosticism is an enriching alternative of ancient Christianity; Robinson may claim that Gnosticism is the left wing of early Christianity. But if they are correct, the bird has a right wing going in one direction and a left in the other. Such a bird cannot even stay in the air, let alone fly anywhere. This hapless avian hybrid will fall on its head. To provide a better overview of just how different the two systems are in every area, I've organized some of the material we have already seen in the form of a chart below. The scholarly accounts of Gnosticism as an alien system to Christianity are confirmed by the comparison of the two pictures of Jesus.

JESUS'	GNOSTIC	BIBLICAL
GOD	Universal, impersonal spirit God in everything hates the blind creator god	God of creation, good father Redeemer, reveals himself Requires obedience to created structures
MESSAGE AND **MINISTRY**	No kingdom because no king Kingdom is within you Created reality is evil Defeat the king	God rules over his creation Rightful king over his people Kingdom not within you Transforms earthly into heavenly
BIRTH	No physical birth for Jesus No family lineage Not born of a woman	Jewish lineage Real baby, born of a real woman Born under the law Born in time and space

JESUS'	GNOSTIC	BIBLICAL
HUMANITY	No interest in history No chronology No context for Jesus' life	Jesus has real body Suffers temptation Knows physical weakness Lives in a body of sin
DIVINITY	All are divine, so Jesus is too Not the master of disciples All are Messiahs	Jesus is the only begotten God Disciples afraid of Jesus Masters the wind and seas With God before creation
SPIRITUALITY	Silence the mind Knowledge, not worship Meditation, not prayer Spirituality by joining opposites	Faith, not gnosis Rational reflection Prays to Father in heaven
SEXUALITY	Spiritual experience Androgyny Ecstatic unity with all things Excess or ascetics	God-created heterosexuality Physical offspring Unity and communion Communication
MORALS	No law, therefore no sin Creator evil We create our own law No king, No master	Sin is judged Sin demands punishment God's law defines sin Righteousness from the Spirit
DEATH	Physical life=rags Death cannot touch divine soul Substitute died for Jesus Jesus' death an illusion	Death is an enemy Jesus' death redeems his people Real, physical death Death defeated by resurrection
RESURRECTION	Resurrection is symbolic Escape from the body's prison Spiritual, not physical	Resurrection is physical Resurrection is transformation New creation miracle

The New Testament scholar, Marcus Borg, as a child knew the biblical Jesus, divine Son of God and Savior of the world. As an adult, he now speaks of "meeting Jesus again for the first time."[44] This Jesus is much more a spiritual guru along the lines of the Buddha.[45] Borg makes a fatal error of judgment that many now make. He speaks of the two contradictory worldviews, "the religious and the secular."[46] However, the secular is but a blip on the graph of human history. The real divide is between two "religious" views of the world—the worship of creation or the worship of the Creator. The proof is that the two pictures of Jesus we have examined share little common ground. In some ways I wish it were not true, but it is impossible to avoid the fact that in the choice for Jesus we are faced with two radically contradictory, irreconcilable *religious* systems.

The debate about the real Jesus is now a dominant theme in contemporary religious discussion. Each version of Jesus shows an internal coherence that flows from its assumptions about the nature of God and the world. This gives the debate not only a certain clarity but also a sharper edge, since there is little or no room for compromise. Faced with questions of truth and historical fact, we must ultimately choose only one answer. If you fill in more than one bubble on the ballot, your vote will not count at the final tally.

Joining the opposites is not the goal of Gnostic spirituality alone. In our time, many in the church are seeking to join the opposites and to reconcile the irreconcilable. The worldwide Anglican Communion is torn apart over the ordination of gay bishops. Commissions and study groups procrastinate, arguing for "big tent" ecclesiology, but there is no reconciliation possible between the opposing camps. Similar gridlock paralyzes other mainline churches like the Presbyterians and the United Methodists. Irenic compromise is impossible because, as the apostle Paul says, "there is no fellowship with light and darkness."[47]

A lesbian minister in a mainline denomination, in a moment of frustration in her struggle with the biblical orthodox wing of her church, gave expression to the problem in an unforgettable one-liner of unusual limpidity. "Maybe," she said, "we are dealing with a different view of God." Finally, some clear thinking!

THE PRESENT SPIRITUAL CONFLICT

You would not have read this far if you are not intensely interested in Jesus. The choice you must make is not a purely personal one. There are implications involved in the contemporary debate about the historical Jesus. For some time progressive spiritualists have predicted the arrival of a spiritual sea change. Already in the 1930s some were speaking of the New Age, of "a new day ... dawning.... The Piscean Age is passing; the Aquarian Age is coming on."[48] The last two thousand years of Western history are now dismissed by some as the "Christian Interlude." If you have not already made your choice of Jesus, remember that the choice must be seen against the backdrop of the big issues of contemporary spirituality. We are living at the beginning of the "third Spiritual Awakening." The Gnostic Jesus has reappeared to celebrate his kind of spiritual revival. There is more going on than the mere discovery of objective historical facts and neutral scholarly interpretations.

The crisis has been evident for some time. When I returned to the States in 1991, I was so struck by the chasm in American religious life between biblical Christianity and a rising "New Spirituality," then called "New Age," that I immediately wrote a book, *The Gnostic Empire Strikes Back: An Old Heresy for the New Age.*[49] My argument back then was that the New Age was not a "Californian cult" that would go the way of the hula hoop, but a return of Gnosticism. Gnosticism is neither a fad nor a cult; it is apostasy.

Apostasy messes with the foundations of the faith, especially with the foundational notion of God. Gnosticism redefined God.

The struggle in the church and in the society is not over details but over essentials. We are not debating the chronological minutia of the Second Coming, but whether there is a Christ who will come or if he has a place from which to come! We are divided today not over minute details of truth, but whether there is such a thing as truth. We are not divided over various attributes of God, but whether God is the God of the Bible or the divine force of paganism.

The Gnostic option is all around us. A keen observer of the culture notes that "the current postmodernist worldview is ... intrinsically Gnostic."[50] Even the philosophy taught in the academy which underlies moral and cultural meltdown has an unmistakable religious inspiration. Take, for example, the father of postmodern deconstructionism, Jacques Derrida, who died in October, 2004. Derrida called into question the whole notion of absolute truth and argued that the essence of deconstruction was to tear down the dualisms and hierarchies embedded in Western thinking—such as good-evil, mind-body, male-female, truth-fiction.[51] These are "false polarities."[52] If the goal of Gnostic spirituality is the "joining of the opposites," then postmodernism fits perfectly with our modern religious yearnings for the morality and spirituality of inclusion—the pantheistic "all is one" wholeness.

The discovery and publication of the Nag Hammadi texts was not merely an interesting event for scholarly research but, according to Hoeller, a "vital opening drama of cosmic proportions."[53] Some of the authors cited above believe that the return of the Gnostic Jesus will bring planetary salvation. Mark Gaffney believes that "the spiritual development of the West has been seriously impeded by Christianity's failure to evolve a detailed understanding of the spiritual body" as the Gnostics understood it.[54] He clearly implies that the impediment must be removed. Stephan Hoeller believes that only Gnosticism will help avert the final catastrophe. He pleads for a wholeness that includes the great world religions like Buddhism and Hinduism. His admirable desire for "wholeness," however, excludes one religious tradition. Hoeller foresees banishing the biblical spirituality that has dominated the West for the last two thousand years. At least Hoeller is honest in his desire to eliminate as toxic the biblical view of Jesus:

> Our spiritual enfeeblement is *not* due to a fall from grace on the part of Adam and Eve ... and our regeneration will not come about by accepting a personal savior [or] by a risen redeemer, but only by the reconciliation of the gods and goddesses within us.[55]

When the chips are down and clear definitions are important, Gnostic inclusivism and unity emerges as disturbingly exclusivist and intolerant.

In a chapter entitled "How the West was Lost: Loss and Recovery of Psychological Spirituality," Hoeller calls Gnosticism the "internalist" religion, declared heretical by "externalist" religion, and driven underground but now reappearing. There is no room in this book to explore at length the influence of Carl Gustav Jung in the growth of Gnostic influence, but his input has been enormous. If "externalist" religion (i.e. biblical religion) is doomed, what will replace it? Jung answers:

> If Christianity is to come into possession of a conception of ... human spirituality that is more appropriate to the psychological process of becoming whole ... it must appropri[ate] and assimil[ate] ... those movements ... it [once] declared heretical.[56]

Names such as Jung and Hoeller are barely known to the general populace, but names like Dan Brown, and even Pagels, are on the front shelves of the bookstores in the malls and airports. Brown clearly expresses his Gnostic spiritual aspirations: "My sincere hope is that *The Da Vinci Code*, in addition to entertaining people, will serve as an open door for readers to begin their own explorations."[57] Brown hopes his readers will seek enlightenment by considering the claims of the esoteric, pagan spirituality promoted in his novel: That spirituality is Gnostic and its first principle is the removal of the God of the Bible. In his novel, while the goddess is everywhere, God the Creator of heaven and earth is nowhere to be found. The repaganization of the West proceeds apace. The title of an article in *The Times* of London proves the point: "Spirited Away: Why the End Is Nigh for Religion."[58] It is the report of a sociological study of religion in England whose studied conclusion declares that "Christianity will be eclipsed by spirituality in thirty years." The article begins:

> In the beginning there was the Church. And people liked to dress up in their best clothes and go there on Sundays and they praised the Lord and it was good. But it came to pass that people grew tired of the Church and they stopped going, and began to be uplifted by new things such as yoga and t'ai chi instead. And, lo, a spiritual revolution was born.

We have noted from time to time how this conflict about Jesus appears at the level of popular entertainment as Gibson's *The Passion* and Dan Brown's *The Da Vinci Code*. Here also we discover the dour pronouncements as to the long-overdue but certain demise of biblical Christianity. Hollywood producer Stephen Simon, a promoter of what he calls "Spiritual Cinema," which seeks to nurture creativity and inner divine power, sees in Gibson's movie not only the last painful hours of Jesus' life, but the final days of biblical Christianity. In his opinion, "The entire film seemed like the dying gasp of an old ultra-religious paradigm that is slowly fading into oblivion ... I was watching the symbolic conclusion to 2000 years of human history.... Gibson has indeed ushered out this chapter of history in a blaze of O'gory."[59]

The old Gnostic Jesus is emerging in our time as brand-new, multipurpose Jesus for contemporary inclusive upbeat spirituality. According to one astute observer of the American religious scene, what is happening in England is and has happened here. He speaks of the "new religious synthesis ... [which is] a radical alternative to the Judeo-Christian traditions" that *"has already eclipsed"* the Judeo-Christian culture of America's past.[60]

Are we seeing a repeat of the history of Gnosticism? As Gnosticism, which early on claimed to be Christian but then in the 4th century AD became the syncretistic world religion of Manichaeism, and took many Christians with it, we seem to be reliving this same history in our time. The Lutheran scholar Frederic Baue asks the question, "What comes after the Postmodern?" He answers, "A phase of Western/world civilization that is innately religious but hostile to Christianity ... or worse, a dominant but false church that brings all of its forces to bear against the truth of God's Word."[61]

Why be aware of this larger context?

It is easy to think that the so-called "new spirituality" is new and therefore superior. It is easy to think that since the cultural elite champions this new view of Jesus that it must be true. By the way, this same cultural elite, which is now winning the hearts and minds of the nation, especially the young, is now rewriting the early history of the church to rehabilitate the Gnostic gospels—and succeeding quite well. The controversial actress, Jane Fonda, tours the country, declaring herself before the national media to be a Christian. However she then makes it clear that she is "a feminist Christian" who reads both the gospel of John and the Gnostic gospels. In her own words, she believes that "people have different ways of approaching The Word. For me, it's metaphor, written by people a long time after Christ died. And interpreted by specific groups. *I read the gospels that aren't included in the Bible. These make me feel good about calling myself a Christian* [emphasis mine]."[62] This ideology is piped into America's living rooms as superior "gospel truth," believed by the good and the beautiful of the cultural elite.

But if, as the modern revisionists say, we must be suspicious of the winners' version of history, then, as they win the culture wars, their new, winning version is equally and certainly suspect. As you make your choice, you must be equally suspicious of it too. Because glamorous cultural winners like Jane Fonda and the media industry of Hollywood affirm such "truth," this does not make it true. According to their own criteria, it makes it highly suspect!

Beyond this, the larger context helps us to see that the choice we need to make is not a choice for a certain kind of fifties America and the compromised Jesus of our cultural, jingoistic past. The choice is between two views of Jesus that are and always have been the only two religious choices on offer.

The two Jesuses refuse to get along, in spite of what Jane Fonda says. You cannot mix the Jesus of John's gospel with the Jesus of *The Gospel of Thomas.* Thus I would go not with Jane but with James, the brother of Jesus, who says, without ambiguity, "Can fresh water and salty water flow from the same spring?"[63] One Jesus is fresh water; the other is brine. One is meat; the other is poison. One day every knee will bow, either to the Jesus of Gnosticism or to the Jesus of the Bible. Either Yahweh will be cast into hell, or Yahweh will do the casting. Before that day arrives, we have a stark and pressing choice, a choice with deep emotional overtones as well as personal, cosmic, and eternal consequences, demanding great personal courage.

Is Jesus a fellow-traveler and guru we meet on our own path to "internalist" enlightenment, personal reconciliation, and self-redemption? If truth is personal power, as postmodernism tells us, then the choice is easy. Go with the flow. Hook up with the Gnostic Jesus. Empower yourself.

Or is he Immanuel, the "external" God, who has come into

human flesh to be with us, achieving for us through his life, death, and resurrection what we can never achieve on our own, namely, reconciliation with the God who made us? If truth is true, and determines not just earthly but eternal existence, then the wise thing to do is to "kiss the Son," as the old Psalm says,[64] embrace his lordship, and receive his grace, whatever the immediate cost.

You can't *not* choose! I have tried as fairly as I can to present the two views of Jesus, but, by now, it has doubtless become obvious which Jesus I have chosen. In the final chapter I would like you to understand why I have chosen the biblical Jesus.

CHAPTER 11

MY CHOICE

The Word became flesh and made his dwelling among us.
We have seen his glory, the glory of the One and Only,
who came from the Father, full of grace and truth.
JOHN 1:14

People meet Jesus in many ways. Mine was typically unspectacular. Born to Christian parents, I grew up in a Christianity that sometimes came quite close to the kind described in the movie *Saved!* The movie describes, sometimes quite brutally, a kind of Bible-quoting evangelicalism that is high on group emotion and personal salvation but woefully inconsistent and shallow on the demands of Christian behavior and biblical thinking. Jesus was preached as the Savior, but I cannot remember any consistent preaching on the gospel accounts of Jesus' life and moral teachings. How many times as a young person did I make my way to the altar rail when the call to conversion was made by visiting evangelists, and, on my knees, with tears, I determined to be a better believer? Clearly those times equaled the number of times when I was quite convinced I was not "saved." In my youthful and superficial way, I kept meeting Jesus and then losing him.

In college, my childish faith died, and I began to work on the serious business of growing up and proving to all (myself included) the significance and importance of my own person. In this project, Jesus had no place.

One day, as an adult, I met Jesus—or should I say, Jesus met me at the beginning of my adult life. In the middle of a PhD. program—ironically in ancient Gnosticism, no less—my life of self-affirmation and success-seeking came to a screeching halt. I was studying religion to be able to put a PhD. after my name, so that I could finally believe in my own significance. The doctorate was not to help people with whatever knowledge I could acquire. It was to help me. But I was running out of gas. Selfish living can drive you nuts, and I was beginning to doubt I had the inner resources to pull off this final effort of self-affirmation.

It was the beginning of the discovery of Jesus, not just as the personal Savior but as the Lord and Creator of the universe, and thus the all-consuming discovery of the Bible's theistic worldview of which Jesus is both the center and the fulfillment. In a profound, emotional experience, I saw Jesus on the cross, in time and space, really dying for my sins, granting me inner cleansing, bringing me reconciliation with my Maker and thus allowing me to accept my real self, giving me the freedom to be finally unconcerned about me and be concerned about him and serving others.

This is the biblical Jesus I know and love, and when I compare him with the Jesus of Gnosticism, only he makes sense of my life. Let me tell you why.

MEETING THE BIBLICAL JESUS

Sometimes, the Gnostic Jesus is presented as "a new Jesus" for a new global era. The fact is, as the comparison above shows, the Gnostic Jesus is just as old as the biblical Jesus. If one is a valid option, then so is the other. Historical distance is no obstacle. A verse in the New Testament, written close to the time of Jesus, says this very eloquently: "Jesus Christ, the same yesterday, today and forever."[1]

The God of Jesus: The God Jesus serves and reveals is the personal, transcendent, good Creator who is the loving Redeemer.

I am drawn to this God because of a deep sense of what the apostle Paul calls "his eternal power and divine nature" revealed "plainly in the things he made."[2] The God of the Bible, Father, Son, and Holy Spirit, mysteriously though certainly, explains the origin of order, beauty, morality, and personhood that I find so essential in my own being. God as the universal spirit inhabiting all things is doubtless, in a certain sense, liberating, but it produces from the pen of a modern Gnostic elder, the following kind of impersonal speech about God: "God will reveal *itself* in full. God is revealing *itself* all of the time [emphasis mine]."[3] To know that I am in a world created by a personal God, not in an impersonal universe where I must find and create my own way, is profoundly satisfying.

Actor and essayist Ben Stein well captures this sentiment: "We are not responsible for the operation of the universe.... God is real, not a fiction, and when we turn over our lives to Him, he takes far better care of us than we could ever do for ourselves. In a word, we make ourselves sane when we fire ourselves as the directors of the movie of our lives and turn the power over to Him."[4]

My soul is drawn to the personal Creator with a sense of utter necessity, knowing that the choice is not academic or merely interesting. The stakes are almost incalculable. The Bible teaches that everyone knows God through his creation, but refusing to recognize him as such, people prefer to worship creation, which is the heart of idolatry and deliberate rebellion. We will all pay eternally in one way or another for this life-defining choice.

The Message of Jesus: The Gnostic Jesus as a spiritual guru, like the Buddha, Lao-tse, and the Sufi masters, offers deep teaching on the meaning and practice of esoteric spirituality. They are techniques that one must follow and very quickly become salvation by works. What I find attractive in the message of the biblical Jesus is that he came not just to teach but also to accomplish a task I cannot accomplish. By his actions alone, in obedience to God his Father, in the amazing drama of grace, Jesus brings about the end-time utopian kingdom, into which people enter by faith as a gift from God. This message of the kingdom holds within it the immense promise of a transformed universe.

The Humanity of Jesus: The biblical Gospels give us much information about Jesus' physical and national origins so that we can interpret his teaching, knowing where he is coming from. I write as a convinced believer, but it seems to me that this biblical testimony of the Jewish/Old Testament background of Jesus certainly holds together as a composite picture. From what we know of the historical data surrounding Jesus, this biblical picture of Jesus makes believable sense. Nobody has ever questioned that the human Jesus was born into a Jewish family at the time the Gospels indicate. The Gnostic account of a mystical guru who appears from nowhere reads much more like the invention of later interpretation and speculation as Christianity spread into the pagan/Greco-Roman empire. In the Gnostic texts, there is no interest in grounding Jesus in a historical Jewish time and place. From all that we know from our own human experience, while the Gnostic Jesus, with no family or historical background, does not ring true, the biblical Jesus is part of my human reality.

This is not just an interesting fact. The historical reality of Jesus as a human being just like me brings to the whole question of religious faith an unparalleled and joyful element of personal communion. The original followers affirm that they know him,[5] that they love him,[6] that they receive him,[7] that they live in his presence,[8] that they have fellowship with him,[9] that he is now interceding for them[10] as their present heavenly advocate,[11] that they are waiting for Jesus,[12] and pray "Come,

Lord Jesus."[13] It is easy to dismiss the simplistic "me and Jesus" discourse of TV Christianity, but it is important not to forget the enormous living presence of the person of Jesus in biblical faith. Without getting bleary-eyed or overly-sentimental and mystical, there is a level of personalized New Testament speech about Jesus that is unparalleled in other religions. Not in Judaism, Islam, Hinduism, ancient Gnosticism nor in the many other religions do you find a person like the biblical Jesus. Jesus is not simply remembered and honored as a founder of a religion, or a great teacher of the past. Neither is he a shaman, channeler, or a vague ethereal presence, where the person of the medium is strictly without importance. In biblical Christianity the person of Jesus is received both as a real human being of the past who, because raised from the dead, is experienced as an objective personal reality in the present. Such an understanding of Jesus is part of the living Christian hope of one day meeting Jesus face to face. Going through a time of bereavement as I write these lines, I cannot tell you how much this aspect of the biblical account commends Jesus as the object of my faith, love, and devotion.

Jesus as a real person mysteriously reveals the personal heart of God assuring me that I am not alone in an impersonal universe.

The Divinity of Jesus: I must be a kid at heart for I love Christmas. There is something in the air, a sense of expectation, a reminder that all is not misery and discouragement. At the heart of this optimism is the biblical message about the baby Jesus, who mysteriously is not just human but also divine. The divinity of Jesus declares that the transcendent God, in gracious condescension, comes to us as Immanuel, "God with us." I do not wish to suggest that this is easy to comprehend. The mystery of the incarnation is certainly too big for my head, but it fits in my heart. The amazing message of the Bible is not to reveal how we can seek God but how God has come to seek and save us. The God who made us, who controls the universe, has come to redeem us. Little wonder the angels were singing!

There is no Christmas in the Gnostic texts. There is Jesus, ethereally poised between earth and heaven, certainly divine, but no more divine than any other well-informed believer. The gifts he brings come from the East alright, but unlike the gifts of the magi, gold, frankincense, and myrrh, which recognize the uniqueness of the baby Jesus, these bring us one more technique for self-realization—what the French call a *cadeau empoisonné*—not a gift that keeps on giving but a gift that keeps on demanding.

Michael Graham, for many years the right-hand man to Swami Muktananda, the Hindu gurus' guru, speaks about this "gift": "Experiences were easy to come by. Somehow they were never 'it'… Really it was a ride on a merry-go-round forever to nowhere … [and] so much … was starting to look the same."[14]

The Spirituality of Jesus: Even those within the movement of the so-called "new spirituality," or revived Gnosticism, describe it as a "celebration of the self." This is necessarily the case. If there are two options, either worship of the Creator or worship of creation, then worship of the creation necessarily involves the worship of the self as a part of creation. When we hear someone say of someone else, "He worships himself," we all are put on our guard. But one must not miss the point that Gnostic spirituality is ultimately narcissistic. Let me say here that I know my own narcissistic tendencies; but I do not like them.

You find the term *gnosis* everywhere on the lips of the Gnostic Jesus. The biblical Jesus uses the term *gnosis* just once, in a different sense, but the term "faith" he uses twenty-four times. For the biblical Jesus, faith is the essence of spirituality, and of prayer in particular, which is rational trusting discourse of the personal creature with the personal Creator, the Father in heaven. As a creature I understand that simple faith is and always will be the normal relationship of a human creature to the majestic and mysterious Creator. Paul says that faith remains, even when the perfect comes. Gnosis is thus finally hubris, because we know that we are God and the mystery is over. The "aha" moment claims to unlock the inscrutable enigma of God, and confers on creatures an "illegitimate certainty" of the knowledge of themselves as divine. Such spirituality removes the wonder from the gospel and trivializes the transcendent mystery of God. After decades of practice, Michael Graham came to see the great gulf between Eastern mysticism and biblical faith. He states:

> Decades of experiential participation in Eastern mysticism, the world of personal development and the New Age movement, have led me to believe that there is nothing to compare in value with classical biblical Christianity.[15]

When I read Graham's testimony I was struck with the simplicity of his faith compared with the complexity of the knowledge of spirituality he had developed for twenty-eight years. Something about the simplicity and the truth of faith draws me to the gospel. If God is who the Bible says he is, then this is the way it must be. At this point, I cannot hide from you the fact that the Bible describes this Gnostic view as "spiritual seduction," promising the moon but delivering ashes.

One more word about spirituality. Gnostic spirituality solves the human plight by flight not fight! It is true that human beings find themselves in a fallen, suffering world. The Gnostics solve the problem by either asceticism or antinomianism, or, to put it in popular terms everyone understands, by either purging or binging, all this overlaid by a spirituality which denies the reality of the physical world, and proposes flight into the viritual world of out-of-body experiences.

Instead of seeking the Creator as Redeemer, the Creator of the real world is dismissed as the Devil, and salvation is understood as disengagement from the real. This is no more evident than in sexuality.

The Sexuality of Jesus: Why is the Gnostic Jesus so interested in promoting abnormal, anything-goes, sexual expressions? I know that some people suffer from sexual dysfunction, but for me, normalizing this dysfunction is the wrong route, as the very nature of the universe suggests. A clinical psychologist argues that the normal is "that which functions according to its design."[16] The design of our bodies, written by the good Creator into the fabric of our biology, is heterosexual. This is an undeniable fact. Unbridled, *self*-fulfilling sex goes against who we are and has produced the breakdown of marriage, an epidemic of STDs, sexual identity confusion, and the spread of sterility. On this diet of selfish individualism, our culture cannot survive.

The Jesus of the Gospels endorses the normal sexuality of creation both as a life-giving and civilization-promoting blessing from God, and as a way of bringing us face to face with created reality, and thus, face to face with the personal Creator.

The Morals of Jesus: I hate to go to the doctor, but I go to get an honest diagnosis of what is going wrong that I know a band-aid will not help. In my better moments I long for moral purity and know that shoving my filthy rags under the rug does not make the world a safer place or calm my guilt. I somehow know that transcending ethical polarities of good and evil and relativizing right and wrong is a rationalization process that does not rid my human heart of the selfishness and evil I always find there. Above I mentioned the article about George Soros with the title, "The 'God' Who Carries Around Some Dangerous Demons." When Soros says, "I do not accept the rules imposed by others," and reserves the right to decide when "normal rules" do not apply, he is following the moral system of the Jesus of Gnosticism. When the Gnostic Jesus tells us we are gods and can do as we please, I begin to worry what fallible, sinful human beings are capable of producing with that false sense of the self— people "divinely empowered" eventually to do evil, deciding (for the good of others, of course) when the rules do not apply. So far, this kind of empowerment has resulted throughout human history not in utopia but in nightmarish gulags and holocausts. Why should the future be any different?

The Jesus of the Bible boldly confronts me with the blinding light of God's moral purity, which is the heart of the God of the Old Testament law, in order that I might begin to hunger and thirst for righteousness and seek outside of myself and my self-justifications the solution to my moral bankruptcy.

The Death of Jesus: In an article on Alzheimer's, described as "a grim, dreadful and devastating disease," we are nevertheless assured by a Zen-practicing Professor at Florida State University's Medical School, that you can look at it another way, through Buddhist eyes. If "Zen Buddhism … is all about clearing your mind, detaching from your thoughts, grounding yourself in the moment.… Well, that's Alzheimer's."[17] I was speechless. We are asked to believe that true religion is actually a "grim, dreadful and devastating disease"—spiritual Alzheimer's that is robbing a person of thought and life. On the other hand, I began to wonder if the professor was more right than he imagined. Gnostic-type views of physical life as worthless illusion and death as friend are akin to the devastating loss of rational thought.

We all have to face the reality of our own death. The Gnostic Jesus has us close our eyes to the ugliness of death, and I am not reassured.

The Gnostic account of death as friend does not ring true in my soul. I find my deep, human foreboding before death expressed in the realism of the biblical Jesus who cries out in anger before the tomb of Lazarus and shudders as he faces his own death on the cross. From the perspective of the human lot of suffering and death, the truly human Jesus who knows pain and suffering surely offers realistic hope to those who seek him.

The earliest recorded phrase of the Christian gospel, probably written in the mid-thirties of the first century AD, is: "Christ died for our sins according to the scriptures."[18] While some modern scholars see in the death of Jesus only a tragic martyrdom, I place my hope on what the earliest martyrs believed about Jesus. They went to their deaths believing that that this was no ordinary death. It was the death of the *Christ*, God's anointed deliverer. They believed it was a death demanded by the Old Testament's understanding of justice and substitution. They believed therefore that it was a death that had profound implications for them—for us. This is the earliest good news, announcing Jesus as our righteous and effective substitute.

The personal, moving character of the death of Jesus was captured for me in the song, "I Thirst."[19] It depicts the moment when Jesus, who had freely given water to all that came to him, now himself, in a moment of great agony for those he will save, calls out for water to slake his burning thirst:

Between the earth and blackened sky
Suspended on a cross to die
The Savior bows his head and cries,
"I thirst."
Is this the wedding Guest who dined
And turned the water into wine
The one who calls himself the Vine?
"I thirst" …
He shared the cup the night before
And now he is the drink that's
poured …
He says to all, "Come drink from Me

The Water that I give is free
Thirst no more ... come unto Me ...
"I thirst" he cries upon the tree
"I thirst" he cries in agony ...
"I thirst."

To my knowledge there is nothing more deeply moving and soul-transforming in all of religious literature and history than the account of my Savior suffering to the death *for me!*

To the realism and courage of the biblical Jesus we can add the victory of his atoning passion, which is the moral defeat of death. When I come to death it is essential to know that Jesus has taken away the sting of death—the guilt of my sin.

The Resurrection of Jesus: The choice we make for the Gnostic or biblical Jesus is never more starkly evident than here. In simple terms, in Gnosticism, Jesus is a teacher; in the Bible he is Savior. In Gnosticism he speaks wisdom;[20] in the Bible he procures redemption from the jaws of physical death and sin by his perfect life and by the miracle of resurrection. In Gnosticism the final significance of Jesus is his revelation of the fact of my uncreated, timeless spiritual existence; in the Bible it is his revelation of a transformed physical universe.

I am won over by this incredible perspective. You might think I am attracted to the physical resurrection of Jesus by mere wish fulfillment, and I understand why you would. Death as an ugly blight on the miracle of human and cosmic life was no more obvious than when I stood before the casket of my beautiful and brilliant sister, cut down at the age of forty-two by brain cancer. The doctors had tried everything they knew. All was to no avail. Death had won. But would we not all love to believe that a truly dead corpse could come back to life?

What I find so appealing about the biblical account of the physical resurrection of Jesus is its deep consistency. It is not simply the claim that a few people once witnessed the weird fact of a man they had seen brutally murdered and buried, then walking around, identifiable but completely transformed, which is amazing enough. What I also find satisfying is the place of physical resurrection in the biblical worldview, grounded in the power of God the Creator.[21]

Already the physical creation lucidly discloses the derived and dependent character of my human situation. I did not create the world in which I so easily and gladly live. It was all here before me—like a luxury hotel room overlooking the ocean, with everything I need, laid on by a wealthy friend for a well-deserved weekend getaway. I did not invent the world of beauty and personality and of sense and significance, without which I could not even open my mouth to communicate in meaningful sentences. I assume it, get on with life, and write books, like this one. It was God through his Spirit who created the world. How much more is this true about the resurrection?[22] This, too, is the work of the same Spirit.[23] I certainly cannot earn resurrection and, since we still have not figured out how original physical life came into existence, it would be sheer folly to think we could produce the miracle that will transfigure it. I keep bumping against an insoluble human impossibility. "Flesh and blood cannot inherit the kingdom of God."[24] Only a divine initiative from outside the created domain by the God who made all things in the first place can bring in the kingdom. God does something *for me* that I cannot do myself. I am very sorry, but that's the way it is! I have a nagging sense that humanly-constructed utopias will always fail. They have all failed in the past and there is no reason to think they will not fail in the future. If there is any hope for the *human* race, it will have to be found here, outside of human possibilities, in the power of the Lord, Creator, and Redeemer.

A British theologian puts it beautifully:

> Before God raised Jesus from the dead, the hope that
> we call Gnostic, the hope for redemption *from* creation

rather than for the redemption *of* creation, might have appeared to be the only possible hope. "But in fact Christ has been raised from the dead ..." (15:20). That fact rules out those other possibilities, for in the second Adam the first is rescued. The deviance of his will, its fateful leaning towards death, has not been allowed to uncreate what God created.[25]

I cannot see it any other way: The resurrection of Jesus is both the turning point and the glorious culmination of human history. The one who understands the truth about the risen Jesus has understood everything about the cosmos entire.

Not all human questions are answered. Many things about God remain clouded in deep mystery—as it should be, if God is God.

Nevertheless, the Jesus I kept meeting as a kid has come to represent for me a fully satisfying way of understanding the world in all its deep personhood, magnificent complexity, and glorious destiny. This perspective takes my breath away. It is more than I can ever hope or imagine. With it I plan to face the reality of my own death.

THE HISTORICAL AUTHENTICITY OF THE BIBLICAL JESUS

In this chapter so far I have related why the biblical Jesus appeals to my deeply felt religious aspirations and sensibilities. To me the biblical Jesus rings true in my understanding of my own humanity. I recognize, however, that my "subjective" preferences may not coincide with yours. But I cannot end this account without dealing with some questions of history. Today, many believe that with the discovery of the Gnostic Gospels we now have objective reasons for revising the traditional approach to the origins of Christianity, and thus of preferring the Gnostic Jesus to the biblical Jesus. It is doubtless a good thing to be forced, in the light of the Nag Hammadi texts, "The Jesus Seminar and Dan Brown's *The Da Vinci Code,* to look again at the "facts" of this traditional account, for those "facts" give weightiness to the biblical picture

of the person of Jesus, facts that move it out of the merely subjective and cause every human being to ask the ultimate question of
real truth.

THE ORIGINALITY OF THE BIBLICAL GOSPEL

It is possible to note certain peripheral parallels between the
Gnostic and the biblical Gospels, as, for instance, a number of
common sayings in *The Gospel of Thomas* and Matthew, Mark,
and Luke.

What you *never* find in the Gnostic scrolls is a statement of
agreement with what the New Testament defines as the *sine qua
non* (without which nothing) of the Christian faith, what it calls
"the gospel."

What is the gospel according to the New Testament? You find
it in a programmatic condensed statement, in prophetic form,
from the mouth of Jesus himself, who, after the divine revelation
of his person, tells the disciples the essence of his mission:

> And he began to teach them that the Son of Man *must*
> suffer many things and be rejected by the elders and
> the chief priests and the scribes and be killed, and
> after three days rise again.[26]

All these elements you then find in creedal, foundational
form[27] from the post-resurrection church, defined as the heart
and essence of the gospel. This "gospel" is introduced solemnly
and formally by Paul as his gospel ("the gospel I preached to
you"), as the believer's ("which you received, in which you
stand, and by which you are being saved"),[28] as well as that
which all the apostles preached—("whether then it was I or they,
so we preach and so you believed").[29] Little wonder Paul can
identify this "gospel" as the defining, essential statement of the
church's faith ("of first importance").[30] Here is the creed:

> That Christ died for our sins in accordance with the
> Scriptures, that he was buried, that he was raised on

> the third day in accordance with the Scriptures, and
> that he appeared to Cephas, then to the twelve.[31]

Both in the case of Jesus before the cross, and the apostles after it, the essence of the mission of Jesus (which is the gospel or "good news"), is defined by his death and resurrection, in fulfillment of the Hebrew Scriptures. This deep agreement between Jesus and the apostles is a powerful proof of the authenticity of the biblical gospel.

THE INSPIRING LIFE OF THE DISCIPLES

As I finish this book, we just came through another nail-biting presidential election. During the campaign there were two groups of Vietnam Swiftboat veterans—one group swearing that Senator John F. Kerry was a fake, the other that he was a brave war hero. Because there were two groups, saying contradictory things, we will never know the truth. This is not the case with the hero of early Christianity and those who followed him.

What is amazing about the earliest followers of Jesus is that they all told the same story, all the time. The atoning death and bodily resurrection of Jesus constitutes a fundamental strand in the tapestry of all the New Testament writings, "undergirding and informing one topic after another."[32] The New Testament documents do not show a variety of beliefs about the various meanings of the term "resurrection" (for instance, the Gnostic notion of "spiritual resurrection," or "disembodied bliss"). Everywhere there is only one view, the physical resurrection and transformation of Jesus' dead body.[33] This is quite extraordinary, according to the considered opinion of New Testament scholar, N. T. Wright. "After his violent and shameful death ... nobody, not even his closest friends and associates would have dreamed of saying that [Jesus] really was the Messiah ... unless something else had happened, to make them think such a thing."[34]

This is what impressed Frank Morison, a hardheaded English lawyer, a pure product of the Western scientific culture, who set about to disprove the resurrection. What struck Morison about the biblical accounts was their realistic description of the utter weakness of the tiny remnant (reduced to three grieving women—Mary Magdalene, Mary, wife of Cleopas, and Salome—and John; see John 19:26–27) at the moment of the crucifixion of their leader, Jesus.[35] All four Gospels agree on this.[36] Those who should have been there— Jesus' male disciples—had all fled in unbelief, panic, or a mixture of both. Only the resurrection can explain the change in behavior and message.

Professor Pinchas Lapide,[37] a Jewish orthodox rabbi who teaches New Testament at the University of Göttingen also cannot escape the powerful evidence of the disciples' transformation. He calls their original experience of the death of Jesus "the valley of despair."[38] "No vision or hallucination is sufficient to explain" that a band of demoralized disciples could overnight be changed into "a world religion."[39] The cause of it all, the bodily resurrection of Jesus, he finds entirely believable in terms of the Jewish and Old Testament worldview according to which God intervenes in order to save his people.[40] "Without the Sinai experience—no Judaism," declares Lapide. But then he follows the logic of his thought: "without the Easter experience—no Christianity."[41]

If the early disciples had created a fictional account about Jesus being bodily raised but knowing all along they had stolen the body, the fact is that their message about the risen Jesus, after years on the road, never changed. Many of them suffered torture and excruciating deaths. Not one of them squealed. On pain of death, not one of them changed the gospel story.

They could have made things easier by preaching the "spiritual resurrection" of Jesus, since most people in the pagan world believed in some version of after-death existence.[42] But then what would have been unique about Christianity to explain its phenomenal success? It was the physical resurrection of Jesus that made their message unique and got them into trouble, for which they were willing to give their lives.

All religions to some extent claim Jesus, either as one of the prophets or as a great religious teacher, but at the resurrection one is faced with an either-or choice. This is not just an old problem. It is a stark choice all must make, ever since that paradigm-bursting event took place "on the third day" some time in the first third of the first century.

But can you trust these biblical documents that contain the gospel?

Before you ditch the Jesus of the Bible in favor of the newly discovered Gnostic one, there is something important you should know. The argument is technical but the stakes are enormous.

THE LATE DATE OF THOMAS

Though, according to the biblical record, all the original disciples held to the above statement as to the nature of the Christian gospel, some critical scholars beg to differ. Rejecting this Christianity-defining gospel/creed, but still claiming to be in some sense "Christians," they have ingeniously sought to create another form of Christianity, one based, not on the death and resurrection of Jesus, but solely on the wise teachings of Jesus. This effort has been enormously helped by the discovery of *The Gospel of Thomas*.

Though you cannot find any kind of statement of this gospel creed in *Thomas*, the religious convictions of liberal scholars draw *Thomas* to Jesus and claim that in *Thomas*, not in the gospel creed, we discover the Master's authentic voice.

As hypotheses go, few are more novel. I wish I could say that this is objective science, but it has much more the marks of an ideologically driven hypothesis, proposed by a handful of New Testament scholars,[43] many associated with "The Jesus Seminar."[44] It is easy to see why. With a deep aversion to the biblical gospel, and having adopted the major ideas of Gnosticism, these scholars seek to show that Jesus and the earliest disciples were Gnostics and thus, that their version of "Christianity" is the authentic one. They do this in two ingenious ways.

1. *Q*: The hypothetical document Q is made to be the first Christian "gospel." What is Q? Q (German *quelle* meaning "source") is the sayings of Jesus that are only found in Matthew and Luke. No one has ever seen the so-called document Q, but for many years scholars have theorized that Matthew and Luke must have had a common sayings source that was unknown to Mark.[45] Matthew and Luke thus used as sources to construct their gospels Mark, Q, and other specific collections from which they took the material only found in either Matthew or Luke.

Readers who are golfers should realize that this is a different kind of "Q school" dealing with eternal truth not mere sporting glory. The pro-Gnostic scholars turn Q into an independent written "gospel," arguing that the first Christian community used Q as their basic text. Q is a list of sayings that, as it turns out, when separated from its context in Matthew and Luke, contains no reference to the atoning death and physical resurrection of Jesus.[46] It is thus argued that the earliest group of disciples did not hold to the gospel we find stated in the creed of 1 Corinthians 15:3–5, which then becomes evidence of a later "orthodox" theological overlay. If the Q reconstruction of original Christianity is true, the earliest disciples saw Jesus rather as a wisdom teacher, very similar to the Jesus of *The Gospel of Thomas*. This Q scholarship has worked diligently to bestow on Q the precious gift of objective existence.[47]

2. *The Gospel of Thomas*: Q therefore "proves" that *Thomas* belongs to this original "Gnostic" faith. New Testament scholar Stevan Davies states, "[*Thomas*] appears to be roughly as valuable a primary source for the teaching of Jesus as Q," and dates *Thomas* prior to all the canonical Gospels.[48] *Thomas*, like the hypothetical document Q, is a list of sayings, has no death and resurrection elements, and reveals Jesus as a wisdom teacher. Two other arguments for the age of *Thomas* are: the sayings of

Jesus in *Thomas* that do not appear in the canonical Gospels have a ring of authenticity; and, the three Greek fragments of *Thomas* that exist independently of the Coptic document *Thomas* found in Nag Hammadi, show that *Thomas* existed in Greek before the complete Coptic version known to us from Nag Hammadi.

This hypothesis, used by Dan Brown in his *The Da Vinci Code* to undermine the claims of historic Christianity, is the reason many people today confidently reject the historicity of the Bible and its picture of Jesus. It must, however, be said that rarely has such a major reinterpretation of one of the most decisive events of human history been made to depend upon such flimsy and speculative "evidence." Jacob Neusner, a Jewish professor of religious studies at the University of Florida and one of the most prolific authors in modern times, and no friend of biblical Christianity, calls this new scholarship "either the greatest scholarly hoax since the Piltdown Man or the utter bankruptcy of New Testament studies—I hope the former."[49]

CURIOUS ABOUT Q?

In our contemporary fascination with hidden or suppressed texts, and our suspicion of all things institutional, many have come to believe that the orthodox, biblical picture of Jesus is the result of a massive and ancient unworthy scam. A recent book tying Freemasonry to the Knights Templar and then to Gnosticism states:

> It was very much in the interests of the rulers of the early Church to accept [the New Testament account of Jesus] as literal truth because of the benefits it conferred on them in the form of an uncontested source of authority.[50]

As postmodern thinking declares—truth is [merely] power. In all of this, Q plays a pivotal role. A certain kind of scholarship has allowed Q to morph from being a simply literary hypothesis, explaining the relationship between Matthew, Mark, and Luke (first suggested in the middle of the nineteenth century), into being a real, objective historical source; and then from a source, it has become a full-fledged "gospel"; and from a gospel among many it has become "the key theological document of a very early Christianity."[51] Q legitimizes all the speculation about suppressed texts and alternate forms of early Christianity.

With regards to Q, there is *no* proof that such a text ever existed as a separate document. There is *no* manuscript evidence. There are *no* independent references to Q in any early document, Christian or Gnostic. Furthermore, Q contains *no* Gnostic teaching such as we find in *Thomas*. Q is not a mystical document but agrees with all the ethical and spiritual teaching of the Jesus we find in the canonical gospel, and has many themes the Gnostics would never touch.[52] Finally, Q may never have existed at all, as has been argued by many scholars. If Luke used Matthew, there is *no separate, independent source.*[53] If what is common to Matthew and Luke is what Luke found in Matthew and subsequently reproduced in his own account, Q disappears into thin air! For reasons like this, a number of scholars have recently argued that "there are no literary or historical data that speak in favor of the existence of Q ... the construct of Q [is] of no historical value whatsoever."[54]

With Q gone, the dating of *Thomas* becomes much more hazardous.

THOMAS, LATE AS USUAL

Like the historical disciple, Thomas, who arrived late to the Upper Room, there are good reasons for thinking that *Thomas*, the Gnostic gospel, was written much later than some claim, and therefore much later than the biblical Gospels.[55]

The actual material on which the Nag Hammadi scrolls were written is dated in the fourth century AD. Though that does not tell us when the actual contents of the documents were written, it is true that, besides *Thomas*, none of the other Gnostic gospels are claimed to be particularly early.[56] For instance, *The Gospel of Philip*, which has recently created such a stir with its statement that Jesus kissed Mary Magdalene on the mouth, is dated in the middle of the third century by its official modern translator.[57] *The Gospel of Mary* is similarly dated, at the earliest, in the third century.[58] In the light of what Dan Brown does with these texts in *The Da Vinci Code*, you would be led to believe that many were dated early. The truth is, of all these Gnostic scrolls, an early date is proposed uniquely for *Thomas*—and you should know that this date is hotly contested.

In other words, since Q (even if it existed) is in no sense Gnostic, the case for a Gnostic Jesus depends entirely upon the early date of one lone text, *The Gospel of Thomas*.

The three independent Greek fragments containing one or two phrases from *Thomas* are generally dated around AD 200. It is impossible to know if these were independent sayings[59] or whether they prove the existence of a complete *Thomas* before AD 200. On the contrary, a serous piece of linguistic detective work argues that *Thomas* was originally composed in Syriac and depends upon the first gospel harmony ever written, the so-called *Diatessaron*, which was written in Syriac, and is dated to around AD 170.[60] This would place *Thomas* at the earliest around AD 200.

Scholars have pointed out that *Thomas* alludes to or quotes more than half the New Testament writings (Matthew, Mark, Luke, John, Acts, Romans, 1 and 2 Corinthians, Galatians, Ephesians, Colossians, 1 Thessalonians, 1 Timothy, Hebrews, 1 John, and Revelation).[61] The merging of all this New Testament material with developed Gnostic ideas that you find in *Thomas*[62] would put *Thomas* into the late second century at the earliest.

For me, the most decisive consideration for the date of *Thomas* in the late second century, at the earliest, is Marcion (died around AD 160). For a hundred years, New Testament scholarship has argued that Marcion, the so-called "proto-Gnostic," was the catalyst that forced the church to define its own scriptural canon.[63] Marcion arrived in Rome in AD 140 and was excommunicated from the church in AD 144 because he rejected the Old Testament revelation of God the Creator and developed his own early form of Gnostic Christianity. Marcion recognized the importance of written Scripture, and rejected the canon the church was following, and so created his own.

What would a mid-second-century Gnostic put in his canon? Apparently, for Marcion, there was not much choice. He had to work with essentially the biblical canon we now know. All he could do was produce a reduction. He dismissed the entire Old Testament, kept the Epistles of Paul, and kept one of the four biblical gospels then recognized as canonical, the gospel of Luke, from which he expunged all references to the Old Testament. Just how early, available, and authoritative the Gnostic writings were in the middle of the second century is shown by the fact that Marcion includes not one of the Gnostic texts we now know from Nag Hammadi. He does not include *The Gospel of Truth*, which was later known at Rome.[64] More to the point, if *The Gospel of Thomas* were the earliest written gospel, it is inexplicable to me why this important Gnostic teacher, Marcion, trying to create a Gnostic canon, had no knowledge of *Thomas*'s existence, and did not make it the very centerpiece of his Gnostic "canon." Without the availability of *Thomas*, Marcion had to go to all kinds of trouble to make for himself a Gnostic gospel like *Thomas*—out of the already existing canonical gospel of Luke! Perhaps Marcion's not very successful attempt to create a "Gnostic"gospel provoked later Gnostics to produce a real one—*Thomas*!

The final reason I believe *Thomas* was written late is the character of the book's theology. Against Pagels[65], who claims that *Thomas* is not Gnostic, there are clear signs in *Thomas* of the later sophisticated Gnosticism of the second century, a Gnosticism more developed even than that of Marcion. Here is my reasoning. The first expressions of emerging Gnosticism appear in the New

Testament, in what Paul calls "so-called gnosis."[66] This early false teaching has to do "only" with the rejection of bodily resurrection and forms of asceticism.[67] Paul sees where this thinking will go and roundly rejects it, but it is still very primitive Gnostic thinking. In Marcion you still find only a primitive, nascent form of the later Gnostic system. In *Thomas*, on the contrary, though clothed in the form of "sayings of Jesus" and mixed with apparently innocuous teaching, you have, in my judgment, full-blown Gnosticism. *Thomas* rejects physical motherhood, gender-distinctions, the goodness of creation, God the Creator, and the whole Old Testament witness to Christ. *Thomas* affirms the practice of esoteric mysticism, spiritual androgyny, pantheism, and the belief in the innate divinity of all Gnostic believers who are no different from Christ. In spite of its "gospel" form, this is, in essence, the Gnosticism of the middle to late second century.[68]

Imagine in your mind the great Egyptian Kahfre pyramid that has stood unmoved for almost six millennia. In the minds of some, the Q-Thomas construction is almost as unassailable. The truth about Q-Thomas may well resemble that ancient pyramid but turned upside-down: impressively massive at the top, but ready to come crashing down at the slightest breeze because it is precariously balanced at the lower apex on a tiny little worthless pebble. No one builds that way, only those who wish at any price to undermine the solid case for the biblical Jesus.

A significant conclusion stares us in the face. If no Gnostic text is early, then they are not genuine historical sources for discovering the real, earthly Jesus. They are rather "pious frauds," like the Jewish pseudepigraphical books, which claim to be by Adam, Enoch, Abraham, Moses, Baruch, or Isaiah, but everyone knew were composed hundreds, sometimes thousands of years later, by pious authors, known or unknown.[69] Everyone knew you did not go to these books for biographical and historical knowledge about Adam or Enoch. Similarly, with the Gnostic texts that claim to be written by Peter, Paul, Philip, Mary, or

Thomas. How many really believed that the biblically-orthodox apostles would actually write such heresy? The fact is, *The Gospel of Thomas*, for instance, is neither a gospel nor written by Thomas. This judgment of "pious frauds" might offend those scholars seeking to argue for the early date of *Thomas* but surely not the original Gnostics. They show no interest in dates and events. The Gnostic scrolls do not claim to be "gospels" in the strict sense of the term, giving historical information from eye-witnesses. The Gnostic teachers were quite sure that history was meaningless and that "true" divine revelation came to anyone at any time without any reference to particular historical events. Their books did not have to be written early in the first century, because the "living Jesus" can and did speak at any time. There was thus no reason why they could not imagine themselves speaking in the name of original apostles.

In view of the effects of "The Jesus Seminar" and Dan Brown's *The Da Vinci Code* in undermining the faith of many in the trustworthiness of the biblical Gospels, it is important to set the record straight. Having looked at the evidence, we need to allow the well-respected historian Philip Jenkins to bring us back to historical sanity: "Far from being the alternative voices of Jesus' first followers, most of the lost gospels should rather be seen as the writings of much later dissidents who broke away from an already established orthodox church."[70] We would simply add, instead of *most—all* of the lost gospels.

THE EARLY DATE OF THE BIBLICAL MESSAGE

I have made my choice for the biblical Gospels because, on the contrary, they make a very convincing case for providing a direct access to the real Jesus of history. They do not claim to be manuals of esoteric spirituality, but exhibit in their own ways the base meaning of the term *gospel*, that is, writings that bring news of significant historical events.[71]

How do they stand as historical sources?

The earliest widely attested and accepted Christian writings come from the pen of the apostle Paul, who wrote from AD 48 to around AD 60. Paul's first writing was sent just *fifteen years* after the crucifixion of Jesus. His epistles constitute the backbone of the New Testament. No reputable scholar today puts this into question. Paul was in Jerusalem during the public ministry of Jesus, pursuing his rabbinic studies, and was converted two or three years after the death of Jesus.[72] Around AD 50 Paul explicitly states that he received from Peter, John, and James, Jesus' brother, and the other original followers,[73] the condensed version of "the gospel," the text we cited above, 1 Corinthians 15:3–5. This condensed, creedal statement, which, according to N. T. Wright, "was formulated within the first two or three years after Easter itself,"[74] reveals what was being preached as the fundamental "gospel" in Jerusalem immediately after the death of Jesus. About the nature of this text, a contemporary scholar says: "This is the sort of data that historians of antiquity drool over."[75] There are no Gnostic texts like this to drool over. N. T. Wright calls this text, "unalterable Christian bedrock … firm, universal and early."[76] If this is not historical, then nothing we have of early Christianity is!

This essential message of the death and resurrection of Jesus found in the teaching of Jesus and the early creeds of the church is reflected in the very literary structure of the Gospels (remember: "passion narratives with long introductions"), and explicitly stated in the very first Christian sermon ever preached, recorded by Luke in Acts.[77] They do not claim to be manuals of esoteric spirituality, but exhibit in their own ways the base meaning of the term "gospel," that is, writings that bring news of significant historical events, in this case, God's actions in history to accomplish redemption.[78]

THE HISTORICAL RELIABILITY OF THE BIBLICAL GOSPELS

In dating the biblical Gospels, *Acts is pivotal*. The reader will recall that Acts is the second volume of a work by the evangelist

Luke, the early church historian. He divides his account in Acts by following the careers of the two great apostles of the early church, Peter who was sent to the Jews,[79] and Paul, the apostle to the pagans.[80] Both end up in Rome and are put to death by Nero around AD 66.

Critical scholarship, which wants to date *Thomas* early in the first century, wants to date Acts at the end of the first century. For such a late date, there are many strange and inexplicable omissions. There is no mention of Paul's letters. Unbelievably, there is no mention of the martyrdom of the book's two heroes, Peter and Paul. How could one write this kind of history at a moment when the church was facing the Domitian persecution at the end of the first century and omit the final, glorious testimony, sealed in blood, of the church's original martyred founders? There is no hint of the Neronian persecution of the sixties, and no mention of the martyrdom in AD 62 of James, brother of Jesus, head of the Jerusalem church from the early days. The oddest omission of all for this supposedly late first-century book is the total silence about the destruction of Jerusalem in AD 70. This one event changed forever the religious history of Judaism and Christianity. The destruction of the temple and the sacking of Jerusalem by the Romans brought about the end of the Jewish state and nation, and in a deep sense vindicated the movement Jesus began. Instead of historical and theological reflections on the change of religious regime, oddly, in the Gospels, in the Acts, and in the Epistle to the Hebrews, the Jewish elders and the Sanhedrin are still exercising positions of authority and social power in Jerusalem and in Jewish national life generally.[81]

These unexplainable considerations caused a radical English bishop, J. A. T. Robinson, whose personal theology was more Buddhist than Christian, to reexamine the dating of the New Testament. Robinson argues, against the current of skeptical scholarship, that every book in the New Testament was written prior to AD 70.[82] He shows convincingly that even though Jesus *predicted* the destruction of the temple, no New Testament book reveals any knowledge of its actual occurrence, nor celebrates in this regard Jesus as a true prophet.

Robinson dates Acts prior to the martyrdom of James in AD 62, which has immediate repercussions for the dates of the Gospels. Since Acts is Luke's second volume, the first volume, the gospel of Luke, must come before Acts. Because it is generally believed that Luke used Matthew and Mark as his sources, Matthew and Mark are necessarily written prior to Luke. As to the gospel of John, it too betrays no knowledge of the destruction of the temple. On the contrary, its narrative of the ministry of Jesus refers to a standing, functioning temple *in the present tense*.[83]

Robinson's conclusion, and I make it mine, is that the four biblical Gospels were written "in the first two decades of the Christian church."[84] I thus believe that no other sources bring us so close to the Jesus of history. So not only do I find deep satisfaction in the person of the biblical Jesus, I also find the biblical accounts of Jesus historically trustworthy.

If, as I wrote in the prologue, there are only two views of Jesus that can make any kind of historical claim on Jesus, then, after examining the historical claims of these two, the Gnostic and the biblical, it seems to me that only one passes muster. You may prefer the Jesus of the Gnostic texts for all kinds of "religious" reasons, but the only Jesus with any kind of historical authenticity is surely the Jesus of the Bible.

Only this Jesus explains the historical phenomenon of early Christianity.

THE UNIQUENESS OF JESUS

I attended the Parliament of the World's Religions in Chicago in 1993. In spite of the thousands of delegates and the hundred or so religions, the colorful robes and the many languages, I still remember my dominant emotional response after listening for seven days to the oft-repeated message of speaker after speaker. It was essentially the same as the message of the Gnostic Jesus—man is divine, greater than the god who created him, and with this knowledge we can change ourselves and the world.[85] My emotion in Chicago was *boredom!* Simply put, every religion was, in different ways, saying the same thing. And the Christianity represented there was of the Gnostic kind, saying the same thing as all the others—just like the "Christian" Gnosticism of the ancient world. The only role of the Gnostic Jesus, like that of many gurus before him and since, like a spiritual weight trainer who nevertheless does not lift the weights for you, is to remind you of your true divine self so that you can make it on your own.

It was thus patently evident that this great crowd of very religious people could not and did not do something I love to do—engage in songs of praise. Gnosticism is ultimately self-praise, and when I look into my heart I know that I am not a worthy object for my own praise. Only the transcendent Lord and condescending Redeemer, mysteriously and gloriously present in Jesus, is the worthy and inspiring object of such heartfelt and soul-inspiring praise.

There is nothing unique about the Jesus of the Gnostic texts. If Gnosticism is but a "Christian" version of pagan spirituality, ancient and modern, it is merely one more variation of the same spiritual technology one finds in human religion generally. That is what I witnessed in Chicago. Indeed, the Gnostic picture of Jesus is a profound diminution of what we find in the Bible, where, against all expectations, the Creator of heaven and earth becomes flesh and brings genuine redemption. For me, the Gnostic picture finally does not explain to my satisfaction the incredible success and vast influence of this simple Jewish construction worker. The Jesus of Gnosticism is merely one of us, to such an extent that there is no uniqueness in his person or decisive significance in his achievement.

Let the reader be apprised! In spite of the enormous interest in Jesus today, I believe that the Gnostic Jesus is now promoted, not because of the real appeal and fascination of his historical person, but because of the present appeal of an alien non-Christian spirituality, of which he is made to be a part, but not even an essential part. Remember what we saw above. The Gnostic texts show no interest in a specific, historical person called Jesus. He serves merely as a cipher for the passing on of timeless Gnostic wisdom. In other words, *Jesus is not indispensable to Gnosticism*, which itself is merely one more "Christianized" variant of the many pagan spiritual techniques of the ancient world by which to gain spiritual "enlightenment." If this is true, Gnosticism cannot account for the unique and explosive effect of the *actual Jesus* on human history.

Napoleon is reputed to have said, "I know men; and I tell you that Jesus Christ is no mere man. Between him and every other person in the world there is no possible term of comparison." The church father Origen (AD 185–254) declares, "Our Jesus, despised for being born in a rural [uncivilized] village ... has been able to shake the entire civilized world ... [his impact surpasses that of] even Pythagoras, Plato, let alone that of any ruler or military leader in the world."[86] Malcolm Muggeridge, converted Marxist and well-known English satirical journalist, said, "The coming of Jesus into the world is the most stupendous event in human history."[87] J. B. Phillips, the translator and paraphraser of the Gospels, wrote, "I have read, in Greek and Latin, scores of myths, but I did not find the slightest flavor of myth here.... No man could have set down such artless and vulnerable accounts as these unless some real Event lay behind them."[88]

Everyone agrees that Jesus is central to the appearance of Christianity, and most give at least lip service to the idea that Jesus was unique. At the same time, however, many modern accounts of Jesus, including the classic Gnostic picture of Jesus, reduce the

revelation of truth Jesus brings to very simple aphorisms comparable to those of other "holy men." As a historical figure, from this
perspective, he is quite uninteresting,[89] and ends up not being
unique at all, so that all the complexity and all the genuine uniqueness of his teaching and his life are removed and laid to the
account of a later generation of admiring, inventive believers.

For my part, I find this judgment rather disappointing and
finally quite unconvincing. If Jesus is the unique person everyone seems to want him to be, then the likelihood of Jesus being
the source of the complex, world-transforming teaching about
the kingdom, about his place within it, and about his divine person seems to be the most convincing historical explanation of all.
When critical Bible scholars leave well enough alone, there
emerges in the biblical Gospels an architectural beauty in the
way in which the complex notions of present and future elements of the kingdom and their relationship with the mysterious
person of Jesus surprisingly but finally combine to produce a
seamless whole.[90] Once scholars begin to pull away various
threads as "later additions," the larger tapestry disintegrates,
and one is left with mere unconnected bits and pieces. But a
larger tapestry is discernable. The mind of Jesus is not found just
in individual sayings and odd deeds but in the way those sayings and deeds communicate a holistic message that makes
fundamental sense of the whole of his life, and indeed of the
whole of biblical revelation. Such a perspective is not the work of
a committee or church councils or of four different evangelists
writing Gospels. It is ultimately the work of a single mind, the
mind of a genius—the mind of the biblical Jesus.

The faith surrounding the biblical Jesus is unlike any other in
the course of religious human history. Its uniqueness surely
explains its success. Here are just a few examples:

- In the Judaism at the time of Jesus "at no point did anyone envisage a Messiah who would die a shameful death,
  let alone be raised from the dead."[91]

- Judaism had a variety of beliefs about what would happen to the dead, but it was totally unprepared for "the new mutation that sprang up," the bodily resurrection of the Messiah.[92]
- "No pagans known to us ever imagined that resurrection could or would really take place."[93]
- A two-stage resurrection was unknown in Judaism.[94]
- "Nobody imagined that any individuals had already been raised or would be raised in advance of the great last day ... there are no traditions about a Messiah being raised to life."[95]
- The transcendent Creator who takes on human form in time and space for the redemption of the creation is not found in any other religion.
- God in the flesh, dying on a cross, atoning for the sins of the world, is a unique idea in the history of religion.

The uniqueness of Jesus is surely (1) the earthshaking claim of Immanuel, God come in human form, added to (2) the declaration of the definitive forgiveness of sins and the defeat of evil, and (3) completed by the proclamation of the physical resurrection of Jesus, the final defeat of death, and the coming transformed cosmos that account for the success of early Christianity. For what more could one ask? In the cross of Jesus, the human problem of sin is resolved. In the resurrection of Jesus, the human inevitability of death is vanquished. In this gospel, God is with us and acts for us. No other religion has ever made such a claim.

In the debate about the identity of Jesus, and the argument regarding the version we can trust, the stakes are enormous. There is no neutral position. You must choose. Is he "the divine/human Savior of the world" or a spiritual guru like many others? Is he a source of timeless wisdom or the bringer of gospel news? I have chosen the biblical Jesus because I sense a deep need, not for a coach or religious technical advisor, but for a righteous and fully trustworthy Savior, who as my Creator and Redeemer does things for me I could never do for myself. To end, this is how the biblical account begins:

"You shall call his name Jesus because he will save his people from their sins."[96]

BIBLIOGRAPHY

Aland, Kurt. *The Problem of the New Testament Canon.* London: Mowbray, 1962.

Aland, Kurt. *Synopsis Quattuor Evangeliorum.* Stuttgart: Württembergische Bibelanstalt, 1964.

Angus, Samuel. *The Mystery-Religions : A Study in The Religious Background of Early Christianity.* New York. Dover Publications, 1975. 14., reprint of *The Mystery-Religions and Christianity.* New York: Scribner, 1966.

Baigent, Michael, Richard Leigh, and Henry Lincoln. *Holy Blood, Holy Grail.* New York: Dell, reissued, 1983.

Bailey, Foster. *The Spirit of Masonry.* London: Lucis Press, 1957.

Baue, Frederic. *The Spiritual Society: What Lurks beyond the Postmodern.* Wheaton, IL: Crossway, 2001.

Bleeker, C. J. "Isis and Hathor, Two Ancient Egyptian Goddesses." In *The Book of the Goddess, Past and Present: An Introduction to Her Religion.* Edited by Carl Olsen. New York: Waveland, 2002.

Blomberg, C. L. "Tradition and Redaction in the Parables of the Gospel of Thomas." In *The Jesus Tradition Outside the Gospels.* Edited by D. Wenham, 177–205. Sheffield: JSOT Press, 1984.

Blomberg, C. L. *The Historical Reliability of the Gospels.* Downers Grove, IL: InterVarsity Press, 1987.

Bloom, Harold. *The American Religion: The Emergence of the Post-Christian Nation.* New York: Simon and Schuster, 1992.

Borg, Marcus J. *Meeting Jesus Again for the First Time: The Historic Jesus and the Heart of Contemporary Faith.* San Francisco: HarperSanFrancisco, 1994.

Borg, Marcus J., and N. T. Wright. *The Meaning of Jesus: Two Versions.* San Francisco: Harper, 1999.

Brashler, James, and Peter A. Dirkse. "The Prayer of Thanksgiving." In *The Nag Hammadi Library in English,* 298–299.

Brashler, James, Peter A. Dirkse, and Duncan M. Parrot, "The Discourse on the Eighth and Ninth: Introduced and Translated." In *The Nag Hammadi Library in English,* 292–297.

Brown, Dan. *The Da Vinci Code.* New York: Doubleday, 2003.

Brown, Raymond. "The Gospel of Thomas and St John's Gospel." *New Testament Studies 9* (1962–63): 155–177.

Burke, George. *Gnostic Christianity: An Introduction.* Geneva, NE: Saint George Press, 1994.

Calvin, John. *Heart Aflame: Daily Readings from the Psalms.* Phillipsburg, NJ: P&R Publishing, 1999.

"Cathari." In *The Oxford Dictionary of the Christian Church*, edited F. L. Cross, Oxford: Oxford University Press, 1958, 1983.

Clowney, Edmund P. *How Christ Transforms the Ten Commandments* Philippsburg, NJ: P&R Publishing, date to be announced.

Corbin, Andrew. "Critics' Betrayal." *World*, March 20, 2004.

Crossan, John Dominic. *The Historical Jesus: the Life of a Mediterranean Jewish Peasant.* New York: Harper Collins, 1992.

Crossan, John Dominic, Johnson, Luke Timothy and Kelber, Werner H. *The Jesus Controversy: Perspectives in Conflict.* Harrisburg, PA: Trinity Press International, 1999.

Culianu, Ioan P. *The Tree of Gnosis: Gnostic Mythology from Early Christianity to Modern Nihilism.* San Francisco: HarperSanFrancisco, 1992.

Davies, Stevan. "The Christology and Protology of the Gospel of Thomas." *Journal of Biblical Literature* lll/4 (1992): 663-382.

Ehrenfeld, Rachel, and Shawn Macomber. "George Soros: The 'God' Who Carries Around Some Dangerous Demons." *Los Angeles Times*, October 4, 2004, B9.

Eliade, Mircea. *Shamanism: Archaic Techniques of Ecstasy.* Princeton, NJ: Princeton University Press, 1972.

———. *The Two and the One.* London: Harvill Press, 1965.

———, ed. *The Encyclopedia of Religion.* Volume I. New York: MacMillan, 1987.

Evans, C. A., R. L. Webb, and R. A. Wiebe. *Nag Hammadi Texts and the Bible: A Synopsis and Index.* Leiden: Brill, 1993.

Farrer, Austin M. "On Dispensing with Q." In *Studies in the Gospels,* 55–88. Edited by D. E. Nineham. Oxford: Oxford University Press, 1955.

France, R. T. *The Evidence for Jesus.* London: Hodder & Stoughton. 1985.

Fox, Matthew. *The Coming of the Cosmic Christ.* San Francisco: HarperSanFrancisco, 1988.

Gaffney, Mark H. *Gnostic Secrets of the Naassenes: The Initiatory Teachings of the Last Supper.* Rochester, VT: Inner Traditions, 2004.

Garlow, James and Peter Jones. *Cracking Da Vinci's Code: You've Read the Fiction, Now Read the Facts.* Colorado Springs: Cook, 2004.

Geering, Lloyd. *Tomorrow's God: How We Create Our Worlds.* Santa Rosa, CA: Polebridge Press, 2000.

Goldenburg, Naomi. *Changing of the Gods: Feminism and the End of Traditional Religion.* Boston: Beacon Press, 1979.

Goodacre, Mark, and Perrin, Nicholas. *Questioning Q: A Multidimensional Critique.* Downers Grove, IL: InterVarsity Press, 2004.

Graham, Michael. *The Experience of Ultimate Truth.* Melbourne, Australia: U-Turn Press, 2001.

Greenlees, Duncan. *The Gospel of the Gnostics.* Madras, India: The Theosophical Publishing House, 1958.

Grof, Stanislav. *Future of Psychology: Lessons from Modern Consciousness Research.* New York: State University of New York Press, 2000.

Habermas, Gary R., and Michael R. Licona. *The Case for the Resurrection of Jesus*. Grand Rapids, MI: Kregel, 2004.

Handelman, Susan A. *The Slayers of Moses: The Emergence of Rabbinic Interpretation in Modern Literary Theory*. Albany, NY: State University of New York Press, 1982.

Hayman, Ronald. *A Life of Jung*. New York: W. W. Norton & Co., 1999.

Herrick, James A. *The Making of the New Spirituality*. Downers Grove, IL: InterVarsity Press, 2003.

Hoeller, Stephan A. "The Genesis Factor." *Quest*, September, 1997.

———. *Jung and the Lost Gospels: Insights into the Dead Sea Scrolls and the Nag Hammadi Library*. Wheaton, IL: Quest Books, 1989.

———. "What Is a Gnostic?" *Gnosis: A Journal of Western Inner Traditions*, 23 (Spring 1992).

Holroyd, Stuart. *The Elements of Gnosticism*. Rockport, MA: Element Books, Ltd., 1994.

Isenberg, Wesley W. "The Gospel of Philip, Introduced and Translated." In *The Nag Hammadi Library in English*, 131–151.

Jacobson, Arland D. *The First Gospel: An Introduction to Q*. Sonoma, CA: Polebridge Press, 1992.

Jenkins, Philip. *Hidden Gospels: How the Quest for Jesus Lost Its Way*. Oxford: Oxford University Press, 2001.

Johnson, Luke Timothy. "The Humanity of Jesus: What's at Stake in the Quest for the Historical Jesus?" In *The Jesus Controversy: Perspectives in Conflict*, 48–74. Harrisburg, PA: Trinity Press International, 1999.

Jonas, Hans. *The Gnostic Religion*. Boston: Beacon, 1958.

———. *Gnosis und spätantiker Geist*, vol I, Göttingen, 1934

Jones, Peter. "1 Corinthians 15:8: Paul the Last Apostle." *Tyndale Bulletin* 36 (1985): 3–34.

———. *Capturing the Pagan Mind: Paul's Blueprint for Thinking and Living in the New Global Culture*. Nashville: Broadman and Holman, 2003.

————. *The Gnostic Empire Strikes Back: An Old Heresy for the New Age.* Phillipsburg, NJ: P&R, 1992.

————. *Spirit Wars: Pagan Revival in Christian America.* Mukilteo, WA: Wine Press, 1997.

Jones, Rebecca. *Does Christianity Squash Women?* Nashville: Broadman and Holman, 2005.

Jung, Carl. *Psychological Types: or the Psychology of Individuation.* Princeton, NJ: Princeton University Press, 1921/1971.

Kloppenborg, John S., Marvin W. Meyer, Stephen J. Patterson, and Michael G. Steinhauser. *Q Thomas Reader.* Sonoma, CA: Polebridge Press, 1990.

Koester, Helmut. *Ancient Christian Gospels: Their History and Development.* Philadelphia: Trinity Press International, 1990.

La Due, William J. *Jesus Among the Theologians: Contemporary Interpretations of Christ.* Harrisburg, PA: Trinity Press International, 2001.

Lapide, Pinchas. *The Resurrection of Jesus: A Jewish Perspective.* Minneapolis, MN: Augsburg Press, 1983.

Levitin, Michael. "International Prayer Research Office Announced." *Science and Theology News,* September, 2004.

Lewis, Theodore J. *Cults of the Dead in Ancient Israel and Ugarit.* Atlanta: Scholars Press, 1989.

Lewis, C. S. *Mere Christianity.* New York: Macmillan Publishing, 1984.

Machen, J. Gresham. *The Virgin Birth of Christ.* Ann Arbor, MI: Baker Book House, 1965 (originally published in 1930).

Mack, Burton L. *The Lost Gospel: The Book of Q and Christian Origins.* San Francisco: Harper, 1993.

MacLaine, Shirley. *Going Within.* New York: Bantam Books, 1989.

MacRae, George W. "The Gospel of Truth: Introduced and Translated." In *The Nag Hammadi Texts in English,* 37–49.

Malachi, Tau. *Gnostic Gospel of St. Thomas: Meditations on the Mystical Teachings.* St. Paul, MN: Llewellyn Publications, 2004.

Markschies, Christoph. *Gnosis: An Introduction.* Edinburgh, Scotland: T&T Clark, 2003.

Marshall, I. Howard. *I Believe in the Historical Jesus.* Grand Rapids, MI: Eerdmans, 1979.

Martin, Luther H. *Hellenistic Religions: An Introduction.* Oxford: Oxford University Press, 1987.

Matthews, Caitlín. *Sophia, Goddess of Wisdom: The Divine Feminine from Black Goddess to World-Soul.* London: The Aquarian Press/Harper Collins, 1992.

Meyer, Marvin. *Secret Gospels: Essays on Thomas and the Secret Gospel of Mark.* Harrisburg, PA: Trinity International Press, 2003.

Meyer, Marvin, and Charles Hughes, eds. *Jesus Then and Now: Images of Jesus in History and Christology.* Harrisburg, PA: Trinity Press International, 2001.

Miller, Ron. *The Gospel of Thomas: A Guidebook for Spiritual Practice.* Woodstock, VT: Skylight Paths Publishing, 2004.

Mohler, Albert. "The Re-Paganization of the West: A Glimpse of the Future." http://www.albertmohler.com.

Morison, Frank. *Who Moved the Stone?* Grand Rapids, MI: Zondervan, 1976.

Mueller, Dieter. "The Prayer of the Apostle Paul: Introduction." In *The Nag Hammadi Library in English*, 27–28.

Muggeridge, Malcolm. *Jesus, the Man Who Lives.* New York: Harper and Row, 1978.

The Nag Hammadi Library in English. Translated by Members of the Coptic Gnostic Library Project of the Institute for Antiquity and Christianity. James M. Robinson, director. San Francisco: Harper and Row, 1977.

Nelson-Pallmeyer, Jack. *Jesus Against Christianity: Reclaiming the Missing Jesus.* Harrisburg, PA: Trinity Press International, 2001.

Nicolosi, Joseph. *A Parent's Guide to Preventing Homosexuality.* Downers Grove, IL: InterVarsity Press, 2002.

Noll, Richard. *The Aryan Christ: The Secret Life of Carl Jung.* New York: Random House, 1997.

———. *The Jung Cult: Origins of a Charismatic Movement.* Princeton, NJ: Princeton University Press, 1994.

O'Donovan, Oliver. *Resurrection and the Moral Order: An Outline for Evangelical Ethics.* Grand Rapids, MI: Eerdmans, 1994.

Pagels, Elaine. *Beyond Belief: The Secret Gospel of Thomas.* New York: Random House, 2003.

———. *The Gnostic Gospels.* New York: Random House, 1979.

———. "'The Mystery of the Resurrection': A Gnostic Reading of 1 Corinthians 15," *Journal of Biblical Literature* 93 (1974): 276–288.

———. *The Origin of Satan.* New York: Random House, 1955.

———. "What Was Lost Is Found: A Wider View of Christianity and Its Roots." In *Secrets of the Code: The Unauthorized Guide to the Mysteries of the Da Vinci Code.* Edited by Dan Burstein. New York: CDS Books, 2004.

Patterson, Stephen J. *The God of Jesus: The Historical Jesus and the Search for Meaning.* Harrisburg, PA: Trinity Press International, 1998.

———. *The Gospel of Thomas and Jesus.* Avalon, PA: Polebridge Press, 1993.

Perrin, Nicholas. *Thomas and Tatian: The Relationship between the* Gospel of Thomas *and the Diatessaron.* Atlanta: Society of Biblical Literature, 2002.

Ridderbos, Herman. *The Authority of the New Testament Scriptures.* Phillipsburg, PA: P&R Publishing, 1963.

———. *The Coming of the Kingdom.* Phillipsburg, PA: P&R Publishing, 1969.

Robinson, James M. "How My Mind Has Changed (or Remained the Same)." *Society of Biblical Literature Seminar Papers Series.* Edited by

K. H. Richards. Atlanta: Scholars Press, 1985.

———. "Introduction: What is the Nag Hammadi Library?" *Biblical Archeologist* 42 (1979): 206–224.

———. "What the Nag Hammadi Texts Tell Us About 'Liberated' Christianity." In *Secrets of the Code: The Unauthorized Guide to the Mysteries of the Da Vinci Code.* Edited by Dan Burstein. New York: CDS Books, 2004.

Robinson, John A. T. *Redating the New Testament.* London: SCM, 1976.

Rudolf, Kurt. *Gnosis: the Nature and History of an Ancient Religion.* Edinburgh, Scotland: T&T Clark, 1977.

Satinover, Jeffrey. *Homosexuality and the Politics of Truth.* Grand Rapids, MI: Baker, 1996.

Seymour-Smith, Martin. *Gnosticism: The Path of Inner Knowledge.* San Francisco: HarperSanFrancisco, 1996.

Shucman, Helen. *A Course in Miracles.* New York: Foundation for Inner Peace, 1975.

Singer, June. *Androgyny: Towards A New Theory of Sexuality.* London: Routledge & Kegan, 1997.

———. *A Gnostic Book of Hours: Keys to Inner Wisdom.* San Francisco: HarperSanFrancisco, 1992.

Sjoo, Monica, and Barbara Mor. *The Great Cosmic Mother: Discovering the Religion of the Earth.* San Francisco: HarperSanFrancisco, 1987.

Smith, Wolfgang. *Teilhardism and the New Religion.* Rockford, IL: Tan, 1989.

Spong, John Shelby. *A New Christianity for a New World: Why Traditional Faith is Dying and How a New Faith is Being Born.* San Francisco: HarperSanFrancisco, 2002.

———. "The Theistic God Is Dead." In *From the Ashes: A Spiritual Response to the Attack on America*, collected by the editors of Beliefnet. Emmaus, PA: Rodale Books, 2001.

Thepsophon, Phra. *Buddhist Morality.* Bangkok: Mahachulalongkornrajavidyalaya University, 2004.

Thiselton, Anthony. "Realized Eschatology in Corinth." *New Testament Studies.* (1978): 510–526.

Tomko, Carrie; Natalie Khorochev and Marilyn Mai, "Indigo Children and the Spiritual Cinema Circle," SCP Newsletter 29:3 (Spring, 2005), 4.

Van Oort, Johannes. "New Light on Christian Gnosis." *Louvain Studies* 23 (1999): 21–39.

Veith, Gene E. "Forging Ahead," *World*, September 25, 2004.

———. "Knownothings." *World*, July, 2004.

Vivekananda, Swami. *Raja Yoga.* New York: Brentano, 1929.

Wilkins, Michael J., and J. P. Moreland, eds. *Jesus Under Fire: Modern Scholarship Reinvents the Historical Jesus.* Grand Rapids, MI: Zondervan, 1995.

Witherington, Ben, III. *The Gospel Code: Novel Claims About Jesus, Mary Magdalene and Da Vinci.* Downers Grove, IL: InterVarsity Press, 2004.

———. *The Jesus Quest: The Third Search for the Jew of Nazareth.* Downers Grove, IL: InterVarsity Press, 1995.

Wright, N. T. *Who Was Jesus?* London. SPCK. 1992.

———. *The Resurrection of the Son of God.* Minneapolis, MN: Fortress Press, 2003.

Yancey, Philip. *The Jesus I Never Knew.* Grand Rapids, MI: Zondervan, 1995.

Yungen, Ray. *A Time of Departing: How a Universal Spirituality Is Changing the Face of Christianity.* Silverton, OR: Lighthouse Trails, 2002.

Ziesler, John, "Historical Criticism and Rational Faith," *Expository Times* 105 (1994): 270–274.

NOTES

PREFACE

1. See the cover of *Newsweek*, September 27, 2004.
2. Fox, Matthew. *The Coming of the Cosmic Christ*. San Francisco: HarperSanFrancisco, 1988.
3. "Jesus 2000," *National Catholic Reporter*, December 1999.
4. *The Daily Record* (London), December 11, 1999.
5. While ancient, the glorification and adoration of the human body and the sex act is very modern. We see it especially in the rise of "porno-chic" in the mainline movie industry. What was once relegated to the "red light district" is now front page viewing.
6. One scholar, Jack Nelson-Pallmeyer (*Jesus Against Christianity*, 140), argues that the real choice is between two "competing, incompatible, and irreconcilable portraits of Jesus" within the biblical Gospels themselves, but he is so obviously picking and choosing what he likes about Jesus—and rejecting what he does not like—that the result is hopelessly subjective. The irreconcilable portraits are those of the Bible and Gnosticism.
7. A number of the Gnostic quotations are taken from a privately commissioned translation of the original Coptic Gnostic texts. Others are taken from what has become the standard translation of these texts, *The Nag Hammadi Library in English*, dir. James M. Robinson, New York: Harper and Row, 1977. All references to the Gnostic texts correspond to the system of numeration that has become formalized in *The Nag Hammadi Library in English*, which readers are encouraged to consult.
8. See *The Nag Hammadi Library in English*, 3, 6, 7, 16, 24.
9. In a popular book on Jesus, as late as 1995, Philip Yancey, in *The Jesus I Never Knew*, can discuss the historical evidence for Jesus without ever mentioning the Gnostic version. See especially, p. 20. Dan Brown has changed all that.

CHAPTER 1

1. Machen, *The Virgin Birth of Christ*, 387.
2. John 14:9.
3. *The Gospel of Thomas* 67.
4. Ibid., 77.
5. *Teaching of Silvanus* 100:10–15.
6. *Allogenes* 63.
7. Ibid., 65–66.
8. *Trimorphic Protennoia* 45:3–4.
9. *The Thunder, Perfect Mind* 13–16.
10. *The Gospel of Truth* 26:29–30.
11. *The Apocryphon of John* 6:8–10. This is a quote from *The Nag Hammadi Library* translation.
12. *The Gospel of Thomas 77*. Such pantheistic notions are not limited to overt statements. The contemporary Gnostic teacher, Tau Malachi, says of Saying 19 (in which Jesus speaks of stones ministering to the disciple): "With such a gnosis, one would realize the Supernal Light of Keter [according to Kabbalah, the first emanation of God] secretly hidden in every particle of matter and would possess the knowledge to actualize this spiritual nuclear energy" (Gnostic Gospel, 64).
13. June Singer, *A Gnostic Book of Hours*, 25.
14. Quoted by Kurt Rudolf, (Gnosis, 14).
15. Hippolytus, *Refutation of All Heresies*, 5:9:10.
16. *The Thunder, Perfect Mind* 16:6–7.
17. Preston, "Goddess Worship," 38.
18. See the description of Sophia in the program of the RE-Imagining Conference as "the place where the entire universe resides." ("The RE-Imagining Conference: A Report,"

The American Family Association, April 1994, 19.)

19. Cited by Sjoo and Mor, *The Great Cosmic Mother*, 253, without reference. This representation of Isis is no doubt correct. Professor Luther H. Martin of the University of Vermont, in his book *Hellenistic Religions*, 79, states that in the Hellenistic world where Gnosticism took root, Isis was no longer seen as a local Egyptian deity tied to her consort Osiris, but becomes the "lunar Queen of heaven … the universal 'Mother of All Things.'"

20. C. J. Bleeker, "Isis and Hathor, Two Ancient Egyptian Goddesses," in *The Book of the Goddess*, 32.

21. Caitlín Matthews notes that "the strong character of Isis the Goddess became the Sophianic touchstone of … Gnosticism" (*Sophia, Goddess of Wisdom*, 67).

22. *Apocalypse of Adam* 75:22.

23. See two stunning exposés by Richard Noll, *The Jung Cult: Origins of a Charismatic Movement* and *The Aryan Christ: The Secret Life of Carl Jung*.

24. Quoted in Stuart Holroyd, *The Elements of Gnosticism*, 114.

25. Orval Wintermute shows that this was justified by assigning the Aramaic meaning ("teacher") to the Hebrew word HYH— "wild animal," of which the serpent was one (Gen. 3:1) ("Gnostic Exegesis of the Old Testament," 252).

26. *On the Origin of the World* 114:3–4. See also the treatment of this theme in Pearson, *Gnosticism, Judaism and Egyptian Christianity*, 43ff. In *The Testimony of Truth*, the Coptic term describing the wisdom of the serpent is stronger than that used in the Bible and means "revealer of wisdom and knowledge." In this literature the serpent is the "teacher of Eve and Eve is the 'teacher' of Adam" (see *On the Origin of the World* 113:33; cp). (*The Hypostasis of the Archons* 89:32; 90:6). Gnosticism clearly makes the role reversals and role confusion an aspect of Gnostic wisdom. In this same document the serpent/teacher is called "the beast"–Gk: *therion* (see 114:3), in this context a title of nobility. Revelation uses this term for a being who is the embodiment of evil (11:7) whom the inhabitants of the earth will worship and who will make war against the saints and conquer them (13:7). His bestial successor is given the number 666 (13:18).

27. I deal at length with this subject of the Gnostic God in my book, *Spirit Wars*, 161–176.

28. In a few Gnostic texts, Christ as the Logos takes the place of Sophia. (See *The Tripartate Tractate* 100:1ff.) The Logos created the various aeons and authorities, over which he placed the chief Archon. "When the archon saw that they are great and good and wonderful, he was pleased and rejoiced, as (101) if he himself in his own thought had been the one to say and do them, not knowing that the movement within him is from the spirit who moves him … he was thinking that they were elements of his own essence."

29. *Sophia of Jesus Christ* 112:19, 114:14–15.

30. *The Gospel of Thomas* 101, according to the reconstruction of T. Lambdin in *The Nag Hammadi Library in English*, 128–129. According to Kurt Aland, the original text reads: "for my [mother] … but in truth she gave me the life" (*Synopsis Quattuor Evangeliorum*, 528). Certainly Lambdin's emendations make sense theologically from a Gnostic point of view, and fit with the general anti-creational theology of *Thomas* (see Sayings 22, 52, 53, 56, and 114).

31. See *Letter of Peter to Philip* 135:16.

32. See also *The Apocryphon of John* 11:15–25.

33. This is the summary of Ioan P Culianu, *The Tree of Gnosis*, 96. For other examples from the Gnostic texts, see *The Apocryphon of John* 11:25–35, 13:5; *The Gospel of the Egyptians* 58:23–26; *The Sophia of Jesus Christ* 108:9–11, 119:9–15; *The Gospel of Philip* 75:1–10; *The Gospel of Truth* 17:10–19.

34. Isa. 45:18.

35. *The Apocryphon of John* 10:19, 10:33–11:3.

36. Cited in Culianu, *Tree of Gnosis*, 94.

37. *Trimorphic Protennoia* 39:21, 40:23, 43:32, 43:35–44:2.
38. *Hypostasis of the Archons* 95:8ff.; cp. *On the Origin of the World* 103:25ff.
39. Geering, *Tomorrow's God*, 130–1.
40. Goldenburg, *Changing of the Gods*, 5.
41. Ibid., 4. On the subject of the Gnostic God, see my *Spirit Wars*, 141–159.
42. John Shelby Spong, "The Theistic God Is Dead," *From the Ashes: A Spiritual Response to The Attack on America* (Emmaus, PA: Rodale Inc, 2001), 55, 58–59.
43. Nelson-Pallmeyer, *Jesus Against Christianity*, 138.
44. Ibid., 86.
45. Ibid., 71.
46. Ibid., 78.
47. Matt. 5:45.
48. Borg and Wright, *The Meaning of Jesus*, 31.
49. Luke 2:46–47.
50. Matt. 3:3.
51. Matt. 21:9.
52. Matt. 22:37.
53. Mark 13:19.
54. Matt. 19:4.
55. Isa. 40:22.
56. Matt. 5:34–35.
57. Matt. 11:25.
58. Ex. 4:22.
59. Ps. 68:5: "Father of the fatherless and protector of widows is God in his holy habitation," cp. Pss. 89:6; 103:13; Isa. 63:16; 64:8; Jer. 3:4, 19; 31:9; Mal. 1:6.
60. Mark 14:36.
61. Matt. 10:29–30.
62. Matt. 10:32.
63. Matt. 6:7–9.
64. Matt. 16:17.
65. Matt. 5:16.
66. Matt. 15:31.
67. Matt. 6:24.
68. See Matt. 6:24 (NKJV).
69. Matt. 4:10.
70. Rom. 1:25 (NIV).
71. Matt. 6:22–23.
72. Matt. 7:13–14.
73. Matt. 4:10.
74. Rev. 12:10–17.

CHAPTER 2

1. The *Apocalypse of James* uses "kingdom of God" ten times and *The Gospel of Philip*, seven. A definitive number is difficult to give because no concordance yet exists for the Nag Hammadi texts.
2. *The Gospel of Thomas* 20.
3. Ibid., 54.
4. Ibid., 57, 76.
5. Ibid., 109–110.
6. Ibid., 96.
7. Ibid., 97.
8. Ibid., 107.
9. Ibid., 99.
10. Ibid., 1.
11. Hoeller, *Jung and the Lost Gospels*, xvii.
12. Hoeller, ibid. See also the Jungian author June Singer, *A Gnostic Book of Hours*; Martin Seymour-Smith, *Gnosticism*; Gnostic Orthodox Abbot George Burke, *Gnostic Christianity*; Mark H. Gaffney, *Gnostic Secrets of the Naasennes*.
13. *The Gospel of Thomas* 108.
14. Malachi, *Gnostic Gospel*, viii.
15. "Keter" in Kabbalah mysticism is the first emanation of divine light-energy—see Malachi, *Gnostic Gospel*, 65.
16. Ibid.
17. Ibid., 66.
18. *The Gospel of Thomas* 3.
19. See *The Gospel of Philip* 82:6.
20. *The Gospel of Thomas* 113.
21. The official name is *The Apocalypse of James*. "Apocryphon" means "secret book."
22. *The Apocalypse of James* 5:1–3.
23. Ibid., 8:25.
24. Ibid., 12:20–30.
25. *The Gospel of Truth* 18:30–33.
26. *The Gospel of Philip* 53:22–23.
27. *The Gospel of Thomas* 16, 23, 49.
28. *The Gospel of Thomas* 27.
29. Ibid., 109–110.
30. See for instance 1 John 2:16.
31. Ibid., 22.
32. Ibid., 46.
33. Ibid., 114.
34. *The Gospel of Philip* 62:30–35.
35. Ibid., 67:26.
36. *On the Origin of the World* 113:22–114:4.
37. Gen. 3:1.
38. Ps. 45:6: "Your throne, O God, is forever and ever. The scepter of your kingdom is a scepter of uprightness."
39. Matt. 6:10, 13. The last phrase is not in some manuscripts.
40. Ex. 19:5.
41. 2 Sam. 7:13. As Wright, *The Meaning and Message of Jesus*, 46, correctly notes, Jesus' kingdom message is "not timeless teaching about religion or morality [and one could add, spirituality]. It is a claim about eschatology … of history reaching its unique climax (ibid., 50)."
42. Isa. 9:6–7.
43. Dan. 2:44.
44. Luke 1:31–33: "And behold, you will conceive in your womb and bear a son, and you shall call his name Jesus. He will be great and will be called the Son of the Most High. And the Lord God will give to him the throne of his father David, and he will

reign over the house of
Jacob forever, and of his
kingdom there will be
no end."
45. Mark 1:14–15 (as I translate and paraphrase it).
46. Lewis, *Mere Christianity*,
56.
47. Mark 3:27.
48. Luke 4:18–19.
49. Luke 4:21.
50. Luke 7:21. John seems to
have been puzzled by
seeing only one side of
Old Testament prophecy
fulfilled. Jesus is healing
the sick and restoring
sight to the blind, but
seems to have no inten-
tion of bringing justice
and judgment. The sub-
tleties of how Jesus was
bringing justice escaped
John, as they did the
apostles, until after
Christ's death and resur-
rection.
51. Luke 7:22–23.
52. Matt. 3:2.
53. Luke 10:9, 11.
54. Matt. 5:10–12.
55. Mark 14:25.
56. Mark 14:62.
57. Matt. 12:39.
58. Mark 3:6.
59. Mark 4:11.
60. Matt.12:28.
61. Jer. 17:9 (NKJV).
62. Mark 9:1.
63. Mark 9:1–7.
64. Mark 4:11.

CHAPTER 3

1. *A Valentinian Exposition*,
23.
2. *The Gospel of Thomas* 15.
3. *Sophia of Jesus Christ*
94:15.
4. *Testimony of Truth* 45:15.
5. *The Gospel of Thomas* 105.
6. Ibid., 101.
7. Luke 14:26. (The biblical
Jesus, in Luke, of course,
is expressing the total
demand of the kingdom,

where believers must be
willing to lose every-
thing—fathers, mothers
children, land, and one's
life—for the sake of the
kingdom. However, in
so doing, these good
things find their rightful
place, for in seeking first
the kingdom of heaven,
says Jesus, we actually
find life.)
8. *The Apocryphon of John*
18:5.
9. Ibid., 24:26–27.
10. *The Book of Thomas the
Contender* 139:8–11,
28–29.
11. *The Dialogue of the Savior*
144:19–20.
12. *The Authoritative Teaching*
23:18–20. See also *The
Gospel of Philip* 56:25,
which teaches that the
soul is precious but
came in "a contemptible
body."
13. *The Paraphrase of Shem*
18:34–35, 27:2–3, and
22:34.
14. *Zostrianos* 131:5–8. See
also *The Testimony of
Truth* 68:6–8. Compare
The Gospel of Philip 82:4
which speaks of the
"marriage of defile-
ment." On this see
Marvin W. Meyer, "Male
and Female," 565.
15. According to the early
Gnostic teacher, Marcion
(d. 160), see Christoph
Markschies, *Gnosis: An
Introduction* (Edinburgh:
T&T Clark, 2003), 88.
16. *The Tripartate Tractate*
113:25–114:1.
17. *The Apocryphon of John*
13:20.
18. *The Apocryphon of John*
11:25–35.
19. For the text, see *The
Second Treatise of the
Great Seth* 62:28–63:30,
*The Nag Hammadi Library
in English*, 335.

20. Gen. 4:25.
21. *The Gospel of the
Egyptians* 56:1–14;
60:1–20.
22. Ibid., 60:25–61:15.
23. Ibid., 65:20.
24. *The Apocalypse of Adam*
82:20.
25. *The Paraphrase of Shem*
29:1–30.
26. Markschies, *Gnosis*, 119.
To be perfectly accurate,
Dan Brown's Jesus is a
hodge-podge of ideas
taken both from the
Gnostic *Gospel of Philip*
and from anti-Christian
notions regarding the
divine nature of Jesus,
inspired by which
Brown says Jesus was a
mere mortal. This Jesus
is part Gnostic, part
merely human, but the
result is the same. In
Brown's history of
Christianity, Jesus'
humanity, as with the
Gnostics, "all but disap-
pears."
27. *The Tripartite Tractate*
113:38–114:31.
28. Markschies, *Gnosis*, 90.
29. Rev. 1:1.
30. MacRae, "The Gospel of
Truth," 37.
31. Marvin Meyer, show
that the term "living
one" also refers to God
and the disciples of Jesus
(*Secret Gospels*, 5).
32. 1 Chron. 10:9; Jer. 20:15.
33. Luke 1:1–4.
34. Matt. 1:1–16.
35. John 1:14.
36. Mark 1:1.
37. Isaiah actually uses the
very term "gospel" to
prophesy the coming in
history of God's
Messiah. See Isa. 40:9,
52:7, and 61:1. The
prophecy of 52:7 con-
cerns the coming of
God's Servant, Isa.
52:13—53:12.

38. Matt. 1:18.

39. Luke 2:6.

40. Luke 2:7.

41. See Luke 3:1–2 for the dating of the beginning of the ministries of John the Baptist and Jesus, locating the events both with regard to world history (the reign of the Roman emperor), the politics of Judea (the Herodian dynasty), and Jewish religious events (the identity of the high priest).

42. Luke 2:1–2. Matt. 2:1 gives the further precision that Jesus' birth occurred during the reign of Herod the Great.

43. Luke speaks of another census in Acts 5:37.

44. Gal. 4:4, cp. Phil. 2:7.

45. John 16:21.

46. John 18:37.

47. Remember that Gnosticism is both a general view of the world and a Christian heresy.

48. Gen. 10:1–32.

49. Luke 1:27.

50. Luke 2:21–24.

51. Luke 2:25–38.

52. Luke 2:39.

53. Matt. 1:19 (NIV).

54. Luke 1:42.

55. Luke 1:32.

56. Luke 1:54–55 (NIV).

57. Matt. 5:17.

58. John 3:2.

59. John 4:22.

60. Matt. 8:11.

61. Matt. 22:32.

62. Luke 13:28.

63. Gen. 12:1–3; 15:1–20; 17:1–8.

64. John 8:56.

65. Mark 11:10.

66. Acts 2:25–29.

67. John 12:41.

68. We know he was extremely knowledge-able of the Scripture, and was obedient to his par-

ents, (Luke 2:47, 51) but that's it. The so-called apocryphal Gospels fill out the details in fictional, unbelievable fashion, as when the boy Jesus, playing by a river, makes balls of mud, throws them in the air, claps his hands, and they fly away as birds.

69. Matt. 11:19 has "glutton and drunkard." See also Luke 15:2.

70. I speak of Joseph as his father, because Jesus was the legal son of Joseph in Jewish society, no matter what the neighbors may have thought about the circumstances of his birth, and though the biblical account makes the virginity of Mary clear.

CHAPTER 4

1. Miller, *The Gospel of Thomas*, xv.

2. *The Gospel of Thomas* 13.

3. Matt. 16:13–20; Mark 8:27–30.

4. Malachi, *Gnostic Gospel*, 1, 7.

5. *The Gospel of Thomas* 30.

6. Matt. 18:20.

7. *The Apocryphon of John* 15–19, cp. 21:30—"And his (man's) thinking was superior to all those who had made him."

8. See *The Prayer of the Apostle Paul* 1 A:26–27.

9. Mark 4:10–12.

10. Jer. 23:5–6 (NKJV).

11. Phil. 2:6.

12. John 1:1–2.

13. John 1:2; 1 Cor. 8:6; Col. 1:15–16; Heb. 1:10.

14. John 1:18.

15. Isa. 40:9.

16. See James Garlow and Peter Jones, *Cracking Da Vinci's Code: You've Read the Fiction, Now Read the*

Facts (Colorado Springs: Cook, 2004).

17. Jesus as lover of Mary is pure speculation, with no basis in historical fact.

18. Matt. 16:13–17.

19. The expression, "the living God," is from the Old Testament: See Deut. 5:26; Josh. 3:10; 1 Sam. 17:26; Ps. 42:2, and many more. Only once, in Hos. 1:10, cited in Rom. 9:26, is the plural "sons" applied to God's people.

20. Mark 6:50. See Isa. 6:1–6.

21. Mark 1:11 and 9:7.

22. Luke 24:49.

23. John 5:18.

24. John 17:5.

25. Luke 10:22.

26. John 15:26, cp. John 14:26.

27. Matt. 28:19.

28. John 1:14.

29. Matt. 1:18.

30. John 20:28.

CHAPTER 5

1. MacLaine, *Going Within*, 224.

2. Falsani, "The Next Great Awakening?" *Chicago Sun Times*, March 18, 2004.

3. Ibid.

4. Yungen, *A Time of Departing*, 15.

5. Ibid., 23.

6. *The Gospel of Thomas* 14.

7. *The Gospel of Philip* 68:9–11, citing Matt. 6:6.

8. *The Gospel of Philip*, Ibid. This gospel about Jesus points out that while Jesus spoke of "my Father in heaven," this is not the true and ultimate Father whom the Gnostic texts called "the Father of the Totalities" or "the fullness" (see ibid).

9. 1 Cor. 2:9.
10. Matt. 6:13.
11. *The Prayer of the Apostle Paul* I A:25–29; I B:5–9.
12. Mueller, "The Prayer of The Apostle Paul," 27.
13. Hippolytus, *Refutation of All Heresies,* 5.27.1–3.
14. *The Prayer of Thanksgiving* 64:19.
15. Brasher and Dirkse, "The Prayer of Thanksgiving," 298.
16. Pagels, *The Gnostic Gospels,* 25.
17. *The Apocryphon of James* 4:19–23.
18. *The Gospel of the Egyptians* III 40:13—41:7.
19. *The Paraphrase of Shem* 1:8–9; 2:27, cp. 34:25–31.
20. Ibid., 41:5–6.
21. Ibid., 41:22–24.
22. Vivekananda, *Raja Yoga,* 51, 59.
23. See the article, "From the New Physics to Hinduism," http://www.karma2grace.org (accessed in 2004).
24. *The Gospel of Truth* 22:39—23:15.
25. Ibid., 23:34.
26. *Apocalypse of Peter* 84:12.
27. Hoeller, *Jung and the Lost Gospels,* 227.
28. Besides "The Discourse on the Eighth and the Ninth," see also *The Gospel of the Egyptians* 44:1–10. For similar nonsense letters, see also *Zostrianos* 118:20; 127:1–5; *Marsanes* 28:1–28; cp. *Allogenes* 53:35—55:11; *Trimorphic Protennoia* 38:28–29.
29. "The Discourse on the Eighth and the Ninth" 56:17–20.
30. Ibid., 4.
31. Grof, *Future of Psychology.*
32. Ibid., 7.
33. See Grof, *Future of Psychology,* 5, for a whole

list of time-honored techniques.
34. See Gaffney, *Gnostic Secrets.* Gaffney, with precious little evidence, identifies this sermon, which the church father Hippolytus preserved in his anti-Gnostic writings, *The Refutation of All Heresies,* written around AD 200, as an original teaching of Jesus.
35. Gaffney, *Gnostic Secrets,* 34.
36. Ibid., 35.
37. Hippolytus, *Refutation of All Heresies* 5.9.4–6, cited in Gaffney, *Gnostic Secrets,* 204.
38. *Zostrianos* VIII 1, 1:10–20.
39. *Allogenes* 60:15–19.
40. *The Gospel of Thomas* 1—2.
41. Ibid., 114.
42. See Gaffney, *Gnostic Secrets.*
43. Ibid., 155.
44. Hoeller, *Jung and the Lost Gospels,* 202.
45. Leonardo took the idea from Vitruvius, a Roman architect who drew the first *Vitruvian Man.* Vitruvius was deeply influenced by Pythagoras, the Greek philosopher and contemporary of Buddha (sixth century BC). Like Buddha, Pythagoras taught his disciples that life is an endless wheel of reincarnations until we purify ourselves and return to our divine source.
46. Hoeller, *Jung and the Lost Gospels,* 211.
47. Ibid., 194.
48. Gaffney, *Gnostic Secrets,* 171.
49. *The Testimony of Truth* 36:21–29.
50. The classic number. See Brashler, Dirkse, and

Parrot, "The Discourse on the Eighth and Ninth," 292.
51. *Marsanes* X 1, 1:1–4:24. See also *Zostrianos* 4:25–26.
52. *The Gospel of Truth* 24:10–15.
53. Gaffney, *Gnostic Secrets,* 33.
54. *The Dialogue of the Savior* 120:24–25.
55. Gaffney, *Gnostic Secrets,* 160.
56. Ibid., 167.
57. *The Gospel of Philip* 53:14–16.
58. Ibid., 53:20–24.
59. Ibid., 68:23–27.
60. *The Gospel of Thomas* 18.
61. Ibid., 22.
62. Helen Shucman, *A Course in Miracles* (New York; Foundation For Inner Peace, 1975), 47, 262.
63. *The Gospel of Mary* 7:12–14.
64. 1 Thess. 1:5.
65. Levitin, "International Prayer Research": 1. The confusion that runs throughout this periodical (the Hindu Deepak Chopra is made part of this interest in prayer—see art. cit) is all the more discouraging, since the editor explicitly identifies himself as "an evangelical Christian"—see art. cit., p. 4.
66. Ibid.
67. Thepsophon, *Buddhist Morality,* 125. Phra Thepsophon is considered one of the leading authorities on Buddhism. He states that the first "main teaching" of Buddhism is "the non-existence of a Creator God." Surely, "prayer" in Buddhist spirituality must not be the same thing as prayer

in the Bible.

68. Matt. 14:23; 26:36; Mark 6:46; Luke 3:21; 6:12.
69. Matt. 6:9–13.
70. Luke 1:35; 4:14; 24:49; Rom. 15:13, 19; 1 Cor. 2:4–5; 6:14; 2 Cor. 13:4; Eph. 1:19; 3:16, 20.
71. 2 Cor. 6:6–7.
72. Matt. 6:7.
73. *Battalogêsête*—to use the same words over and over, stammer/stutter—*Bible Works Lexicon*.
74. Matt. 26:41.
75. Matt. 6:12.
76. Matt. 19:13.
77. Mark 11:25.
78. Luke 6:28.
79. Mark 11:24; Luke 11:1.
80. Stephan Hoeller, *Jung and the Lost Gospels*, 5.
81. Mark 10:15.
82. Luke 11:13.
83. Matt. 5:44.
84. 1 Cor. 4:20.
85. John 7:39.
86. Mark 1:8.
87. Acts 1:4 (NIV).
88. According to Herman Ridderbos, "The temptation is not merely described as an event that took place under the leading of God's providence, but as an encounter of the divinely appointed Messiah, equipped by the Holy Spirit, with the great adversary. Jesus being driven and being filled with the Spirit also explains that the tempter's assault was fore-doomed to failure. It is the secret of Jesus' word of power after the third temptation: 'Get thee hence, Satan.'" (*The Coming of the Kingdom*, 87).
89. Luke 4:14.
90. Mark 1:15.
91. Luke 4:18–19.
92. Luke 4:21 which cites

Isa. 61:1–2. See also Matt. 12:18 where another text from Isa. 42:1–4 is applied to Jesus: "Behold, my servant whom I have chosen, my beloved with whom my soul is well pleased. I will put my Spirit upon him, and he will proclaim justice to the Gentiles."
93. Matt. 12:28.
94. Mark 9:1.
95. This is the exact same Greek term as in Mark 9:1.
96. Rom. 1:4.
97. Gen. 1:2.
98. See especially John 16:13, "When the Spirit of truth comes, he will guide you into all the truth, for he will not speak on his own authority, but whatever he hears he will speak, and he will declare to you the things that are to come," but also John 14:15–16.
99. John 3:5.
100. Rom. 1:21.

CHAPTER 6

1. Brown, *The Da Vinci Code*, 309.
2. Ibid., 328.
3. Ibid., 308–9.
4. *Zostrianos* 131:5–8.
5. I would agree that some church fathers took a dim view of women, insisting that they were the chief reason for the existence of sexual sin. They could have been unduly influenced by the Gnosticism around them, but whatever the reason, it is clearly unbiblical.
6. *The Apocryphon of John* 112.
7. *The Gospel of Philip*

56:26–26.
8. *The Gospel of Thomas* 79.
9. Ibid., 101.
10. Hoeller, *Jung and the Lost Gospels*, 190. This statement raises an interesting debate in our time, where some wish to radically separate mothering from womanhood. The other side notes that while it is true that not all women are mothers, it is true that all mothers are women, and that ingrained within the woman is the whole ethos of the maternal, so that woman can be mothers in different ways.
11. Frederik Wisse, "The Apocryphon of John: Introduced and Translated," *The Nag Hammadi Library in English*, 98.
12. *The Book of Thomas the Contender* 139:28–29.
13. *The Dialogue of the Savior* 144:19–20.
14. *The Book of Thomas the Contender* 144:9–10.
15. James Dobson, *Marriage Under Fire: Why We Must Win this Battle* (Sisters, OR: Multnomah, 2004).
16. *The Gospel of Philip* 69:22–25. In Philip there are actually five sacraments—baptism, chrism [anointing], Eucharist, redemption and bridal chamber, see 67:27–29.
17. Ibid., 65:30.
18. Brown, *The Da Vinci Code*, 308–9.
19. *The Gospel of Philip* 59:1–4.
20. Ibid., 59:8–9.
21. Ibid., 63:35–37.
22. Ibid., 64:1–3.
23. Ibid., 69:1–4.
24. Ibid., 71:16–23; 72:20.
25. Singer, *Hours*, 13. Singer notes here that, according

to the Gnostic myth, the original "feminine principle," Sophia, in the mists of the atemporal past, desired a "perfect child" but by accident she produced a "monstrous demiurge," the Creator of matter and thus of physical childbirth.

26. Singer, *Androgyny*, 203.
27. *The Gospel of Philip* 78:25–79:5.
28. Ibid., 82:4–85:8.
29. Ibid., 56:31–32.
30. Ibid., 70:18.
31. Hippolytus, *Refutation of All Heresies*, 5.8.44.
32. *The Gospel of Philip* 70:6.
33. See Markschies, *Gnosis*, 112.
34. Epiphanius, *Medicine Chest*, 26.4.8, and see Markschies, *Gnosis*, 113.
35. Gaffney, *Gnostic Secrets*, 155.
36. Ibid., 269. Gaffney believes that this chalice proves that "the Grail was an invention of Gnostic Christianity."
37. *The Gospel of Philip* 82:23–26, indicates that the sacrament of the bridal chamber is indeed a communal celebration.
38. See Jones, *Spirit Wars*, 200.
39. Epiphanius, *Medicine Chest*, 26.4.4, speaks of Gnostics as using sexual intercourse exclusively for pure pleasure, not for procreation. One is reminded of Dan Brown's ritual sex scene where sex is for spiritual ecstasy.
40. *The Exegesis on the Soul* 127:22–24; 132:13–14. See also the introduction by William C. Robinson, Jr., *The Nag Hammadi Library in English*, 180.
41. Mircea Eliade, a leading expert in the History of Religions and editor in chief, *The Encyclopedia of Religion*, volume I (New York: MacMillan, 1987), 276, argues that androgyny as a religious universal or archetype appears virtually everywhere and at all times. Religions with the myth of a bisexual Creator are to be found in ancient Mesopotamia, the ancient Indo-European world, as well as in the myths of Australian Aborigines, African tribes, South American Indians, and Pacific islanders, still surviving today.
42. Eliade, *Shamanism*, 352.
43. Isenberg, "The Gospel of Philip," 131. See also *EuGnostos* 104:6–20.
44. *On the Origin of the World* 117:33.
45. *Exegesis of the Soul* 127:23–24.
46. *The Gospel of Philip* 68:23–24.
47. *On the Origin of the World* 109:20–25.
48. *The Gospel of Thomas* 22.
49. *The Gospel of Philip* 68:23–24.
50. *The Gospel of Thomas* 61.
51. *The Gospel of Philip* 62.
52. *The Gospel of Mary* 9:19–20.
53. Hippolytus, *Refutations*, 5.10.9.
54. O'Flaherty notes that for Jung, spiritual androgyny symbolizes "the integration of the opposites or the state of individuation of the autonomous individual" (*Women, Androgynes, and Other Mythical Beasts*, 294). Satinover notes how Jung saw the spiritual aspect of homosexuality, and perceptively associates homosexuality with the rise of neo-paganism— (*Homosexuality and the Politics of Truth*, 46–47), see ibid., 229–242.
55. Eliade, *The Two and the One*, 118.
56. Ibid. In Buddhism also the true human, the archetype, is androgynous. See Lama Surya Das, *Awakening the Buddha Within: Tibetan Wisdom for the Western World* (New York: Broadway Books, 1997), 140, cp. 384. Regarding homosexuality, Das notes that in the past, Buddhism "looked askance at … homosexual sex. Yet most contemporary Dharma teachers feel [such] behavior … within bounds and karmically workable" (209).
57. Singer, *Androgyny*, 182–3.
58. Ibid., 190, 306.
59. Ibid., 189.
60. Ibid., 190.
61. Ibid., 205.
62. Jon Ward, "Board OKs Sex-ed Program," *The Washington Times* (November 19, 2004).
63. Singer, *Androgyny*, 207, 267, 275.
64. Ibid., 124.
65. See also Rebecca Jones, *Does Christianity Squash Women?* (Nashville: Broadman and Holman, 2005).
66. John 16:21.
67. Luke 2:51 (NIV).
68. *The Gospel of Thomas* 101.
69. John 19:25–27.
70. Luke 18:16.
71. Mark 9:36.
72. Matt. 15:38; Mark 5:43; Luke 8:54–55.
73. Matt. 7:11.
74. Matt. 19:4.

75. Gen. 1:1.
76. Gen. 1:27.
77. Gen. 1:31.
78. Matt. 9:5 citing Gen. 2:24.
79. Ex. 20:12; Deut. 27:16.
80. Luke 14:26. Jesus here is teaching that no created thing, however good, can stand in the way of the coming kingdom.
81. John 2:1–12.
82. 1 Cor. 9:4–6.
83. Matt. 19:10–12.
84. 1 Cor. 7:7, 26–35.
85. 1 Cor. 9:5.
86. Ibid.
87. Luke 20:27–36.
88. There is no hint here of androgyny, and it is permissible to think that in the new heavens and earth sexual differences, like everything else, will be transformed, not obliterated.

CHAPTER 7

1. Ehrenfeld and Macomber, "George Soros."
2. *The Gospel of Mary* 9:1–4.
3. In the Greek it is one word, *abasileutos*, quite literally, "kingless."
4. Bloom, *The American Religion*, 57.
5. *The Gospel of Thomas* 13.
6. *The Gospel of Philip* 61:29–32.
7. Jonas, *The Gnostic Religion*, 68.
8. *The Apocryphon of John* 4:28–5:20.
9. Ibid., 10:8–30.
10. See the account of the Naassene Gnostics' beliefs in Irenaeus, *Against Heresies* 1.30.7. See also the discussion in Jonas, *The Gnostic Religion*, 93.
11. *The Testimony of Truth* 47:1–49:7. See Pagels, *The Origin of Satan*, 160.

Interestingly, in the thought of the modern Gnostic psychologist, C. J. Jung, Satan was Christ's elder brother. See Hayman, *A Life of Jung*, 441. Pagels argues that paganism at the time of the New Testament was essentially "monotheistic" in the sense of the generalized belief that all the gods were really just expressions of the one divine force (*The Origin of Satan*, 142). What bothered pagans about Christians was their belief in Satan, thereby introducing the notion of religious difference and conflict (ibid., 143). Pagels sides with paganism's unified view of religion. With ad hominem arguments, claiming to know the deep motivations of people, Pagels accuses Christians and Jews of inventing the figure of Satan merely to demonize their opponents. In her other books, she makes the same kind of ad hominem arguments against the church fathers who, she claims, gained and held ecclesiastical authority from motivations of macho male dominance rather than from considerations of religious truth. See my review of her book, *Beyond Belief*, posted on my web site, http://www.cwipp.org.
12. Gen. 3:1.
13. Evil is purely the responsibility of God the Creator.
14. Jon Ward, *The Washington Times* (April 15, 2005).

15. *The Thunder, Perfect Mind* 13:17–18.
16. *Hypostasis of the Archons* 95:8ff, cp. *On the Origin of the World* 103:25ff. Little is said of the fate of non-Gnostic believers, of which there are two kinds, *psychics* and *hylics*. The *hylics* are the purely fleshly ones who will doubtless disappear when the illusion of matter is finally exposed; the *psychics* hover between the *hylics* and the *pneumatics* (the true Gnostic believers) with the possibility of conversion/transformation to the Gnostic state or annihilation along with the *hylics*.
17. Matt. 4:17.
18. Matt. 5—7.
19. Deut. 4:8.
20. Matt. 5:17–18.
21. Matt. 5:20. See also v. 19.
22. Mark 7:10.
23. Mark 10:19.
24. Mark 12:28–34. See also the quest for the kingdom of the rich young ruler, and Jesus' emphasis on law-keeping, Mark 10:17–24.
25. Matt. 5:21–48.
26. Matt. 5:48.
27. It is interesting that when Jesus speaks from the mountain, God tells the disciples, "This is my beloved son. Hear him!" God defines the law to be the voice and commands of Jesus.
28. See Gen. 39:1–23, and see especially v. 12.
29. See Isa. 43:1: "I am the Lord, your Holy One, the Creator of Israel, your King."
30. Matt. 4:3–11.
31. Matt. 4:1.
32. Mark 1:12.
33. Gen. 2:15–17.

34. Matt. 4:4, citing Deut. 8:3. The Devil may well be alluding to another passage in the same chapter in Deuteronomy from which Jesus took his answer. For God promises to his faithful children, who are being tested in the wilderness in Deut. 8:9, "a land in which you will eat bread without scarcity, in which you will lack nothing, a land whose stones are iron, and out of whose hills you can dig copper." With this allusion, is the Devil perhaps suggesting that God would change this desert place of stones into the promised land where bread is plentiful? Certainly Jesus knew of God's ability to turn stones into "children of Abraham" (Matt. 3:9), and "make stones … to cry out" in order to praise him (Luke 19:40).
35. Here the Devil quotes at length, and out of context, Ps. 91:11, 12.
36. Gen. 3:1.
37. Matt. 4:7, citing Deut. 6:16.
38. See my treatment of this in *Capturing the Pagan Mind*, 143.
39. Luke 4:13 (NIV).
40. Calvin, *Heart Afflame*, 1.
41. Deut. 8:3.
42. Heb. 4:15.
43. Heb. 5:8.
44. Heb. 2:17.
45. Heb. 2:18.
46. Isa. 53:4.
47. Heb. 4:15.
48. Matt. 3:6.
49. Matt. 13:41.
50. John 8:34.
51. John 16:8.
52. Matt. 7:23.
53. John 8:24.
54. Ps. 9:4, 8; Ps 9:19; Ps.

58:11; Ps. 96:13; Isa. 2:4.
55. Matt. 5:22; Matt. 11:22; Matt. 12:36; Matt. 25:32, 34.
56. Matt. 26:29.
57. Matt. 8:11.
58. Luke 23:43.
59. Matt. 19:28.
60. Matt. 25:34.
61. Matt. 8:12.
62. Matt. 25:41.
63. Matt. 9:6.
64. Matt. 1:21.
65. John 1:29.

CHAPTER 8

1. Malachi, *Gnostic Gospel*, 2.
2. The notion of "twin" is important in Gnosticism, hence the importance of "Thomas," who is also "Didymus," which means "twin." According to the *Gospel of Thomas*, it is clearly implied that Thomas is the twin of Jesus—see Saying 13.
3. Singer, *Androgyny*, 19.
4. This because of the claim to eyewitness testimony of "the Majesty," phrases you find in 2 Pet. 1:16–17.
5. *The Apocryphon of James* 4:20.
6. Ibid., 5:1–3.
7. Ibid., 5:31.
8. Ibid., 6:15.
9. Ibid., 8:35.
10. Ibid., 6:15–16.
11. *The Gospel of Truth* 17:10–20.
12. Ibid., 18:30–34.
13. *The Tripartate Tractate* 113:29–115:15, and see especially 115:9–10.
14. *The Gospel of Truth* 20:1–33.
15. *First Apocalypse of James* 31:15–21.
16. *The Second Treatise of the Great Seth* 55:30—56:19.
17. *Apocalypse of Peter*

81:5–24. The Koran also states that Jesus did not die on the cross.
18. Ibid., 82:18–83:1.
19. 1 John 4:7; 2 John 1:7.
20. *The Gospel of Thomas* 51.
21. Ibid., 56.
22. Ibid., 71.
23. Ibid., 2, 85.
24. Ibid., 111.
25. Corbin, "Critics' Betrayal," 12.
26. Ibid.
27. Mark 3:1–6.
28. Luke 9:51.
29. John 8:40.
30. John 1:29.
31. This, of course, is not Paul's invention. Even before his conversion, the evangelist Philip explains to the Ethiopian government official how Isa. 53, concerning the death of the Servant, is actually speaking of the Christ—see Acts 8:32–35.
32. 1 Cor. 15:3.
33. Otherwise, one believes in vain—see 1 Cor. 15:2.
34. 1 Cor. 15:3.
35. Jer. 31:12.
36. Jer. 30:9.
37. Jer. 33:5.
38. Jer. 30:15.
39. Jer. 33:8.
40. Jer. 33:15.
41. Jer. 31:34.
42. Jer. 30:22.
43. See Dan. 2:29; Matt. 17:10; 24:6; 26:53–54.
44. Matt. 16:21.
45. Mark 14:48–49.
46. At the beginning, in Luke 4:21, and at the end, concerning his entire work, see Luke 24:44.
47. Luke 22:37.
48. Isa. 53:5–10.
49. See for instance, Mark 8:3; 9:12; 10:45.
50. John 19:28.
51. John 19:24.
52. John 19:37.
53. John 19:36.

54. See Isa. 53.
55. Matt. 26:27–28.
56. Isa. 53:12.
57. Mark 8:31.
58. Mark 8:33.
59. Matt. 27:41–43.
60. Mark 8:31. Because this text does not fit his Gnostic picture of Jesus, Marcus Borg simply dismisses these "passion predictions ... as post-Easter creations"—see Borg and Wright, *The Meaning of Jesus*, 81. Once you begin to tinker with the biblical record the way Borg and other New Testament critical scholars do, you are left merely with a Jesus that fits each individual's take on what Jesus might have done. In Borg you find many phrases that begin, "I think ..." or "I am skeptical that ..." Such phrases are useful for a biography of Borg but not for a biography of Jesus.
61. Mark 9:1.
62. Matt. 21:42.

CHAPTER 9

1. *The Gospel of Thomas* 71.
2. *The Treatise on the Resurrection* 44:15–26.
3. Ibid., 49:1ff; 45:15–30, alluding to Rom. 8:17 and Eph. 2:5–6.
4. Ibid., 46:35–38.
5. Ibid., 48:15.
6. 1 Cor. 15:46.
7. *The Gospel of Thomas* 51.
8. 2 Tim. 2:18, cited by Malcom Peel, in *The Nag Hammadi Library in English*, 50. See *The Treatise on the Resurrection* 49:23–24.
9. According to Elaine Pagels, the Gnostics believed in the resurrec-

tion but not the way the church understood it (Pagels, 1974, 278). The Gnostic way is not simply another way. It is the very "antithesis" of the truth.
10. 1 Tim. 6:20, which states "... turn away from ... the opposing ideas of what is falsely called knowledge."
11. 2 Tim. 2:17.
12. 2 Tim. 2:19.
13. 1 Cor. 15:34.
14. *The Gospel of Thomas* 71.
15. *The Gospel of Philip* 56:25–26.
16. *Book of Thomas the Contender* 139:6–8.
17. *The Gospel of Philip* 56:15–17.
18. This is a citation of the apostle Paul, found in 1 Cor. 15:50. See also, *The Gospel of Philip* 56:27–30. Paul, of course, does not mean that "flesh and blood" will be left behind when the kingdom comes. On the contrary, the mortal will put on immortality, and the physical will be transformed by the spiritual. He is simply stating that "flesh and blood," meaning humanity, unaided by the power of God, cannot bring about the kingdom. New creation, like the original creation, is an act of God.
19. *The Exegesis of the Soul* 134:14.
20. Hoeller, "The Genesis Factor."
21. John Irving, "A Prayer for Owen Meany," cited in Yancey, 207.
22. 1 Cor. 15:12; 1 Cor. 4:8. See Thiselton, "Realized Eschatology in Corinth," 510–526.
23. 2 Tim. 2:18–19.

24. Theodore J. Lewis, *Cults of the Dead in Ancient Israel and Ugarit* (Atlanta: Scholars Press, 1989), 42, says: "[There is] no need to resort to Gnosticism or Hellenistic mystery religions—they simply failed to grasp the connection between them and Christ, and how a dead person could be with God."
25. That is, the transformation of his flesh into a new resurrection body, leaving behind an empty tomb.
26. 1 Cor. 15:15.
27. Ibid.
28. 1 Cor. 15:34.
29. Ibid.
30. Rom. 1:18–20, cp. see also 2 Pet. 2:15.
31. *Wisdom of Solomon* 13:1.
32. Rom 1:18.
33. 2 Cor. 4:4.
34. Eph. 2:12.
35. 1 Tim. 4:1.
36. 1 Tim. 4:3, italics mine. The refusal of creation with a lack of thanksgiving is typically pagan—see Rom. 1:21.
37. 1 Tim. 4:4.
38. 1 Tim. 6:20.
39. 1 Cor. 15:46.
40. N. T. Wright makes the same point: "The *pneumatikos* state [the spiritual] is not simply an original idea in the mind of the Creator, from which the human race fell sadly away; this model of humanity is the future reality, the reality which will swallow up and replace mere *psychikos* [natural, earthly] life" (*The Resurrection*, 355).
41. Matt. 22:29.
42. Matt. 22:31; Luke 20:35. Luke uses it in Acts 4:2; 17:32; 23:6; 24:21.

43. Acts 17:32, cp. Rom. 1:4; 1 Cor. 15:12, 21, 42; Phil. 3:11, cp. Heb. 6:2; 1 Pet. 1:3.
44. Ps. 12:5, italics in this and subsequent Scriptural passages are mine.
45. Ps. 35:2.
46. War Scroll 4:12: "Extermination of God for all the nations of vanity" cp. 6:6; 9:9 ("the seven nations of vanity").
47. Ps. 41:8.
48. Ps. 41:10.
49. Ps. 88:10.
50. Ps. 16:8–10.
51. Acts 2:24–29.
52. Job 19:26.
53. Isa. 53:10.
54. Luke 24:45.
55. 1 Cor. 15:4.
56. Mark 8:31.
57. Mark 9:1.
58. Acts 9:3.
59. The apostle Peter, in his second letter, 2 Pet. 1:18ff, does indeed see the transfiguration that way.
60. Mark 8:31.
61. Mark 9:9.
62. Mark 9:10.
63. Mark 9:1.
64. This is the exact same Greek term as in Mark 9:1.
65. Rom. 1:4.
66. Ps. 20:14; 53:3; 68:28.
67. Ps. 74:13.
68. Luke 4:36.
69. Luke 24:36–43; Acts 10:41.
70. 1 Cor. 15:52–54.
71. Ps. 145:13.
72. Matt. 4:23.
73. Matt. 5:3–5.

CHAPTER 10

1. "The Everlasting Gospel" (1810).
2. Opinions vary about the accuracy or appropriateness of this movie. I only wish to point out that it accepts as historically accurate the biblical account of Jesus' last hours.
3. *USA Today*, June 14, 2004, 4D. The movie's caricature of Christianity is, unfortunately, all too true to life in some circles. However, it fails to include even one sound and sane Christian, of which there are many.
4. Robinson, *The Nag Hammadi Library in English*, 3.
5. Robinson, "What the Nag Hammadi Texts Tell Us About 'Liberated' Christianity," 99.
6. Pagels, "What Was Lost Is Found," 100.
7. Pagels, *Gnostic Gospels*.
8. This is the phrase James Robinson uses to describe the church fathers.
9. Pagels, *Beyond Belief*, 73.
10. Mohler, "The Re-Paganization of the West."
11. Dan Brown relied heavily on this book for much of his *The Da Vinci Code*.
12. Baigent, *Holy Blood, Holy Grail*, 408.
13. Pagels, *Beyond Belief*, 80–81.
14. Habermas and Licona, *Case for the Resurrection of Jesus*, 23.
15. On this see Stephen Hoeller, "What Is a Gnostic?" *Gnosis: A Journal of Western Inner Traditions* (No. 23, Spring 1992).
16. Singer, *Hours*, 6–7.
17. Singer, *Hours*, vii.
18. See Borg, *Meeting Jesus Again for the First Time*.
19. Robinson, *Nag Hammadi Library in English*, 1. See also Robinson, "How My Mind Has Changed (Or Remained the Same)," 482.
20. Hoeller, *Jung and the Lost Gospels*, xvii.
21. Pagels, *Beyond Belief*, 31, 74–75.
22. Singer, *Hours*, xii. According to the webpage of the Association of Transpersonal Psychology (atpweb.org), the ATP draws its methods "from traditional spiritual practices, both Eastern and Western. The antecedents of Transpersonal Psychology can be found in Eastern spiritual traditions, such as Buddhist, Sufi, Taoist, and Vedanta traditions; in spiritual practices of the monks and saints from the Catholic and Eastern Orthodox religions; in the American Transcendentalist movement, represented by Emerson, Thoreau, and the religious democracy of the Quakers and other early American Protestant denominations; and in the pioneers of modern cross-cultural psychology and psychology of religion, Carl Jung and William James."
23. Elaine Pagels, *The Gnostic Gospels*. (New York: Random House, 1979), 149.
24. Greenlees, *Gospel of the Gnostics*, vii. See my *Spirit Wars*, chapter 5.
25. Jonas, *Gnostic Religion: The Message of the Alien God and The Beginnings of Christianity*. (Boston: Beacon Press, 1958).
26. Rudolf, *Gnosis: The*

Nature and History of Ancient Religion (Edinburgh: T&T Clark, 1977).

27. Jonas, *Gnostic Religion*, 23.

28. Jonas builds upon the work of Simon Angus at the beginning of the twentieth century.

29. To say it another way, quoting Angus, "From the fourth century BC on, Greek rationalism gave way with increasing docility to the mystic and psychic cults of the East.... As the Greeks Hellenized the East, they became conscious of individual spiritual needs that were more and more met by [the Eastern] Mystery Religions [of personal redemption]," Angus, Samuel, *The Mystery-Religions : A Study in The Religious Background of Early Christianity* (New York: Dover Publications, 1975), 14, reprint of *The Mystery-Religions and Christianity* (New York: Scribner, 1966).

30. Rudolf, *Gnosis*, 276.

31. Ibid., 55.

32. See above, p. 11.

33. See Elaine Pagels, *The Gnostic Gospels*, xviii, 6, 34, 142, 149.

34. Dan Brown, *The Da Vinci Code*, 124, 234.

35. L. Brent Bozell. *The National Ledger* (April 23, 05).

36. Markschies, *Gnosis.*, 120. There is evidence of Manichaeism in Iran, Turkey, Egypt, North Africa, Spain, Gaul, Italy, the Balkans, and even China—see Rudolf, *Gnosis*, 230–240. See also van Oort, "New Light on

Christian Gnosis," 27.

37. Markschies, *Gnosis.*, 120.

38. Pagels, *Beyond Belief*, 31, 74–75. Roshi began life as Richard Baker, an American who, like many in the sixties, went East seeking spirituality. Baker landed in Kyoto, Japan where he became a disciple of the Zen master Shunryu Suzuki Roshi.

39. Gaffney, *Gnostic Secrets* , 4.

40. Singer, *Hours*, xx–xxi.

41. Pagels, "What Was Lost Is Found," 94.

42. Ibid., 93.

43. Ibid.

44. Borg, *Meeting Jesus Again for the First Time.*

45. Borg and Wright, *The Meaning of Jesus*, 60, where Borg describes Jesus as a shaman with essentially Gnostic powers. See also p. 68 for a comparison with Buddha.

46. Ibid., 9.

47. 2 Cor. 6:14.

48. Bailey, *The Spirit of Masonry*, 55.

49. Jones, *The Gnostic Empire Strikes Back.*

50. Veith, "Knownothings," 50.

51. See the obituary by Elaine Woo, "Jacques Derrida," 74: Intellectual founded Controversial Deconstructionist Movement," *Los Angeles Times,* (October 10, 2004), B16. Some scholars even wonder whether, at a deep level, Derrida was not following the Kabbalah, a Jewish form of Gnosticism—see Handelman, *The Slayers of Moses.*

52. Ibid.

53. Hoeller, *Jung and the Lost Gospels*, x.

54. Gaffney, *Gnostic Secrets*, 170.

55. Hoeller, *Jung and the Lost Gospels*, 10.

56. Ibid., 8.

57. See *The Da Vinci Code "FAQs"*: *Dan Brown's Official Website,* www.danbrown.com.

58. Carol Midgley, "Spirited Away: Why the End Is Nigh for Religion," *The Times Online.* http://www.timesonline.co.uk/article/0,,7–1342587,00.html.

59. Carrie Tomko, Natalie Khorochev, and Marilyn Mai, "Indigo Children and the Spiritual Cinema Circle," *SCP Newsletter* 29:3 (Spring, 2005), 4.

60. Herrick, *Making of the New Spirituality.*

61. Baue, *The Spiritual Society*, 16.

62. Liz Smith, "Fonda on Faith and Politics," *New York Post Online Edition* (May 13, 2005).

63. James 3:11.

64. Ps. 2:12.

CHAPTER 11

1. Heb. 13:8.

2. Rom. 1:19–20.

3. Malachi, *Gnostic Gospel*, 17. Compare the Gnostic June Singer, who says: "Before there was matter or any created thing ... or Creator ... there was Mystery ... It cannot be described, as It had no qualities ..." (*Androgyny*, 158).

4. Ben Stein, *Monday Night at Morton's*, E-online, www.eonline.com (Nov 4, 2004), his last column! Stein is an extremely well-known actor in movies, TV, and commercials. His part of the boring teacher in *Ferris*

Bueller's Day Off was recently ranked as one of the fifty most famous scenes in American film. Starting in July of 1997, he has been the host of the Comedy Central quiz show, "Win Ben Stein's Money." The show has won seven Emmies. He appears regularly on the Fox News Channel talking about finance.

5. 1 Cor. 2:2.
6. Eph. 6:24; Phil. 3:8.
7. Col. 2:6.
8. 1 Tim. 5:21; 2 Tim. 4:1.
9. 1 Cor. 1:9.
10. Rom. 8:24.
11. 1 John 2:1.
12. 1 Cor. 1:7; Phil. 3:20; 2 Thess. 1:7; 2:1; Titus 2:13; 1 Peter 1:7.
13. Rev. 22:20.
14. Graham, *Experience of Ultimate Truth*, 146–7.
15. Ibid., 218.
16. Nicolosi, *A Parent's Guide to Preventing Homosexuality*, 17. Elsewhere he states: "The human race was designed male and female; there is no third gender," 12.
17. Lauren Kessler, "Dancing with Rose: A Strangely Beautiful Encounter with Alzheimer's Patients Challenges the Way We View the Disease," *The Los Angeles Times Magazine* (August 22, 2004), 12–13.
18. 1 Cor. 15:3.
19. Pamela Martin, lyrics, Craig Courteney, music, *I Thirst*. (Columbus, OH: Beckenhorst Press, 2003).
20. Among those who would relegate Jesus to being merely a wise man are such notable historical figures as Thomas

Jefferson with his "scissors and paste Bible which eliminated all miracles"; the great nineteenth-century liberal, Albert Schweitzer who declared, "The glorified body of Jesus is to be found in his sayings" (see Meyer, *Secret Gospels*, 170); and Rudolf Bultmann, the giant of twentieth-century German New Testament scholarship, for whom Jesus "rose" in the faith of his disciples.
21. N. T. Wright says of Paul that his entire worldview, which is solidly grounded in Judaism, is "dramatically rethought around Jesus … and his resurrection" (*Resurrection*, 274).
22. Gen. 1:2; 2:7; Ps. 8:4–6.
23. Rom. 1:4; 1 Tim. 3:16.
24. 1 Cor. 15:50.
25. O'Donovan, *Resurrection and the Moral Order*, 14.
26. Mark 8:31. Notice that Jesus uses the little word "must" (*dei*) meaning "the fulfillment of Scripture, which ties this prophecy to the creedal statement below."
27. See Jones, "1 Cor. 15:8," 3–34.
28. 1 Cor. 15:1–2.
29. 1 Cor. 15:11.
30. 1 Cor. 15:3.
31. 1 Cor. 15:3–5.
32. Wright, *Resurrection*, 271, 274.
33. Ibid., 209.
34. Ibid., 244.
35. Frank Morison, *Who Moved The Stone?* (Grand Rapids, MI: Zondervan, 1976), 69.
36. Morison's approach does call on the reader to give a fair hearing to the four accounts, and not reject them out of hand, "a

course which I am convinced no honest and critical reader … will refuse" (ibid., 77). Morison could not have imagined the radical lengths to which later liberal scholarship would go.
37. Lapide, *Resurrection of Jesus*.
38. Ibid., 85.
39. Ibid., 125.
40. Ibid., 44–65.
41. Ibid., 92.
42. Wright, *The Resurrection*, 314.
43. Michael J Wilkins and J. P. Moreland, (eds.), *Jesus Under Fire: Modern Scholarship Reinvents the Historical Jesus* (Grand Rapids, MI: Zondervan, 1995), 19–20, show how ingrown this group of scholars is. See also Ben Witherington, III, *The Jesus Quest: The Third Search for the Jew of Nazareth* (Downers Grove, IL: InterVarsity Press, 1995), 43–44.
44. John Dominic Crossan argues that a first version of *Thomas* dates from the fifties of the first century, and a second, fuller version from the sixties (*The Historical Jesus*, 427). Pagels states that her old professor, Helmut Koester of Harvard believes that "*The Gospel of Thomas* comes from about the year 50, and so is the earliest of the New Testament Gospels"— see the same Beliefnet conversation with Ben Witherington. See also New Testament scholar Stevan Davies, who says, "'[*Thomas*]' appears to be roughly as valuable a primary source for

the teaching of Jesus as Q." ("The Christology and Protology of the Gospel of Thomas," 663). Elaine Pagels dates *Thomas* later in the first century (*Beyond Belief*, 29).

45. It is generally believed that Matthew and Luke used the gospel of Mark, it being most probably the first gospel written. Readers should know, however, that this whole area of the relationship of the individual gospels has been debated for two hundred years and we are still only dealing with theories.

46. Arland D. Jacobson even says that "Q is not a Christian document" (*The First Gospel*, 2).

47. In addition to the above references see also Mack, *The Lost Gospel*; Kloppenborg, Meyer, Patterson, and Steinhauser, *Q Thomas Reader*.

48. Davies, "The Christology and Protology of the Gospel of Thomas," 663.

49. Quoted in *Time* (January 10, 1994).

50. Christopher Knight and Robert Lomas, *The Hiram Key: Pharoahs, Freemasons and the Discovery of the Secret Scrolls of Jesus* (New York: Barnes and Noble, 1996), 39. As proof, these authors cite Elaine Pagels' comments in her book, *The Gnostic Gospels* (New York: Random House, 1979), 26–27. See also her chapter, "One God, One Bishop: the Politics of Monotheism," pp. 28–47. See also for a similar approach Michael

Baigent, Richard Leigh and Henry Lincoln, *Holy Blood, Holy Grail* (New York: Dell, reissued, 1983).

51. N. T. Wright, "Foreword," in Mark Goodacre and Nicholas Perrin, eds., *Questioning Q: A Multidimensional Critique*. (Downers Grove, IL: InterVarsity Press, 2004), xi.

52. Q contains material that could never be found in a Gnostic document: the prophecy concerning Jesus baptizing with the Spirit; the narrative of the temptation; a number of healings; a statement of high Christology, making Jesus unique; the Lord's Prayer; the binding of the strong man and the struggles against evil spirits; the sign of Jonah prophesying the resurrection; a final judgment; the coming of the Son of Man; the future inclusion of the Gentiles; rejection of divorce; and insistence of faith.

53. Farrer, "On Dispensing with Q."

54. Mark Goodacre and Nicholas Perrin, *Questioning Q*, 165, 173.

55. There are many recognized scholars who make this claim. See for instance Blomberg, "Tradition and Redaction in the Parables of the Gospel of Thomas"; Brown, "The Gospel of Thomas and St John's Gospel."

56. N. T. Wright, *The Resurrection*, 587, describes Nag Hammadi Gnosticism as "small and late." In 1979 James M. Robinson observed

that *The Gospel of Thomas* "alone would make the Nag Hammadi library a very important discovery ..." See James M. Robinson, "Introduction: What is the Nag Hammadi Library?" *Biblical Archeologist* 42 (1979), 202. It turns out *Thomas* is also the *only* one, and that is highly contested.

57. Isenberg, *The Nag Hammadi Library in English*, 131.

58. MacRae and Wilson, *The Nag Hammadi Library in English*, 471.

59. Helmut Koester describes them as "independent developments" (*Ancient Christian Gospels*, 77).

60. Perrin, *Thomas and Tatian*.

61. On this see Evans, Webb, and Wiebe, *Nag Hammadi Texts and the Bible*, 88–144.

62. *Thomas* 75, 104, mention the "bridal chamber," a notion unknown to the New Testament and fully developed in the third-century *Gospel of Philip*. On this see Luke Timothy Johnson, "The Humanity of Jesus," 56, n. 29.

63. This is a classic liberal account of the history of the canon. See for instance, Kurt Aland, *The Problem of the New Testament Canon*, 14. For a dissenting view on the importance of Marcion's "canon" for the New Testament canon, see Ridderbos, *The Authority of The New Testament Scriptures*, 43–44.

64. George W. MacRae dates *The Gospel of Truth* "in the middle or second

half of the second century" (*The Nag Hammadi Library in English*, 37).

65. See her discussion with Ben Witherington on *Beliefnet.com*. One has to wonder about Pagels's criteria when she finds *The Testimony of Truth's* view of Christ as Satan, as perfectly Christian. See her *The Origin of Satan*, 159–160.

66. 1 Tim. 6:20.

67. 1 Tim. 4:1–5.

68. Markshies, *Gnosis*, x. Markschies states: "[*The Nag Hammadi Library* texts] certainly do not come from the period before the end of the second century" (p. 58).

69. See also Gene Edward Veith, "Forging Ahead," *World* (September 25, 2004), 29.

70. Philip Jenkins, Distinguished Professor of History and Religious Studies, Pennsylvania State University, "Nag Hammadi Documents …" For a resume of his book, *Hidden Gospels*, see the web site *The Bible and Interpretation* of the Laramie County Community College, Cheyenne, WY.

71. 1 Chron. 10:9; Jer. 20:15. "Gospel" in the literature of the Greco-Roman empire refers to the proclamation of real, datable events that change the course of world history, like the birth of an emperor or a significant military victory.

72. William J. La Due gives the date of AD 33–35 (*Jesus Among the Theologians*, 31).

73. 1 Cor. 9:5; Gal. 1:19; 2:8. He calls them "pillars" (Gal. 2:8), that is, the foundational, eye-witness figures (1 Cor. 15:5) on whom Jesus built the church (Matt. 16:16; Eph. 2:20).

74. Wright, *Resurrection*, 319.

75. John Rodgers, Dean of Trinity Episcopal School for Ministry, in Richard Ostling's "Who Was Jesus?" *Time Magazine*, 15 (August, 1988), 41. Also cited in Gary R. Habermas and Michael R. Licona, *The Case for the Resurrection of Jesus* (Grand Rapids, MI: Kregel, 2004), 53.

76. Wright, *Resurrection*, 322.

77. Peter's sermon in Acts 2, which, according to Luke, was preached five weeks after the crucifixion and resurrection—in Jerusalem!

78. See note 71.

79. Gal. 2:7.

80. Acts 13:47; Rom. 11:13; Gal. 2:7.

81. In the Book of Hebrews, the priests are still entering the Holy of Holies, administering the sacrificial system entirely dependent on the temple.

82. Robinson, *Redating the New Testament*, 88.

83. Ibid., 277–278.

84. Ibid., 296.

85. Jonas, *Gnosis und spätantiker Geist* I, Ergänzungsheft, *Die mythologigische Gnosis* (Göttingen, 1934), 383: "the exaltation of man" into a supramundane [otherworldly] God more exalted than the Demiurge [God the Creator]."

86. Origen, *Contra Celsum* 1:29, cited in Pagels, *The Origin of Satan*, 140.

87. Muggeridge, *Jesus, the Man Who Lives*, 7.

88. Cited in Philip Yancey, *The Jesus I Never Knew*, 20.

89. John Ziesler, "Historical Criticism and Rational Faith," *Expository Times* (October 5, 1994), 270, makes the point that precisely because Jesus is truly historical, he is vulnerable to historical attack, but this makes him more believable, not less. On the historicity of Jesus, see I. Howard Marshall, *I Believe in the Historical Jesus*. (Grand Rapids, MI: Eerdmans, 1979); R. T. France, *The Evidence for Jesus*. (London: Hodder & Stoughton, 1985); Craig Blomberg, *The Historical Reliability of the Gospels* (Downers Grove, IL: InterVarsity Press, 1987).

90. I refer again to the brilliant work of Hermann Ridderbos, *The Coming of the Kingdom* for a full scale and convincing treatment of this theme.

91. Wright, *Resurrection*, 243.

92. Ibid., 206.

93. Ibid., 272.

94. Ibid., 315.

95. Ibid., 205.

INDEX